THE VIEW FROM NOWHERE

THE VIEW
FROM NOWHERE

THOMAS NAGEL

New York   Oxford
OXFORD UNIVERSITY PRESS
1986

Oxford University Press

Oxford New York Toronto
Delhi Bombay Calcutta Madras Karachi
Petaling Jaya Singapore Hong Kong Tokyo
Nairobi Dar es Salaam Cape Town
Melbourne Auckland

and associated companies in
Beirut Berlin Ibadan Nicosia

Oxford is a registered trademark of Oxford University Press

Published by Oxford University Press, Inc.,
200 Madison Avenue, New York, New York 10016

Library of Congress Cataloging-in-Publication Data
Nagel, Thomas.
The view from nowhere.
Bibliography: p. Includes index.
1. Objectivity—Addresses, essays, lectures.
2. Mind and body—Addresses, essays, lectures.
3. Ethics—Addresses, essays, lectures.
4. Life—Addresses, essays, lectures. I. Title.
BD220.N34 1986   121'.4   85-31002
ISBN 0-19-503668-9

Printing (last digit): 9 8 7 6 5 4 3 2 1

Printed in the United States of America

To A.L.H.

ACKNOWLEDGMENTS

This book was begun in 1978–79 during a sabbatical from Princeton University and completed in 1984–85 during a sabbatical from New York University—with the support in each case of a fellowship from the National Endowment for the Humanities.

Chapters 2, 8, and 9 are descended from the Tanner Lectures given in May 1979 at Brasenose College, Oxford, and published as "The Limits of Objectivity" in *The Tanner Lectures on Human Values, volume I.* Chapter 4 derives from my contribution to *Knowledge and Mind*, a volume honoring Norman Malcolm. An earlier version of chapter 7 was presented in August 1981 to an International Philosophy Symposium in Oaxaca sponsored by the Instituto de Investigaciones Filosóficas.

Many friends, colleagues, and students have had an influence on my thoughts. Apart from references in the text, let me here thank Rogers Albritton, Thompson Clarke, Ronald Dworkin, Gilbert Harman, Shelly Kagan, Frances Myrna Kamm, John Rawls, Thomas M. Scanlon, Samuel Scheffler, Barry Stroud, Peter Unger, and Susan Wolf. I am particularly grateful to Simon Blackburn and Derek Parfit, each of whom produced valuable comments on the entire manuscript.

New York   T.N.
February 1985

CONTENTS

THE VIEW FROM NOWHERE

I

INTRODUCTION

This book is about a single problem: how to combine the perspective of a particular person inside the world with an objective view of that same world, the person and his viewpoint included. It is a problem that faces every creature with the impulse and the capacity to transcend its particular point of view and to conceive of the world as a whole.

Though it is a single problem, it has many aspects. The difficulty of reconciling the two standpoints arises in the conduct of life as well as in thought. It is the most fundamental issue about morality, knowledge, freedom, the self, and the relation of mind to the physical world. Our response or lack of response to it will substantially determine our conception of the world and of ourselves, and our attitude toward our lives, our actions, and our relations with others. By tracing this element through a number of philosophical problems, I hope to offer a way of seeing them that others may also find natural.

If one could say how the internal and external standpoints are related, how each of them can be developed and modified in order to take the other into account, and how in conjunction they are to govern the thought and action of each person, it would amount to a world view. What I have to say about these questions is not unified enough to deserve that title; one of my claims will be that often the pursuit of a highly unified conception of life and the world leads to philosophical mistakes—to false reductions or to the refusal to recognize part of what is real.

3

Still, I want to describe a way of looking at the world and living in it that is suitable for complex beings without a naturally unified stand-point. It is based on a deliberate effort to juxtapose the internal and external or subjective and objective views at full strength, in order to achieve unification when it is possible and to recognize clearly when it is not. Instead of a unified world view, we get the interplay of these two uneasily related types of conception, and the essentially incompletable effort to reconcile them. The transcendent impulse is both a creative and a destructive force.

I find it natural to regard life and the world in this way—and that includes the conflicts between the standpoints and the discomfort caused by obstacles to their integration. Certain forms of perplexity—for exam-ple, about freedom, knowledge, and the meaning of life—seem to me to embody more insight than any of the supposed solutions to those prob-lems. The perplexities do not result from mistakes about the operation of language or thought, and there is no hope of a Kantian or Wittgen-steinian purity, to be attained if we avoid certain tempting missteps in the employment of reason or language.

Objectivity is a method of understanding. It is beliefs and attitudes that are objective in the primary sense. Only derivatively do we call objective the truths that can be arrived at in this way. To acquire a more objective understanding of some aspect of life or the world, we step back from our initial view of it and form a new conception which has that view and its relation to the world as its object. In other words, we place our-selves in the world that is to be understood. The old view then comes to be regarded as an appearance, more subjective than the new view, and correctable or confirmable by reference to it. The process can be repeated, yielding a still more objective conception.

It will not always yield a result, and sometimes it will be thought to yield a result when it really doesn't: then, as Nietzsche warned, one will get a false objectification of an aspect of reality that cannot be better understood from a more objective standpoint. Although there is a con-nection between objectivity and reality—only the supposition that we and our appearances are parts of a larger reality makes it reasonable to seek understanding by stepping back from the appearances in this way—still not all reality is better understood the more objectively it is viewed. Appearance and perspective are essential parts of what there is, and in some respects they are best understood from a less detached standpoint. Realism underlies the claims of objectivity and detachment, but it sup-ports them only up to a point.

Though I shall for convenience often speak of two standpoints, the subjective and the objective, and though the various places in which this opposition is found have much in common, the distinction between more subjective and more objective views is really a matter of degree, and it covers a wide spectrum. A view or form of thought is more objective than another if it relies less on the specifics of the individual's makeup and position in the world, or on the character of the particular type of creature he is. The wider the range of subjective types to which a form of understanding is accessible—the less it depends on specific subjective capacities—the more objective it is. A standpoint that is objective by comparison with the personal view of one individual may be subjective by comparison with a theoretical standpoint still farther out. The standpoint of morality is more objective than that of private life, but less objective than the standpoint of physics. We may think of reality as a set of concentric spheres, progressively revealed as we detach gradually from the contingencies of the self. This will become clearer when we discuss the interpretation of objectivity in relation to specific areas of life and understanding.

I shall offer a defense and also a critique of objectivity. Both are necessary in the present intellectual climate, for objectivity is both underrated and overrated, sometimes by the same persons. It is underrated by those who don't regard it as a method of understanding the world as it is in itself. It is overrated by those who believe it can provide a complete view of the world on its own, replacing the subjective views from which it has developed. These errors are connected: they both stem from an insufficiently robust sense of reality and of its independence of any particular form of human understanding.   *perceived?*

The fundamental idea behind both the validity and the limits of objectivity is that we are small creatures in a big world of which we have only very partial understanding, and that how things seem to us depends both on the world and on our constitution. We can add to our knowledge of the world by accumulating information at a given level—by extensive observation from one standpoint. But we can raise our understanding to a new level only if we examine that relation between the world and ourselves which is responsible for our prior understanding, and form a new conception that includes a more detached understanding of ourselves, of the world, and of the interaction between them. Thus objectivity allows us to transcend our particular viewpoint and develop an expanded consciousness that takes in the world more fully. All this applies to values and attitudes as well as to beliefs and theories.

Every objective advance creates a new conception of the world that includes oneself, and one's former conception, within its scope; so it inevitably poses the problem of what to do with the older, more subjective view, and how to combine it with the new one. A succession of objective advances may take us to a new conception of reality that leaves the personal or merely human perspective further and further behind. But if what we want is to understand the whole world, we can't forget about those subjective starting points indefinitely; we and our personal perspectives belong to the world. One limit encountered by the pursuit of objectivity appears when it turns back on the self and tries to encompass subjectivity in its conception of the real. The recalcitrance of this material to objective understanding requires both a modification of the form of objectivity and a recognition that it cannot by itself provide a complete picture of the world, or a complete stance toward it.

Both the content of an objective view and its claims to completeness are inevitably affected by the attempt to combine it with the view from where we are. The reverse is also true; that is, the subjective standpoint and its claims are modified in the attempt to coexist with the objective. Much of what I have to say will concern the possibilities of integration; I shall discuss the proper form, and the limits, of objectivity with respect to a range of issues. But I shall also point out ways in which the two standpoints cannot be satisfactorily integrated, and in these cases I believe the correct course is not to assign victory to either standpoint but to hold the opposition clearly in one's mind without suppressing either element. Apart from the chance that this kind of tension will generate something new, it is best to be aware of the ways in which life and thought are split, if that is how things are.

The internal-external tension pervades human life, but it is particularly prominent in the generation of philosophical problems. I shall concentrate on four topics: the metaphysics of mind, the theory of knowledge, free will, and ethics. But the problem has equally important manifestations with respect to the metaphysics of space and time, the philosophy of language, and aesthetics. In fact there is probably no area of philosophy in which it doesn't play a significant role.

The ambition to get outside of ourselves has obvious limits, but it is not always easy to know where they are or when they have been transgressed. We rightly think that the pursuit of detachment from our initial standpoint is an indispensable method of advancing our understanding of the world and of ourselves, increasing our freedom in thought and action, and becoming better. But since we are who we are, we can't get outside of ourselves completely. Whatever we do, we remain subparts of the world with limited access to the real nature of the rest of it and of ourselves. There is no way of telling how much of reality lies beyond the reach of present or future objectivity or any other conceivable form of human understanding.

Objectivity itself leads to the recognition that its own capacities are probably limited, since in us it is a human faculty and we are conspicuously finite beings. The radical form of this recognition is philosophical skepticism, in which the objective standpoint undermines itself by the same procedures it uses to call into question the prereflective standpoint of ordinary life in perception, desire, and action. Skepticism is radical doubt about the possibility of reaching any kind of knowledge, freedom, or ethical truth, given our containment in the world and the impossibility of creating ourselves from scratch.

One of my concerns will be to consider the appropriate attitude to these different forms of skepticism, given that they cannot be ruled out as nonsensical without adopting spurious reductionist analyses of truth, freedom, or value. In general, I believe that skepticism is revealing and not refutable, but that it does not vitiate the pursuit of objectivity. It is worth trying to bring one's beliefs, one's actions, and one's values more under the influence of an impersonal standpoint even without the assurance that this could not be revealed from a still more external standpoint as an illusion. In any case, we seem to have no choice but to make the attempt.

The limit of objectivity with which I shall be most concerned is one that follows directly from the process of gradual detachment by which objectivity is achieved. An objective standpoint is created by leaving a more subjective, individual, or even just human perspective behind; but there are things about the world and life and ourselves that cannot be adequately understood from a maximally objective standpoint, however much it may extend our understanding beyond the point from which we started. A great deal is essentially connected to a particular point of view, or type of point of view, and the attempt to give a complete account of the world in objective terms detached from these perspectives inevitably leads to false reductions or to outright denial that certain patently real phenomena exist at all.

This form of objective blindness is most conspicuous in the philosophy of mind, where one or another external theory of the mental, from physicalism to functionalism, is widely held. What motivates these views is the assumption that what there really is must be understandable in a certain way—that reality is in a narrow sense objective reality. For many philosophers the exemplary case of reality is the world described by physics, the science in which we have achieved our greatest detachment from a specifically human perspective on the world. But for precisely that reason physics is bound to leave undescribed the irreducibly subjective character of conscious mental processes, whatever may be their intimate relation to the physical operation of the brain. The subjectivity of consciousness is an irreducible feature of reality—without which we couldn't do physics or anything else—and it must occupy as fundamental a place in any credible world view as matter, energy, space, time, and numbers.

The ways in which mental phenomena are related to the brain, and personal identity to the biological persistence of the organism, are matters that cannot now be settled, but the possibilities are appropriate subjects for philosophical speculation. I believe it is already clear that any correct theory of the relation between mind and body would radically transform our overall conception of the world and would require a new understanding of the phenomena now thought of as physical. Even though the manifestations of mind evident to us are local—they depend on our brains and similar organic structures—the general basis of this aspect of reality is not local, but must be presumed to inhere in the general constituents of the universe and the laws that govern them.

There is a problem of excess objectivity also in ethics. Objectivity is the driving force of ethics as it is of science: it enables us to develop new motives when we occupy a standpoint detached from that of our purely personal desires and interests, just as in the realm of thought it enables us to develop new beliefs. Morality gives systematic form to the objective will. But escaping from oneself is as delicate a matter with respect to motives as it is with respect to belief. By going too far one may arrive at skepticism or nihilism; short of this there is also a temptation to deprive the subjective standpoint of any independent role in the justification of action.

Some impersonal moral theories embrace this conclusion, holding that we should try so far as possible to transform ourselves into instruments for the pursuit of the general good, objectively conceived (though our own interests play their part along with everyone else's in defining that good). But while transcendence of one's own point of view in action is the most important creative force in ethics, I believe that its results cannot completely subordinate the personal standpoint and its prereflective motives. The good, like the true, includes irreducibly subjective elements.   *ethics*   *science*

The question is how to combine objective and subjective values in the control of a single life. They cannot simply exist side by side without interference, and it seems impossible to give the authority to either in deciding conflicts between them. This problem is the analogue in ethics to the problem in metaphysics of combining into some conception of a single world those features of reality that are revealed to different perspectives at different levels of subjectivity or objectivity. A realist, antireductionist theory of anything is bound to be faced with a problem of this form. The mind-body problem is one example and the problem of how to design ethics for individual human life is another. A third is the problem of the meaning of life, which arises because we are capable of occupying a standpoint from which our most compelling personal concerns appear insignificant.

What really happens in the pursuit of objectivity is that a certain element of oneself, the impersonal or objective self, which can escape from the specific contingencies of one's creaturely point of view, is allowed to predominate. Withdrawing into this element one detaches from the rest and develops an impersonal conception of the world and, so far as possible, of the elements of self from which one has detached. That creates the new problem of reintegration, the problem of how to incorporate these results into the life and self-knowlege of an ordinary human being. One has to *be* the creature whom one has subjected to detached examination, and one has in one's entirety to *live* in the world that has been revealed to an extremely distilled fraction of oneself.

It is necessary to combine the recognition of our contingency, our finitude, and our containment in the world with an ambition of transcendence, however limited may be our success in achieving it. The right attitude in philosophy is to accept aims that we can achieve only fractionally and imperfectly, and cannot be sure of achieving even to that extent. It means in particular not abandoning the pursuit of truth, even though if you want the truth rather than merely something to say, you will have a good deal less to say. Pursuit of the truth requires more than imagination: it requires the generation and decisive elimination of alternative possibilities until, ideally, only one remains, and it requires a habitual readiness to attack one's own convictions. That is the only way real belief can be arrived at.

This is in some respects a deliberately reactionary work. There is a significant strain of idealism in contemporary philosophy, according to which what there is and how things are cannot go beyond what we could in principle think about. This view inherits the crude appeal of logical positivism even though that particular version of idealism is out of date. Philosophy seems regularly to generate announcements that what past philosophers were trying to do was impossible or nonsensical, and that a proper appreciation of the conditions of thought will lead us to see that all those deep questions about its relation to reality are unreal.

Philosophy is also infected by a broader tendency of contemporary intellectual life: scientism. Scientism is actually a special form of idealism, for it puts one type of human understanding in charge of the universe and what can be said about it. At its most myopic it assumes that everything there is must be understandable by the employment of scientific theories like those we have developed to date—physics and evolutionary biology are the current paradigms—as if the present age were not just another in the series.

Precisely because of their dominance, these attitudes are ripe for attack. Of course, some of the opposition is foolish: antiscientism can degenerate into a rejection of science—whereas in reality it is essential to the defense of science against misappropriation. But these excesses shouldn't deter us from an overdue downward revision of the prevailing intellectual self-esteem. Too much time is wasted because of the assumption that methods already in existence will solve problems for which they were not designed; too many hypotheses and systems of thought in philosophy and elsewhere are based on the bizarre view that we, at this point in history, are in possession of the basic forms of understanding needed to comprehend absolutely anything.

I believe that the methods needed to understand ourselves do not yet exist. So this book contains a great deal of speculation about the world and how we fit into it. Some of it will seem wild, but the world is a strange place, and nothing but radical speculation gives us a hope of coming up with any candidates for the truth. That, of course, is not the same as coming up with the truth: if truth is our aim, we must be resigned to achieving it to a very limited extent, and without certainty. To redefine the aim so that its achievement is largely guaranteed, through various forms of reductionism, relativism, or historicism, is a form of cognitive wish-fulfillment. Philosophy cannot take refuge in reduced ambitions. It is after eternal and nonlocal truth, even though we know that is not what we are going to get.

The question of how to combine the external view of this embarrassing but unavoidable activity with the view from inside is just another instance of our ubiquitous problem. Even those who regard philosophy as real and important know that they are at a particular and, we may hope, early stage of its development, limited by their own primitive intellectual capacities and relying on the partial insights of a few great figures from the past. As we judge their results to be mistaken in fundamental ways, so we must assume that even the best efforts of our own time will come to seem blind eventually. This lack of confidence should be an integral part of the enterprise, not something that it needs a historical argument to produce. We also have to recognize that philosophical ideas are acutely sensitive to individual temperament, and to wishes. Where the evidence and the arguments are too meager to determine a result, the slack tends to be taken up by other factors. The personal flavor and motivation of each great philosopher's version of reality is unmistakable, and the same is true of many lesser efforts.

But we can't let this standpoint take over: we can't either engage in the subject or understand the work of others if we look at it only from outside, in a historicist or clinical mood. It is one thing to recognize the limitations that inevitably come from occupying a particular position in the history of a culture; it is another to convert these into nonlimitations by embracing a historicism which says there is no truth except what is internal to a particular historical standpoint. I think that here, as elsewhere, we are stuck with the clash of standpoints. Absurdity comes with the territory, and what we need is the will to put up with it.

Even if philosophical problems were mere manifestations of our particular historical situation or of the accidental forms of our language, we probably wouldn't be able to free ourselves of them. If you are inside something like a language, the external view doesn't supplant the internal view or make it any less serious. (I can't read the words "is comprised of" without disgust even though I fully expect that in another hundred years the tide of misuse will have raised them to grammatical respectability and a place in the best dictionaries.) Recognition of the objective contingency of a language does nothing to diminish its normative reality for those who live in it. But philosophy is not like a particular language. Its sources are preverbal and often precultural, and one of its most difficult tasks is to express unformed but intuitively felt problems in language without losing them.

The history of the subject is a continual discovery of problems that baffle existing concepts and existing methods of solution. At every point it faces us with the question of how far beyond the relative safety of our present language we can afford to go without risking complete loss of touch with reality. We are in a sense trying to climb outside of our own minds, an effort that some would regard as insane and that I regard as philosophically fundamental. Historicist interpretation doesn't make philosophical problems go away, any more than the earlier diagnoses of the logical positivists or the linguistic analysts did. To the extent that such no-nonsense theories have an effect, they merely threaten to impoverish the intellectual landscape for a while by inhibiting the serious expression of certain questions. In the name of liberation, these movements have offered us intellectual repression.

But that leaves a question. If the theories of historical captivity or grammatical delusion are not true, why have some philosophers felt themselves cured of their metaphysical problems by these forms of therapy? My counterdiagnosis is that a lot of philosophers are sick of the subject and glad to be rid of its problems. Most of us find it hopeless some of the time, but some react to its intractability by welcoming the suggestion that the enterprise is misconceived and the problems unreal. This makes them receptive not only to scientism but to deflationary metaphilosophical theories like positivism and pragmatism, which offer to raise us above the old battles.

This is more than the usual wish to transcend one's predecessors, for it includes a rebellion against the philosophical impulse itself, which is felt as humiliating and unrealistic. It is natural to feel victimized by philosophy, but this particular defensive reaction goes too far. It is like the hatred of childhood and results in a vain effort to grow up too early, before one has gone through the essential formative confusions and exaggerated hopes that have to be experienced on the way to understanding anything. Philosophy is the childhood of the intellect, and a culture that tries to skip it will never grow up.

There is a persistent temptation to turn philosophy into something less difficult and more shallow than it is. It is an extremely difficult subject, and no exception to the general rule that creative efforts are rarely successful. I do not feel equal to the problems treated in this book. They seem to me to require an order of intelligence wholly different from mine. Others who have tried to address the central questions of philosophy will recognize the feeling.

II

MIND

1. Physical Objectivity

The natural place to begin is with our own position in the world. One of the strongest philosophical motives is the desire for a comprehensive picture of objective reality, since it is easy to assume that that is all there really is. But the very idea of objective reality guarantees that such a picture will not comprehend everything; we ourselves are the first obstacles to such an ambition.

To the extent that the world is objectively comprehensible—comprehensible from a standpoint independent of the constitution of this or that sentient being or type of sentient being—how do sentient beings fit into it? The question can be divided into three parts. First, does the mind itself have an objective character? Second, what is its relation to those physical aspects of reality whose objective status is less doubtful? Third, how can it be the case that one of the people in the world is *me*?

I shall take up these questions in order, in this chapter and the two following. The second question is the mind-body problem. The third question, how it is possible to be anyone in particular, expresses in purest form the difficulty of finding room in the world for oneself. How can it be? Am I, or are you, really the sort of thing that could be one of the particular creatures in the world? But I shall begin with the first question—whether the mind itself can be objectively understood. It under-

13

lies the mind-body problem, which arises because certain features of mental life present an obstacle to the ambitions of one very important conception of objectivity. No progress can be made with the mind-body problem unless we understand this conception and examine its claims with care.

For convenience I shall refer to it as the *physical* conception of objectivity. It is not the same thing as our idea of what physical reality is actually like, but it has developed as part of our method of arriving at a truer understanding of the physical world, a world that is presented to us initially but somewhat inaccurately through sensory perception.

The development goes in stages, each of which gives a more objective picture than the one before. The first step is to see that our perceptions are caused by the action of things on us, through their effects on our bodies, which are themselves parts of the physical world. The next step is to realize that since the same physical properties that cause perceptions in us through our bodies also produce different effects on other physical things and can exist without causing any perceptions at all, their true nature must be detachable from their perceptual appearance and need not resemble it. The third step is to try to form a conception of that true nature independent of its appearance either to us or to other types of perceivers. This means not only not thinking of the physical world from our own particular point of view, but not thinking of it from a more general human perceptual point of view either: not thinking of how it looks, feels, smells, tastes, or sounds. These secondary qualities then drop out of our picture of the external world, and the underlying primary qualities such as shape, size, weight, and motion are thought of structurally.

This has turned out to be an extremely fruitful strategy. The understanding of the physical world has been expanded enormously with the aid of theories and explanations that use concepts not tied to the specifically human perceptual viewpoint. Our senses provide the evidence from which we start, but the detached character of this understanding is such that we could possess it even if we had none of our present senses, so long as we were rational and could understand the mathematical and formal properties of the objective conception of the physical world. We might even in a sense share an understanding of physics with other creatures to whom things appeared quite different, perceptually—so long as they too were rational and numerate.

The world described by this objective conception is not just centerless; it is also in a sense featureless. While the things in it have properties, none of these properties are perceptual aspects. All of those have been relegated to the mind, a yet-to-be-examined domain. The physical world as it is supposed to be in itself contains no points of view and nothing that can appear only to a particular point of view. Whatever it contains can be apprehended by a general rational consciousness that gets its information through whichever perceptual point of view it happens to view the world from.[1]

Powerful as it has proven to be, this bleached-out physical conception of objectivity encounters difficulties if it is put forward as the method for seeking a complete understanding of reality. For the process began when we noticed that how things appear to us depends on the interaction of our bodies with the rest of the world. But this leaves us with no account of the perceptions and specific viewpoints which were left behind as irrelevant to physics but which seem to exist nonetheless, along with those of other creatures—not to mention the mental activity of forming an objective conception of the physical world, which seems not itself capable of physical analysis.

Faced with these facts one might think the only conceivable conclusion would be that there is more to reality than what can be accommodated by the physical conception of objectivity. But remarkably enough this has not been obvious to everyone. The physical has been so irresistibly attractive, and has so dominated ideas of what there is, that attempts have been made to beat everything into its shape and deny the reality of anything that cannot be so reduced. As a result, the philosophy of mind is populated with extremely implausible positions.

I have argued elsewhere[2] against the various forms of reductionism— behavioristic, causal, or functionalist—that have been offered by those seeking to make the mind safe for physical objectivity. All these theories are motivated by an epistemological criterion of reality—that only what can be understood in a certain way exists. But it is hopeless to try to analyze mental phenomena so that they are revealed as part of the "external" world. The subjective features of conscious mental processes—as opposed to their physical causes and effects—cannot be captured by the purified form of thought suitable for dealing with the physical world that underlies the appearances. Not only raw feels but also intentional mental states—however objective their content—must be

1. There is an excellent account of this idea in Williams (7), pp. 64–8. He calls it the *absolute* conception of reality.
2. Nagel (3). Since it's never too late for an acknowledgment, let me record that two years earlier Timothy Sprigge had proposed as the essential condition of consciousness that there must be "something it is like to be" the creature in question (Sprigge, pp. 166–8). And B. A. Farrell asked, "What would it be like to be a bat?" in 1950, though he dismissed the difficulty for materialism. (When I wrote, I hadn't read Sprigge and had forgotten Farrell.)

capable of manifesting themselves in subjective form to be in the mind at all.

The reductionist program that dominates current work in the philosophy of mind is completely misguided, because it is based on the groundless assumption that a particular conception of objective reality is exhaustive of what there is. Eventually, I believe, current attempts to understand the mind by analogy with man-made computers that can perform superbly some of the same external tasks as conscious beings will be recognized as a gigantic waste of time. The true principles underlying the mind will be discovered, if at all, only by a more direct approach.

But merely to deny the possibility of psychophysical reduction does not end the problem. There is still a question about how we are to conceive of the inclusion of subjective mental processes in the world as it really is. And there is the question of whether they can be in some other way objectively understood. Physicalism, though unacceptable, has behind it a broader impulse to which it gives distorted and ultimately self-defeating expression. That is the impulse to find a way of thinking about the world as it is, so that everything in it, not just atoms and planets, can be regarded as real in the same way: not just an aspect of the world as it appears to us, but something that is *really there*.

I think part of the explanation of the modern weakness for physicalist reduction is that a less impoverished and reductive idea of objectivity has not been available to fill out the project of constructing an overall picture of the world. The objectivity of physics was viable: it continued to yield progressively more understanding through successive application to those properties of the physical world that earlier applications had discovered.

It is true that recent developments in physics have led some to believe that it may after all be incapable of providing a conception of what is really there, independent of observation. But I do not wish to argue that since the idea of objective reality has to be abandoned because of quantum theory anyway, we might as well go the whole hog and admit the subjectivity of the mental. Even if, as some physicists think, quantum theory cannot be interpreted in a way that permits the phenomena to be described without reference to an observer, the ineliminable observer need not be a member of any particular species like the human, to whom things look and feel in highly characteristic ways. This does not therefore require that we let in the full range of subjective experience.

The central problem is not whether points of view must be admitted to the account of the *physical* world. Whatever may be the answer to that question, we shall still be faced with an independent problem about the mind. It is the phenomena of consciousness themselves that pose the clearest challenge to the idea that physical objectivity gives the general form of reality. In response I want not to abandon the idea of objectivity entirely but rather to suggest that the physical is not its only possible interpretation.

2. Mental Objectivity

Even if we acknowledge the existence of distinct and irreducible perspectives, the wish for a unified conception of the world doesn't go away. If we can't achieve it in a form that eliminates individual perspectives, we may inquire to what extent it can be achieved if we admit them. Persons and other conscious beings are part of the natural order, and their mental states are part of the way the world is in itself. From the perspective of one type of being, the subjective features of the mental states of a very different type of being are not accessible either through subjective imagination or through the kind of objective representation that captures the physical world. The question is whether these gaps can be at least partly closed by another form of thought, which acknowledges perspectives different from one's own and conceives of them not by means of the imagination. A being of total imaginative flexibility could project himself directly into every possible subjective point of view, and would not need such an objective method to think about the full range of possible inner lives. But since we can't do that, a more detached form of access to other subjective forms would be useful.

There is even a point to this in the case of our own minds. We assume that we ourselves are not just parts of the world as it appears to us. But if we are parts of the world as it is in itself, then we ought to be able to include ourselves—our minds as well as our bodies—in a conception that is not tied exclusively to our own point of view. We ought, in other words, to be able to think of ourselves from outside—but in mental, not physical terms. Such a result, if it were possible, would qualify as an objective concept of mind.

What I want to do is to explain what a natural objective understanding of the mind along these lines would be—an understanding as objective as is compatible with the essential subjectivity of the mental. I believe it has its beginnings in the ordinary concept of mind, but that it can be developed beyond this. The question is, how far beyond?

As a practical matter, I have no idea how far. But I believe that there is no objection in principle to such a development, and that its possibility should already be allowed for in our conception of our own minds. I believe we can include ourselves, experiences and all, in a world conceivable not from a specifically human point of view, and that we can do this without reducing the mental to the physical. But I also believe that any such conception will necessarily be incomplete. And this means that the pursuit of an objective conception of reality comes up against limits that are not merely practical, limits that could not be overcome by any merely objective intelligence, however powerful. Finally, I shall claim that this is no cause for philosophical alarm, because there is no reason to assume that the world as it is in itself must be objectively comprehensible, even in an extended sense. Some things can only be understood from the inside, and access to them will depend on how far our subjective imagination can travel. It is natural to want to bring our capacity for detached, objective understanding as much into alignment with reality as we can, but it should not surprise us if objectivity is essentially incomplete.

The aim of such understanding, the deeper aim it shares with the reductionist views which I reject, is to go beyond the distinction between appearance and reality by including the existence of appearances in an elaborated reality. Nothing will then be left outside. But this expanded reality, like physical reality, is centerless. Though the subjective features of our own minds are at the center of *our* world, we must try to conceive of them as just one manifestation of the mental in a world that is not given especially to the human point of view. This is, I recognize, a paradoxical enterprise, but the attempt seems to me worth making.

The first requirement is to think of our own minds as mere instances of something general—as we are accustomed to thinking of particular things and events in the physical world as instances and manifestations of something general. We must think of mind as a phenomenon to which the human case is not necessarily central, even though our minds are at the center of our world. The fundamental idea behind the objective impulse is that the world is not our world. This idea can be betrayed if we turn objective comprehensibility into a new standard of reality. That is an error because the fact that reality extends beyond what is available to our original perspective does not mean that all of it is available to some transcendent perspective that we can reach from here. But so long as we avoid this error, it is proper to be motivated by the hope of extending our objective understanding to as much of life and the world as we can.

By a general concept of mind I don't mean an anthropocentric concept which conceives all minds on analogy with our own. I mean a concept under which we ourselves fall as instances—without any implication that we are the central instances. My opposition to psychophysical reduction is therefore fundamentally different from that of the idealist or phenomenological tradition. I want to think of mind, like matter, as a general feature of the world. In each case we are acquainted with certain instances in our small spatiotemporal neighborhood (though in the case of matter, not only with those instances). In each case there is no guarantee as to how far beyond the initial acquaintance our understanding can go, by processes of abstraction, generalization, and experiment. The necessary incompleteness of an objective concept of mind seems fairly clear. But there is also no reason to assume that everything about the *physical* world can be understood by some possible development of our physical conception of objectivity: physical science is after all just an operation of our minds, and we have no reason to assume that their capacities in these respects, remarkable as they are, correlate fully with reality.

In both cases an expanded understanding, to the extent that we can achieve it, not only gives us access to things outside our immediate neighborhood, but should also add to our knowledge of the things with which we are already acquainted and from which the inquiry starts. This is clear with respect to familiar physical objects, which we all now think of in terms of physics and chemistry and not just phenomenally or instrumentally. With respect to mental phenomena our objective understanding is undeveloped, and it may never develop very far. But the idea of such an objective view, coming through the pursuit of a general conception of mind, is to provide us with a way of thinking that we could also bring back home and apply to ourselves.

3. Other Minds

A simpler version of the problem of placing ourselves in a world of which we are not the center appears in philosophy independently of the ambition to form a general nonidealistic conception of reality. It appears at the individual level as the problem of other minds. One might say that the wider problem of mental objectivity is an analogue at the level of mental types to the problem of other minds for individuals: not, "How can I conceive of minds other than my own?" but, "How can we conceive of minds subjectively incommensurable with our own?" In both cases we must conceive of ourselves as instances of something more general in order to place ourselves in a centerless world.

The interesting problem of other minds is not the epistemological problem, how I can know that other people are not zombies. It is the conceptual problem, how I can *understand* the attribution of mental states to others. And this in turn is really the problem, how I can con-

ceive of my own mind as merely one of many examples of mental phenomena contained in the world.

Each of us is the subject of various experiences, and to understand
that there are other people in the world as well, one must be able to
conceive of experiences of which one is not the subject: experiences that
are not present to oneself. To do this it is necessary to have a general
conception of subjects of experience and to place oneself under it as an
instance. It cannot be done by extending the idea of what is immediately
felt into other people's bodies, for as Wittgenstein observed, that will
only give you an idea of having feelings in their bodies, not of *their* having feelings.

Though we all grow up with the required general conception that
allows us to believe in genuinely other minds, it is philosophically problematic, and there has been much difference of opinion over how it
works. The problem is that other people seem to be part of the external
world, and empiricist assumptions about meaning have led various philosophers to the view that our attribution of mental states to others must
be analyzed in terms of the behavioral evidence, or as parts of some
explanatory theory of what produces observable behavior. Unfortu-
nately, this seems to imply that mental attributions do not have the same
sense in the first person as in the third.

Clearly, there must be some alternative to the assumption that anything said about other persons has to be given a reading which places it
firmly in the familiar external world, comprehensible by means of the
physical conception of objectivity. That leads straight to solipsism: the
inability to make sense of the idea of real minds other than one's own.

In fact, the ordinary concept of mind contains the beginnings of an
entirely different way of conceiving objective reality. We cannot make
sense of the idea of other minds by construing it in a way which becomes
unintelligible when we try to apply it to ourselves. When we conceive of
the minds of others, we cannot abandon the essential factor of a point
of view: instead we must generalize it and think of ourselves as one point
of view among others. The first stage of objectification of the mental is
for each of us to be able to grasp the idea of all human perspectives,
including his own, without depriving them of their character as perspectives. It is the analogue for minds of a centerless conception of space for
physical objects, in which no point has a privileged position.

The beginning of an objective concept of mind is the ability to view
one's own experiences from outside, as events in the world. If this is
possible, then others can also conceive of those events and one can conceive of the experiences of others, also from outside. To think in this
way we use not a faculty of external representation, but a general idea

of subjective points of view, of which we imagine a particular instance and a particular form. So far the process does not involve any abstraction from the general forms of our experience. We still think of experience in terms of the familiar point of view we share with other humans. All that is involved in the external conception of mind is the imaginative use of this point of view—a use that is partly present in the memory and expectation of one's own experiences.

But we can go further than this, for the same basic method allows us to think of experiences that we can't imagine. To represent an experience from outside by imagining it subjectively is the analogue of representing an objective spatial configuration by imagining it visually. One uses ordinary appearance as a medium. What is represented need not resemble the representation in all respects. It must be represented in terms of certain general features of subjective experience—subjective universals—some instances of which one is familiar with from one's own experience. But the capacity to form universal concepts in any area enables one not only to represent the present situation from without but to think about other possibilities which one has not experienced and perhaps never will experience directly. So the pretheoretical concept of mind involves a kind of objectivity which permits us to go some way beyond our own experiences and those exactly like them.

The idea is that the concept of mind, though tied to subjectivity, is not restricted to what can be understood in terms of our own subjectivity— what we can translate into the terms of our own experience. We include the subjectively *un*imaginable mental lives of other species, for example, in our conception of the real world without betraying their subjectivity by means of a behaviorist, functionalist, or physicalist reduction. We know there's something there, something perspectival, even if we don't know what it is or even how to think about it. The question is whether this acknowledgment will allow us to develop a way to think about it.

Of course one possibility is that this particular process can go no further. We can have a concept of mind general enough to allow us to escape solipsism and ethnocentrism, but perhaps we cannot transcend the general forms of human experience and the human viewpoint. That viewpoint permits us to conceive of experiences we have not had, because of the flexibility of the human imagination. But does it allow us to detach the concept of mind from a human perspective?

The issue is whether there can be a general concept of experience that extends far beyond our own or anything like it. Even if there can, we may be unable to grasp it except in the abstract, as we are presumably unable to grasp now concepts of objective physical reality which will be developed five centuries hence. But the possibility that there is such a concept would be sufficient motive for trying to form it. It is only if we are convinced in advance that the thing makes no sense that we can be justified in setting the limits of objectivity with regard to the mind so close to our own ordinary viewpoint.

4. Consciousness in General

So far as I can see the only reason for accepting such limits would be a Wittgensteinian one—namely, that such an extension or attempted generalization of the concept of mind takes us away from the conditions that make the concept meaningful. I don't know whether Wittgenstein would actually have made this objection, but it seems a natural development of his views. He observed that while experiential concepts are applied in the first person from within, not on the basis of behavioral, circumstantial, or any other kind of evidence, they also require outward criteria. To mean anything in application to oneself in the first person they must also be applicable to oneself and others on circumstantial and behavioral grounds that are not just privately available. This he took to be a consequence of a general condition of publicity that must be met by all concepts, which in turn derives from a condition that must be met by any rule of whatever kind: that there must be an objective distinction between following it and breaking it, which can be made only if it is possible to compare one's own practice with that of one's community.

I am doubtful about the final "only", and though I have no alternative theory to offer, it seems to me dangerous to draw conclusions from the argument "How *else* could it be?" But I don't wish to deny that the experiential concepts we use to talk about our own minds and those of other human beings more or less fit the pattern Wittgenstein describes. Provided Wittgenstein is not understood, as I think he should not be, as saying that behavior and so forth is what there really is and mental processes are linguistic fictions, his view that the conditions of first- and third-person ascription of an experience are inextricably bound together in a single public concept seems to me correct, with regard to the ordinary case.[3]

The question is whether the concept of experience can be extended beyond these conditions without losing all content. A negative answer would limit our thought about experience to what we can ascribe to ourselves and to others in the specified ways. The objection is that beyond these limits the distinction between correct and incorrect application of

---

3. Wittgenstein (2), secs. 201 ff. On the status of criteria in Wittgenstein and why they aren't offered as *analyses* of meaning see Kripke (2).

the concept is not defined, and therefore the condition of significance is not met.

In a well known passage (sec. 350) Wittgenstein says I can't extend the application of mental concepts from my own case merely by saying others have the same as I have so often had. "It is as if I were to say: 'You surely know what "It is 5 o'clock here" means; so you also know what "It's 5 o'clock on the sun" means. It means simply that it is just the same time there as it is here when it is 5 o'clock.'" This is a fair reply to someone who is trying to explain what he means by saying that the stove is in pain. But could it be used to argue against all extensions of the concept beyond the range of cases where we know how to apply it? Does the general concept of experience really lose all content if an attempt is made to use it to think about cases in which we cannot now and perhaps even never could apply it more specifically? I think not. Not all such cases are like that of the time of day on the sun. That example is much more radical, for it introduces a direct contradiction with the conditions that determine the time of day—namely, position on the surface of the earth relative to the sun. But the generalization of the concept of experience beyond our capacity to apply it doesn't *contradict* the condition of application that it tries to transcend, even if some examples, like the ascription of pain to a stove, do pass the limits of intelligibility.

Admittedly, *if* someone has the concept of a type of conscious mental state and also has that mental state with any frequency, he will be able to apply it from within and without, in the way Wittgenstein describes. If he couldn't, it would be evidence that he didn't have the concept. But we don't ascribe such states only to creatures who have mental concepts: we ascribe them to children and animals, and believe that we ourselves would have experiences even if we didn't have the language. If we believe that the existence of many of the experiences we can talk about doesn't depend on the existence of these concepts, why can't we conceive at one remove of the existence of types of experience of which we don't have and perhaps could never have a complete conception and the capacity for first- and third-person ascription?

Consider first, cases where we have strong evidence that experience is present, without either knowing what its character is or being in a position to hope ever to reach an understanding of its character that will include the capacity for self-ascription. This is true of at least some of the experiences of all animals not very close to us in structure and behavior. In each case there is rich external evidence of conscious inner life, but only limited application of our own mental concepts—mostly general ones—to describe it.[4]

4. Skeptics should read Jennings.

It is the ordinary prephilosophical concept of experience that leads to this result. We have not simply left it behind and taken off with the *word*. And the extension is not part of a private language but a natural idea shared by most human beings about what sorts of things occupy the world around them. We are forced, I think, to conclude that all these creatures have specific experiences which cannot be represented by any mental concepts of which we could have first-person understanding. This doesn't mean that we can't think about them in that general way, or perhaps in more detail but without first-person understanding—provided that we continue to regard them as subjective experiences rather than mere behavioral dispositions or functional states.

But it seems to me that we can in principle go further. We can use the general concepts of experience and mind to speculate about forms of conscious life whose external signs we cannot confidently identify. There is probably a great deal of life in the universe, and we may be in a position to identify only some of its forms, because we would simply be unable to read as behavior the manifestations of creatures sufficiently unlike us. It certainly means something to speculate that there are such creatures, and that they have minds.

These uses of the general concept of mind exemplify a theoretical step that is commonplace elsewhere. We can form the idea of phenomena that we do not know how to detect. Once the conception of a new physical particle is formed, defined in terms of a set of properties, those properties may then allow experiments to be devised which will permit its detection. In this way the progress of physical discovery has long since passed to the formation of physical concepts that can be applied only with sophisticated techniques of observation, and not by means of unaided perception or simple mechanical measurement.

Only a dogmatic verificationist would deny the possibility of forming objective concepts that reach beyond our current capacity to apply them. The aim of reaching a conception of the world which does not put us at the center in any way requires the formation of such concepts. We are supported in this aim by a kind of intellectual optimism: the belief that we possess an open-ended capacity for understanding what we have not yet conceived, and that it can be called into operation by detaching from our present understanding and trying to reach a higher-order view which explains it as part of the world. But we must also admit that the world probably reaches beyond our capacity to understand it, no matter how far we travel, and this admission, which is stronger than the mere denial of verificationism, can be expressed only in general concepts whose extension is not limited to what we could in principle know about.

It is the same with the mind. To accept the general idea of a perspective without limiting it to the forms with which one is familiar, subjectively or otherwise, is the precondition of seeking ways to conceive of particular types of experience that do not depend on the ability either to have those experiences or to imagine them subjectively. It should be possible to investigate in this way the quality-structure of some sense we do not have, for example, by observing creatures who do have it—even though the understanding we can reach is only partial.

But if we could do that, we should also be able to apply the same general idea to ourselves, and thus to analyze our experiences in ways that can be understood without having had such experiences. That would constitute a kind of objective standpoint toward our own minds. To the extent that it could be achieved, we would be able to see our minds as not merely part of the human world, something we can already do with regard to our bodies. And this would serve a natural human goal, for it is natural to seek a general understanding of reality, including ourselves, which does not depend on the fact that we *are* ourselves.

5. The Incompleteness of Objective Reality

In the pursuit of this goal, however, even at its most successful, something will inevitably be lost. If we try to understand experience from an objective viewpoint that is distinct from that of the subject of the experience, then even if we continue to credit its perspectival nature, we will not be able to grasp its most specific qualities unless we can imagine them subjectively. We will not know exactly how scrambled eggs taste to a cockroach even if we develop a detailed objective phenomenology of the cockroach sense of taste. When it comes to values, goals, and forms of life, the gulf may be even more profound.

Since this is so, no objective conception of the mental world can include it all. But in that case it may be asked what the point is of looking for such a conception. The aim was to place perspectives and their contents in a world seen from no particular point of view. It turns out that some aspects of those perspectives cannot be fully understood in terms of an objective concept of mind. But if some aspects of reality can't be captured in an objective conception, why not forget the ambition of capturing as much of it as possible? The world just *isn't* the world as it appears to one highly abstracted point of view that can be pursued by all rational beings. And if one can't have complete objectivity, the goal of capturing as much of reality as one can in an objective net is pointless and unmotivated.

I don't think this follows. The pursuit of a conception of the world that doesn't put us at the center is an expression of philosophical realism, all the more so if it does not assume that everything real can be reached by such a conception. Reality is not just objective reality, and any objective conception of reality must include an acknowledgment of its own incompleteness. (This is an important qualification to the claims of objectivity in other areas as well.) Even if an objective general conception of mind were developed and added to the physical conception of objectivity, it would have to include the qualification that the exact character of each of the experiential and intentional perspectives with which it deals can be understood only from within or by subjective imagination. A being with total imaginative power could understand it all from inside, but an ordinary being using an objective concept of mind will not. In saying this we have not given up the idea of the way the world really is, independently of how it appears to us or to any particular occupant of it. We have only given up the idea that this coincides with what can be objectively understood. The way the world is includes appearances, and there is no single point of view from which they can all be fully grasped. An objective conception of mind acknowledges that the features of our own minds that cannot be objectively grasped are examples of a more general subjectivity, of which other examples lie beyond our subjective grasp as well.

This amounts to the rejection of idealism with regard to the mind. The world is not my world, or our world—not even the mental world is. This is a particularly unequivocal rejection of idealism because it affirms the reality of aspects of the world that cannot be grasped by any conception I can possess—not even an objective conception of the kind with which we transcend the domain of initial appearances. Here it can be seen that physicalism is based ultimately on a form of idealism: an idealism of restricted objectivity. Objectivity of whatever kind is not the test of reality. It is just one way of understanding reality.

Still, even if objective understanding can be only partial, it is worth trying to extend it, for a simple reason. The pursuit of an objective understanding of reality is the only way to expand our knowledge of what there is beyond the way it appears to us. Even if we have to acknowledge the reality of some things that we can't grasp objectively, as well as the ineliminable subjectivity of some aspects of our own experience which we can grasp only subjectively, the pursuit of an objective concept of mind is simply part of the general pursuit of understanding. To give it up because it cannot be complete would be like giving up axiomatization in mathematics because it cannot be complete.

In trying to explain how minds are to be included in the real world that simply exists, I have distinguished between reality and objective reality, and also between objectivity and particular conceptions of objectivity. The physical conception of objectivity is inappropriate for increasing our understanding of the the mind; and even the kind of objectivity that is appropriate for this purpose will not permit us to form a complete idea of all the various incompatible mental perspectives. These conclusions in the philosophy of mind suggest a more general principle that applies in other areas as well: one should pursue the kind of objectivity appropriate to the subject one is trying to understand, and even the right kind of objectivity may not exhaust the subject completely.

The problem of bringing together subjective and objective views of the world can be approached from either direction. If one starts from the subjective side, the problem is the traditional one of skepticism, idealism, or solipsism. How, given my personal experiential perspective, can I form a conception of the world as it is independent of my perception of it? And how can I know that this conception is correct? (The question may also be asked from the point of view of the collective human perspective rather than from that of an individual.) If on the other hand one starts from the objective side, the problem is how to accommodate, in a world that simply exists and has no perspectival center, any of the following things: (a) oneself; (b) one's point of view; (c) the point of view of other selves, similar and dissimilar; and (d) the objects of various types of judgment that seem to emanate from these perspectives.

It is this second version of the problem that particularly interests me. It is the obverse of skepticism because the *given* is objective reality—or the idea of an objective reality—and what is problematic by contrast is subjective reality. Without receiving full acknowledgment this approach has been very influential in recent analytic philosophy. It accords well with a bias toward physical science as a paradigm of understanding.

But if under the pressure of realism we admit that there are things which cannot be understood in this way, then other ways of understanding them must be sought. One way is to enrich the notion of objectivity. But to insist in every case that the most objective and detached account of a phenomenon is the correct one is likely to lead to reductive conclusions. I have argued that the seductive appeal of objective reality depends on a mistake. It is not the given. Reality is not just objective reality. Sometimes, in the philosophy of mind but also elsewhere, the truth is not to be found by travelling as far away from one's personal perspective as possible.

III

MIND AND BODY

1. Dual Aspect Theory

If we believe that a true conception of the mental world, however much objectivity it attains, must admit the mind's irreducibly subjective character, we still have to fit the mind into the same universe with that physical world which can be described in accordance with the physical conception of objectivity. Our bodies and in particular our central nervous systems belong to that physical world, as do the bodies of all other organisms capable of mental activity. We have reason to think that the connection between mental life and the body is very close, and that no mental event can occur without a physical change in the body—in vertebrates the brain—of its subject.

There is nothing unique in the physical composition of our bodies; only their chemical and physiological structure is unusual. An animal organism is composed of ordinary elements, which are in turn composed of subatomic particles found throughout the known physical universe. A living human body can therefore be constructed out of a sufficient quantity of anything—books, bricks, gold, peanut butter, a grand piano. The basic constituents just have to be suitably rearranged. The only way of actually producing such a rearrangement is by the natural biological process of nourishment and growth, beginning with conception, but this does not alter the fact that the materials can come from anywhere.

28

Given our objective understanding of physical reality, the question arises, how does such an arrangement of basic physical materials, complex as it is, give rise not only to the remarkable physical capacities of the organism but also to a being with a mind, a point of view, a wide range of subjective experiences and mental capacities—none of which can be accommodated by the physical conception of objective reality? If no form of psychophysical reductionism is right, what is left?

One answer is that a physical organism by itself obviously can't have a mind: there is no way of constructing subjectivity out of two hundred pounds of subatomic particles. So something else must be added, which may as well be called the soul, and this is the bearer of mental properties, the subject of mental states, processes, and events. No matter how closely it interacts with the body, it is something different.

Dualism of this form is usually adopted on the ground that it must be true, and often rejected on the ground that it can't be true. I myself believe that though the truth of dualism of mind and body is conceivable, it is implausible. There are better alternatives, even if the best hasn't been thought of yet. I argued in the last chapter that reality can't be just physical reality. Still, the relation between the mental and the physical is probably more intimate than it would be if dualism were true.

The main objection to dualism is that it postulates an additional, nonphysical substance without explaining how *it* can support subjective mental states whereas the brain can't. Even if we conclude that mental events are not simply physical events, it doesn't follow that we can explain their place in the universe by summoning up a type of substance whose sole function is to provide them with a medium. There are two points here. First, postulating such a substance doesn't explain how it can be the subject of mental states. If there were a thing that lacked mass, energy, and spatial dimensions, would that make it easier to understand how there could be something it was like to *be* that thing? The real difficulty is to make sense of the assignment of essentially subjective states to something which belongs to the objective order. Second, no reason has been given to think that if we could find a place for mental states in the world by attaching them to a nonphysical substance, we could not equally well find a place for them in something that also has physical properties.

The fact that mental states are not physical states because they can't be objectively described in the way that physical states can doesn't mean that they must be states of something different. The falsity of physicalism does not require nonphysical substances. It requires only that things be true of conscious beings that cannot, because of their subjective character, be reduced to physical terms. Why should the possession of physical properties by the body not be compatible with its possession of mental properties—through some very close interdependence of the two? (Perhaps, as Spinoza believed, the properties are ultimately the same, but that would have to be at a level deeper than either the mental or the physical.)

I suppose I should also consider the "no-ownership" view according to which mental events are not properties or modifications of anything, but simply occur, neither in a soul nor in the body—though they are causally related to what happens in the body. But I don't really find this view intelligible. *Something* must be there in advance, with the potential of being affected with mental manifestations, if lighting a match is to produce a visual experience in a perceiver. This potential must have a preexisting basis: experiences can't be created out of nothing any more than flames can. Of course this 'medium' might be of any kind: it might even be an all-pervading world soul, the mental equivalent of space-time, activated by certain kinds of physical activity wherever they occur. No doubt the correct model has never been thought of.

Nevertheless, I want to proceed on a less adventurous track. Because of the apparent intimacy of the relation between the mental and its physical conditions, and because of a continued attachment to the metaphysics of substance and attribute, I am drawn to some kind of dual aspect theory. This is probably due to lack of imagination, but I still want to explore the possibilities and problems of a theory of this type. Though it is probably nothing more than pre-Socratic flailing about, I believe it will be useful to see what happens if we try to think about the mind in these terms.[1]

To talk about a dual aspect theory is largely hand waving. It is only to say roughly where the truth might be located, not what it is. If points of view are irreducible features of reality, there is no evident reason why they shouldn't belong to things that also have weight, take up space, and are composed of cells and ultimately of atoms. One can formulate the view by saying that the brain has nonphysical properties, but that is just a label for the position and one must be careful to recognize that it doesn't by itself increase our understanding any more than the postulation of a nonphysical substance does. The main question, how anything in the world can have a subjective point of view, remains unanswered.

I want to talk about certain problems that face a dual aspect theory. Behind them all is one that I don't really know how to formulate. Despite

---

1. Though it isn't always clear what should count as a dual aspect theory, versions of the view have been held by several contemporary philosophers: Strawson (1); Hampshire (2); Davidson (2); O'Shaughnessy.

my defense of mental ontology in the last chapter, I can't shake the feeling that Wittgenstein may have been right when he famously said that
the decisive move in the conjuring trick has been made when we talk of
mental states and processes and leave their nature undecided—later we
will learn more about them (Wittgenstein (2), sec. 308). It may be a complete mistake to think that we can learn more about the true constitution
of thoughts and sensations, as we can about the true constitution of heat
or light. There is something deeply suspect about the whole enterprise
of fitting subjective points of view smoothly into a spatiotemporal world
of things and processes, and any dual aspect theory is committed to that
goal and that picture—the picture of appearances as part of reality.

But I can't say what might be wrong with it. The mind is after all a
biological product. When the cat hears the doorbell, this *must* be something going on, literally, in its head, not just in its furry little mind. Anyway, I won't directly attack this unformulated problem, which is as much
a problem for dualism or physicalism as it is for a dual aspect theory—
for they, too, are motivated by the desire for an integrated conception
of a single reality in which the mental and the physical are located in a
clear relation to one another.

Instead I'll discuss some problems that are more specifically about
dual aspect theory—problems about the intelligibility of the view that
one thing can have two sets of mutually irreducible essential properties,
mental and physical. The theory says that we are subjective organisms,
but this naturally gives rise to certain doubts. How can I be a complex
physical object? How can my subjective identity over time be determined
by the objective identity of an organism? How can experiences inhere in
something with physical parts? How can sensations have physical properties? Given the identifying characteristics of the mind—its special type
of unity both at a time and over time, and the subjectivity of its states—
it is not clear how there is room for the further objective characteristics
that dual aspect theory says it also has.

The irreducible subjectivity of the mental can make it seem radically
independent of everything else, so that if one rejects psychophysical
reductionism one is committed to the denial of any necessary connection
between the mental and the physical. But reduction is not the only form
of connection, and some of the things which make it appear that the
mental is independent from everything else are illusions.

There are two types of problems here, both deriving from the subjectivity of the mental. One has to do with the attribution to mental entities
and events of properties not entailed by mental concepts. The other has
to do with properties that seem incompatible with mental concepts.
Obviously the first type of problem is easier to deal with than the second,

since there is no reason why a concept need include all the essential properties of the thing to which it applies. So in dealing with problems apparently of the second type, it is worth asking whether they may not really be of the first type. In some cases, though not in all, I believe it turns out that apparent incompatibilities between the subjective and the physical can be resolved, and that our mental concepts leave room for this possibility.

Like all other concepts, mental concepts have their own form of objectivity which permits them to be applied in the same sense by different persons, in different situations, to different subjects. Mental phenomena belong to the world, and a given mental subject or mental state can be identified from different positions in the world. They are located, despite their subjectivity, in the objective order. Indeed, some mental concepts describe the subjective aspect of objectively observable states of affairs in a very direct way—such as the concepts of action, perception, and orientation. Gareth Evans (ch. 7) points out that we can be aware of these things in our own case without having to identify their subject, just as we can with more "inner" phenomena. Clearly, action has both mental and physical aspects.

However, this kind of objectivity does not settle the question of whether a dual aspect theory of the kind I have described might be correct—that is, whether the brain could be the subject of mental states. We have to consider whether the objectivity that attaches to mental subjects and subjective mental phenomena *as such* leaves open the possibility that they might also be characterized by physically objective properties of the kind the brain has. Certainly it doesn't entail anything of the kind. Having drawn a fundamental distinction in the last chapter between physical and mental objectivity, we must regard this as a serious problem.

I propose to approach it by considering first a particularly difficult mental concept, that of personal identity over time. I shall come to the traditional mind-body problem eventually—the problem of the relation between mental processes and brain processes. But the case of personal identity is a good place to begin, because of the vividness with which the self can appear to be quite independent of everything else: perfectly simple and purely subjective. It will allow us to present and criticize conceivability arguments for the independence of the mental, which also appear elsewhere.

2. The Self as Private Object

The concept of the self seems suspiciously pure—too pure—when we look at it from inside. The self is the ultimate private object, apparently lacking logical connections to anything else, mental or physical. When I consider my own individual life from inside, it seems that my existence in the future or the past—the existence of the same 'I' as this one—depends on nothing but itself. To capture my own existence it seems enough to use the word "I", whose meaning is entirely revealed on any occasion of its use. "I know what I mean by 'I.' I mean *this*!" (as one might think that the concept of a phenomenological quality like sweetness is fully captured in the thought "the same as *this*").

My nature then appears to be at least conceptually independent not only of bodily continuity but also of all other subjective mental conditions, such as memory and psychological similarity. It can seem, in this frame of mind, that whether a past or future mental state is mine or not is a fact not analyzable in terms of any relations of continuity, psychological or physical, between that state and my present state. The migration of the self from one body to another seems conceivable, even if it is not in fact possible. So does the persistence of the self over a total break in psychological continuity—as in the fantasy of reincarnation without memory. If all these things really are possible, I certainly can't be an organism: I must be a pure, featureless mental receptacle.

The apparently strict, perfect, and unanalyzable identity of the self has tempted some to objectify its existence by postulating a similarly disconnected soul designed expressly for the purpose, and otherwise characterized negatively. But such a thing seems inadequate to bear the weight of personal identity, which seems to escape all attempts to define it. We can see this in the classical debates about personal identity between Locke on the one hand and Reid and Butler on the other. Both sides seem to be right in their rejection of the other side, but wrong in their positive theories.

Locke (ch. 27) seems right in asserting that a divergence of same self from either same soul or same body is conceivable. This reflects the truth that the self cannot be defined as a kind of object, either physical or nonphysical, but must be understood as same subjective consciousness.[2] What Locke claimed was that if a soul were postulated as the individual that gave identity to the self, it would drop out as irrelevant to the actual operation of that idea. Kant makes a similar point in the third paralogism (Kant (1), pp. 362–6).

On the other hand, Butler[3] and Reid[4] seem right in arguing that sameness of self cannot be adequately defined in terms of memory continuity. And even more sophisticated analyses in terms of qualitative psycholog-

2. See Wachsberg, ch. 1.
3. Appendix 1, "Of Personal Identity."
4. "Of Memory," ch. 4.

ical continuity seem not to capture the essence of the idea of same consciousness, which seems to be something additional and not complex at
all. Discontinuity in the self seems compatible with any amount of continuity in psychological content, and vice versa. But Reid and Butler are
wrong in thinking that a nonphysical substance is therefore what the self
must be. That after all is just another occupant of the objective order.
An individual consciousness may depend for its existence on either a
body or a soul, but its identity is essentially that of a psychological subject, and not equivalent to anything else—not even anything else
psychological.

At the same time it seems to be something determinate and noncon-
ventional. That is, the question with regard to any future experience,
"Will it be mine or not?" seems to require a definite yes or no answer
(see Williams (2)). And the answer must be determined by the facts, and
not by an externally motivated and optional decision about how a word
is to be used or how it is convenient to cut up the world into pieces (as
might be possible with 'same nation', 'same restaurant', or 'same
automobile').

This seems to leave us with the conclusion that being mine is an irreducible, unanalyzable characteristic of all my mental states, and that it
has no essential connection with anything in the objective order or any
connection among those states over time.[5] Even if it is causally dependent on something else, such as the continued existence of my brain,
there is no way of finding this out on the basis of the idea of the self.
The question of whether a future experience will be mine or not
demands a definite answer without providing any way of determining
what that answer is, even if all other facts are known.

There must be something wrong with this picture, but it is not easy to
say what or to suggest a better one that admits essential connections
between personal identity and anything else. Like other psychological
concepts, the ordinary concept of the self breeds philosophical illusions
that are difficult to resist without falling into errors that are at least as
bad, and often shallower.

The apparent impossibility of identifying or essentially connecting the
self with anything comes from the Cartesian conviction that its nature is
fully revealed to introspection, and that our immediate subjective conception of the thing in our own case contains everything essential to it,
if only we could extract it. But it turns out that we can extract nothing,
not even a Cartesian soul. And the very bareness and apparent complete-

---

5. The conclusion is accepted by Madell. What unites all my experiences, he says, is simply
that they all have the irreducible and unanalyzable property of "mineness."

ness of the concept leaves no room for the discovery that it refers to something that has other essential features which would figure in a richer account of what I really am. Identification of myself with an objectively persisting thing of whatever kind seems to be excluded in advance.

The first step in resisting this conclusion is to deny that the concept of myself, or any other psychological concept, is or could be as purely subjective as the Cartesian assumption takes it to be. As I said earlier, picking up a famous point of Wittgenstein's, even subjective concepts have their appropriate objectivity. In the previous chapter I discussed the possibility of extending the idea of mental objectivity to cover more than the range of mental phenomena with which we are subjectively familiar, but here I want to concentrate on the more limited objectivity that characterizes even those ordinary mental concepts, including personal identity, which we can all apply in the first person to ourselves.

Some of the more radical experiments of imagination that lead to the apparent detachment of the self from everything else result from delusions of conceptual power. It is an error, though a natural one, to think that a psychological concept like personal identity can be understood through an examination of my first-person concept of self, apart from the more general concept of 'someone' of which it is the essence of 'I' to be the first-person form. I would add only that the full conditions of personal identity cannot be extracted from the concept of a person at all: they cannot be arrived at a priori.

The concept of 'someone' is not a generalization of the concept of 'I'. Neither can exist without the other, and neither is prior to the other. To possess the concept of a subject of consciousness an individual must be able in certain circumstances to identify himself and the states he is in without external observation. But these identifications must correspond by and large to those that can be made on the basis of external observation, both by others and by the individual himself. In this respect 'I' is like other psychological concepts, which are applicable to states of which their subjects can be aware without the observational evidence used by others to ascribe those states to them.

As with other concepts, however, we cannot immediately infer the nature of the thing referred to from the conditions of our possession of the concept. Just as adrenalin would exist even if no one had ever thought about it, so conscious mental states and persisting selves could exist even if the concepts didn't. Given that we have these concepts, we apply them to other beings, actual and possible, who lack them. The natural (and treacherous) question then becomes, what *are* these things, apart from the concepts which enable us to refer to them? In particular, what is this self which I can reidentify without the observational evidence used by others to reidentify it? The problem, with regard to the self as with regard to sensations, is how to avoid the error of false objectification, or objectification of the wrong form, of something that does not conform to the physical conception of objective reality.

There must be a notion of objectivity which applies to the self, to phenomenological qualities, and to other mental categories, for it is clear that the idea of a mistake with regard to my own personal identity, or with regard to the phenomenological quality of an experience, makes sense. I may falsely remember making a witty remark that in fact was made in my presence by someone else; I may think falsely that the way something tastes to me now is the same as it tasted to me yesterday; I may think that I am someone I am not. There is a distinction between appearance and reality in this domain as elsewhere. Only the objectivity underlying this distinction must be understood as objectivity with regard to something subjective—mental rather than physical objectivity.

In the case of sensation, the reality is itself a form of appearance, and the distinction one between real appearance and apparent appearance. This cannot be captured by something which is just like an ordinary object or physical property, except that it is visible to only one person. But the correct account of it is extremely difficult, because the conditions of objectivity in the application of psychological concepts do not enter noticeably into each application of those concepts, especially in the first person. They are hidden, because the concepts seem perfectly simple.

When a mental concept seems simple and unanalyzable, there is a philosophical temptation to interpret it as referring to a privately accessible something, which the subjective appearance of the self, or of phenomenological sameness, is the appearance *of*. I believe Wittgenstein in the *Investigations* has made a convincing case that if we construe mental concepts this way, the private something drops out as irrelevant, which shows that there is something wrong with the construal (secs. 200–300, approximately). His argument was offered with respect to sensations: it was designed to show that sensation terms were not the names of private features or objects of experience such as sense data were supposed to be. Similarity or difference of sensations is similarity or difference of sensory appearances, not of something that appears.

The argument is in part a *reductio*: Even if every sensation were the perception of a private object or feature, the sensation would be not the thing itself but its appearing to us in a certain way. Even if the thing changed, the sensation would be the same if it appeared the same. Thus the object drops out as irrelevant to the operation of the concept. (This need not imply incorrigibility with regard to our sensations, since there can be divergence between an appearance and our beliefs about it. It is the appearance itself to which the sensation term refers.)

The other aspect of the argument—the general private language argument—is too complex to discuss adequately here. Wittgenstein claims that there could be no concept of a necessarily private object of experience—that is, a type of thing that was in principle detectable by only one person—since no distinction could exist between the correct and incorrect sincere application of such a concept: adherence to or deviation from the rule for its application by its sole user. All concepts, including concepts of how things appear to us, must admit this distinction. The rule for their use cannot collapse into the individual user's sincere application of them. Otherwise there is nothing he is *saying about* a thing in applying the term to it. To mean something by a term I must be able to make sense of the possibility that my actual use of the term has deviated from that meaning without my knowing it. Otherwise my use doesn't bring with it any meaning apart from itself.

Wittgenstein believes that psychological concepts meet the condition of being governed by objective rules, in virtue of the connection between first-person and third-person ascription. That is the sort of objectivity appropriate to what is essentially subjective.

Whether or not we accept his positive account, with its famous obscurity and reticence, I believe his point that mental concepts are sui generis is correct. They refer not to private objects like souls and sense data but to subjective points of view and their modifications—even though the range of mental phenomena is not limited to those we ourselves can identify subjectively. The question is how to apply to the problem of personal identity this general idea that mental concepts do not refer to logically private objects of awareness.

3. Personal Identity and Reference

Identity is not similarity. The conditions of objectivity for sensations cannot be directly transferred to the self, because being mine is not a phenomenological quality of my experiences and, as with other types of thing, qualitative similarity is here neither a necessary nor a sufficient condition of numerical identity. Still, some sort of objectivity must characterize the identity of the self, otherwise the subjective question whether a future experience will be mine or not will be contentless: *nothing* will make an answer right or wrong. What kind of objectivity can this be?

There are two possible types of answer. One explains the identity of the self in terms of other psychological concepts, thus making its objectivity parasitic on theirs. This is the family of explanations of personal identity in terms of some form or other of psychological continuity—psychological continuity broadly conceived to include action, emotion, and intention as well as thought, memory, and perception. The other type of answer treats personal identity as an independent psychological concept, so that the self is something that underlies the psychological continuities where they exist but has no necessary or sufficient conditions specifiable in terms of them.

This second type of answer is what I shall defend. I believe that whatever we are told about continuity of mental content between two stages of experience, the issue logically remains open whether they have the same subject or not. In addition, it is clearly part of the idea of my identity that I could have led a completely different mental life, from birth. This would have happened, for example, if I had been adopted at birth and brought up in Argentina. The question is how this idea of the same subject can meet the conditions of objectivity appropriate for a psychological concept: how it can express an identity that is subjective (not merely biological) but at the same time admits the distinction between correct and incorrect self-identification.

Even if such a thing cannot be defined in terms of psychological continuities, it will be closely connected with them. Most of my self-reidentifications, and most reidentifications of me by others, refer to stages linked to the present directly or indirectly by memory, intention, and so forth. But here as elsewhere the reality can diverge from the evidence. The idea of myself is the idea of something to which memory and externally observable continuity of mental life stand in an evidential relation—something which can at one time subjectively reidentify itself in memory, expectation, and intention, and can be observationally reidentified as the same person by others, but which *is* something in its own right. In other words, I am rejecting the view that the person is merely the grammatical or logical subject of mental and physical predicates ascribed on the usual grounds. Those grounds provide only evidence of personal identity, rather than criteria of it.

The question is whether this reach of the concept beyond the introspective and observational evidence and the correlation between them permits us to interpret it as referring to something with still further features—something with a nature of its own. If so, then those features can supply further conditions of personal identity which may determine an answer to the question whether someone will be me, in cases where the usual psychological evidence leaves the question unsettled. The idea is that the ordinary conditions of application of the concept point to something further to which the concept refers but whose essence it does not capture.

This is possible only on the assumption that the concept of the self does not tell us fully what kind of things we are. But that assumption seems to me to be true. Our idea of ourselves is one whose exact extension is determined in part by things we don't necessarily know simply in virtue of, or as a condition of, having the concept: our true nature and the principle of our identity may be partly hidden from us. This is a familiar enough situation with regard to other concepts. It is obviously true of definite descriptions, and Kripke and Putnam have argued that it is also true of proper names and natural kind terms, even if they cannot be analyzed as definite descriptions in disguise.[6] But it is harder to accept with respect to the self, because of the apparent subjective completeness of that idea. It does not immediately seem, like the concept of 'gold' or the concept of 'cat' or the concept of 'Cicero', to have any blank space which can be filled in by discoveries as to the true internal constitution of the thing. Nothing seems to correspond here to our general idea of a kind of substance or a kind of living creature whose complete nature we do not know. The idea of the self seems not to be a partial specification of anything.

In general, when a term refers to something whose real nature is not fully captured by the subjective conditions for the term's application, those conditions will nevertheless dictate what kind of thing it is about the world that determines the real nature of the referent. Thus before the development of chemistry, gold already referred to a type of metal, and this determined which kinds of further discoveries about its material composition would reveal the true nature of gold. Specifically it determined that certain common observable properties of gold would have to be explained by its true nature, and that the explanation would have to be uniform for different samples of gold, in terms of something of which they were all composed.

What might perform the function of the idea of a 'type of metal', or 'type of material substance' in the case of ourselves? Subjects of experience are not like anything else. While they do have observable properties, the most important thing about them is that they are subjects, and it is their subjective mental properties that must be explained if we are

---

6. Kripke (1); Putnam (1); see Searle for an argument that this view doesn't involve as big a departure from the Fregean tradition of analysis of sense and reference as is often supposed.

to be able to identify them with anything in the objective order. As with gold, there is also an implication of generality—that the self in my case is something of the same kind as it is for other persons.

I suggest that the concept of the self is open to objective "completion" provided something can be found which straddles the subjective-objective gap. That is, the concept contains the possibility that it refers to something with further objective essential features beyond those included in the psychological concept itself—something whose objective persistence is among the necessary conditions of personal identity—but only if this objectively describable referent is in a strong sense the basis for those subjective features that typify the persistent self.

This is where dual aspect theory comes in. The concept of the self does not of course imply the truth of dual aspect theory. The concept implies only that if it refers at all, it must refer to something essentially subjective, often identifiable nonobservationally in the first person and observationally in the third, which is the persisting locus of mental states and activities and the vehicle for carrying forward familiar psychological continuities when they occur. So far as the *concept* is concerned, this might turn out to be any of a number of things or there might be no such thing. But if dual aspect theory is correct, then it is as a matter of fact the intact brain—customarily found in a living animal of a certain kind but not in principle inseparable from it. I could lose everything but my functioning brain and still be me, and it might even be possible by some monstrosity of genetic engineering to produce a brain that had never been part of an animal but was nevertheless an individual subject.

Let me repeat that this is not offered as an analysis of the concept of the self but as an empirical hypothesis about its true nature. My concept of myself contains the blank space for such an objective completion, but does not fill it in. I am whatever persisting individual in the objective order underlies the subjective continuities of that mental life that I call mine. But a type of objective identity can settle questions about the identity of the self only if the thing in question is both the bearer of mental states and the cause of their continuity when there is continuity. If my brain meets these conditions then the core of the self—what is essential to my existence—is my functioning brain. As things are, the rest of my body is integrally attached to it and is also part of me, so I am not just my brain: I weigh more than three pounds, am more than six inches high, have a skeleton, etc. But the brain is the only part of me whose destruction I could not possibly survive. The brain, but not the rest of the animal, is essential to the self.

Let me express this with mild exaggeration as the hypothesis that I am my brain, and let me leave aside for now problems that could be raised about what counts as the same brain (for example, about its dependence on the sameness of the organism). On the evidence, the intact brain seems to be responsible for the maintenance of memory and other psychological continuities and for the unity of consciousness. If in addition the mental states are themselves states of the brain, which is therefore not just a physical system, then the brain is a serious candidate for being the self—even though, as I shall admit, it does not meet all the intuitive conditions on the idea of the self.

What I am is whatever is in fact the seat of the person TN's experiences and his capacity to identify and reidentify himself and his mental states, in memory, experience, and thought, without relying on the sort of observational evidence that others must use to understand him. That I am a person requires that I have this capacity, but not that I know what makes it possible. In fact, I do not know in any detail what is responsible for it, and others need not know it either in order to know that I am a person. So far as their concept of me and my conception of myself as a self are concerned, the possibility of my subjective identification of myself could depend on a soul, or on the activity of a part of my brain, or on something else that I can't even imagine. If it depended on a soul, then my identity would be the identity of that soul, so long as the soul persisted in the condition which, when it occupies TN, allows it to undergo TN's experiences and enables TN to identify himself and his states subjectively. If it could persist thus after the death of the body, I could exist after death. (Perhaps I could even exist without memory of my present life.)

If, on the other hand, my mental life depends entirely on certain states and activities of my brain, and if some form of dual aspect theory is correct, then that brain in those states (not just in its physical states) is what I am, and my survival of the destruction of my brain is not conceivable. However, I may not know that it is not conceivable, because I may not know the conditions of my own identity. That knowledge is not provided by my subjective idea of myself. It is not provided by the idea others have of me either. Something is left open by the idea which has to be discovered.

The point is a familiar one, taken from Kripke's views about reference. The essence of what a term refers to depends on what the world is actually like, and not just on what we have to know in order to use and understand the term. I may understand and be able to apply the term "gold" without knowing what gold really is—what physical and chemical conditions anything must meet to be gold. My prescientific idea of gold, including my knowledge of the perceptible features by which I identify samples of it, includes a blank space to be filled in by empirical discov-

eries about its intrinsic nature. Similarly I may understand and be able
to apply the term "I" to myself without knowing what I really am. In
Kripke's phrase, what I use to *fix the reference* of the term does not tell
me everything about the nature of the referent.

This can give rise to those illusions, discussed earlier, concerning the
detachability of the self from everything else. Since I do not know what
I really am, it seems possible so far as what I *do* know is concerned—
epistemically possible—that I may really be any of a variety of things
(soul, brain, etc.) that could underlie my capacity for subjective self-identification. Various accounts of my real nature, and therefore various
conditions of my identity over time, are compatible with my concept of
myself as a self, for that concept leaves open the real nature of what it
refers to. This is equally true of other people's concept of me as a self,
since it is true of the concept of a self or continuing subject of consciousness in general.

Now this may lead me to think I can imagine myself surviving the
death of my brain even if that is not in fact imaginable. On the other
hand, it may equally well lead me to think I can imagine myself surviving
the destruction of my soul—or anything else. What I imagine may be
possible so far as what I know about my nature is concerned, but may
not be possible so far as my actual nature is concerned. In that case I
will not have imagined *myself* surviving the death of my brain, but will
merely have confused epistemic with metaphysical possibility. In trying
to conceive of my survival after the destruction of my brain, I will not
succeed in referring to myself in such a situation if I am in fact my brain.
Even if I conceive of a soul with the appropriate memories surviving the
death of my body, that will not be to conceive of myself surviving, if in
fact I am not a soul.[7]

It is the mistake of thinking that my concept of myself alone can reveal
the objective conditions of my identity that leads to the giddy sense that
personal identity is totally independent of everything else, so that it
might even be possible for you and me to switch selves although *nothing*
else changed, either physically, or psychologically, or in any other
respect. Adding in the third person and second person conditions of
application of the concept doesn't complete the specification of its reference either, though. The fact that I can reidentify persons by looking
at them, tracing their movements, and listening to what they say does
not mean that I know their true nature. I do not know it (though I may
conjecture about it), unless I know not only what makes them the organisms they are, but also what makes them capable of subjective, nonob-

7. Cf. Williams (1), p. 44: "At least with regard to the self, the imagination is too tricky a
thing to provide a reliable road to the comprehension of what is logically possible."

servational self-knowledge extending over time. Without this information, the concept of personal identity will not tell me what I am or what they are.

4. Parfit

This approach to personal identity is not without its problems. If what we are depends not only on our concept of ourselves but on the world, the possibility arises that nothing in the world satisfies the concept perfectly. The best candidate may be in various ways defective.

To what extent could it turn out that our true nature diverges from our intuitive conception of ourselves? More specifically, does the hypothesis that I am my brain require the abandonment of central features of my conception of myself; and if so, does this cast doubt on the hypothesis? If the best candidate for what I am is my brain, the best candidate may not be good enough; in that case the proper conclusion would be that the self which we intuitively take ourselves to be does not exist at all.

The problems I have in mind are those which have led Derek Parfit to conclude that the most natural prereflective concept of the self does not apply to us. To say that I am, as a matter of fact rather than of definition, essentially my brain does not solve those acute puzzles he has posed, concerning the apparent unique simplicity and indivisibility of the self.

Parfit begins by describing a natural conception of the self which he calls the Simple View.[8] This says that nothing can be me unless (a) it determines a completely definite answer to the question whether any given experience—past, present, or future—is mine or not (the all-or-nothing condition); and (b) it excludes the possibility that two experiences both of which are mine should occur in subjects that are not identical with each other (the one-one condition). Subjectively, these seem like nonnegotiably essential features of myself.

But the brain is a complex organ, neither simple nor indivisible. While there are no examples of gradual replacement of its cells over time, for example by grafting, there are the famous examples of its division by commissurotomy, with striking psychological effects.[9] As Parfit points out, if my survival depends on the continued functioning of my brain, it seems that I might be able to survive as two distinct selves, not identical with each other, and this would violate the one-one condition. Similarly, he has observed, if the cells of my brain could be gradually replaced, with

8. This term appears in Parfit (1), and I shall use it for convenience here, even though in the much more elaborate treatment of Parfit (2), several different non-reductionist views are distinguished. See p. 210, for example.
9. Parfit (2), sec. 87. I have discussed these cases in Nagel (2).

accompanying gradual transformation of my personality and memories, then a future experience might belong to someone about whom there was *no answer* to the question whether he was me or not, and this would violate the all-or-nothing condition (Parfit (2), secs. 84–6).

Parfit himself concludes that the conditions of the ordinary concept of personal identity cannot be met if such things are possible. Our ordinary concept is so tied to the Simple View that it can actually apply only if the mental life of each of us has a subject that makes such things impossible—something like a simple, indivisible soul. If, as appears to be the case, the subject of our mental lives is a complex, divisible brain, then it is not a suitable bearer of the identity of the self, and we should adopt instead a more complex view of our own nature. His suggestion is that we should withdraw our special self-interested concern from the identity of the organ that underlies our mental lives, and be concerned instead about the psychological continuities themselves, however they are produced, which may hold to different degrees and need not be one-one.

I believe, however, that the actual cause is what matters—even if it doesn't satisfy the conditions of the Simple View. This would be one of those cases where some of our most important beliefs about the referent of one of our concepts may be false, without its following that there is no such thing. In ordinary circumstances, the brain satisfies the one-one and all-or-nothing conditions, but it does not do so necessarily. Nevertheless, it seems to me to be something without which I could not survive—so that if a physically distinct replica of me were produced who was psychologically continuous with me though my brain had been destroyed, it would not be me and its survival would not be as good (for me) as my survival. This assumes that there can be an empirically discoverable answer to the question what I in fact am which falsifies some of my fundamental beliefs about what kind of thing I am.[10]

The difficult issue is whether the answer I propose falsifies such fundamental beliefs that it is disqualified. The brain does not guarantee an absolutely definite and unique answer to the question whether any of the centers of consciousness existing at some past or future time are mine or not. The possibility of its being split or partially replaced implies this. It is therefore hard to internalize a conception of myself as identical with my brain: if I am told that my brain is about to be split, and that the left

---

10. My position is rather like Mackie's, except that he recommends it as a conceptual reform, inconsistent with our present concept of personal identity. He also thinks that further reform might be in order if it turned out that we could produce exact physical and psychological replicas of people: then even brain identity could be dropped as a condition of personal identity. See Mackie (1), pp. 201–3.

half will be miserable and the right half euphoric, there is no form that my subjective expectations can take, because my idea of myself doesn't allow for divisibility—nor do the emotions of expectation, fear, and hope.

It might be asked, if I am prepared to abandon the Simple View over such resistance, why not go all the way with Parfit and abandon the identification of the self with the typical underlying cause of the mental life—regarding psychological continuity, however maintained, as what is really important? What is the advantage of continuing to identify myself with a *thing* whose survival need be neither one-one nor all-or-nothing? Why isn't it enough to identify myself as a person in the weaker sense in which this is the subject of mental predicates but not a separately existing thing—more like a nation than a Cartesian ego?

I don't really have an answer to this, except the question-begging answer that one of the conditions that the self should meet if possible is that it be something in which the flow of consciousness and the beliefs, desires, intentions, and character traits that I have all take place—something beneath the contents of consciousness, which might even survive a radical break in the continuity of consciousness. If there were no such thing, then the idea of personal identity would be an illusion, but we are not in that situation. Even if nothing can be found to fill this role which satisfies the condition of the Simple View, the brain with its problematic conditions of identity in certain cases is still better than nothing. And it is a possible hypothesis that I am my brain, since it is not ruled out by the apparent subjective conceivability of my moving to a different brain. That seems conceivable, to the extent that it does, only so far as what my incomplete concept of myself tells me; and that isn't a reliable basis for deciding what is possible. If a dual aspect theory is correct, then it is not possible for my mental life to go on in a different brain.[11]

11. I have not begun to do justice here to the Proustian exhaustiveness of Parfit's arguments. Among other things, he comments in sec. 98 on some remarks in an earlier draft of the present chapter which I have since abandoned—having to do with possible "series-persons" whose bodies are destroyed and replicated regularly. I said there that they could reasonably regard replication as survival, though we could not. Parfit replies that we can choose what type of beings to think of ourselves as—and he defines "Phoenix Parfit" as the individual he is who *would* survive replication. This is an ingenious suggestion, but there must be some objective limits to the freedom to reconstrue oneself, or it will become hollow. I can't defeat death by identifying myself as "Proteus Nagel", the being who survives if *anyone* survives. "Phoenix Parfit" seems to me also an abuse, though clearly a lesser one, of the privilege of choosing one's own identity.

But I also think now that the series-persons themselves, if they were of human origin, might simply be deluded to think they survive replication—and that like us, they would not be entitled to the "Phoenix" concept of themselves. (For discussion of some related cases, see Shoemaker, secs. 10 and 16.)

5. Kripke

Let me return finally to the mind-body problem more widely conceived. Something analogous to these conclusions about the self applies to the relations between mental events and the brain in general. Even though the concept of a mental event implies that it is something irreducibly subjective, the possibility remains that it is also something physical, because the concept doesn't tell us everything about it.

One consequence is that Kripke's conceivability argument against materialism (Kripke (1), pp.144–55) can't prove that mental events aren't also physical events, in the sense required by dual aspect theory. Since dual aspect theory is not a form of materialism by Kripke's definition (it does not hold that a physical description of the world is a complete description of it), Kripke's arguments were not specifically directed against it. Moreover, in his views about the necessary connection between personal identity and biological origin he seems close to a dual aspect theory himself (see p. 155n).

Still, dual aspect theory does hold that mental processes are identical with physical processes, and so might be thought vulnerable to modal arguments that work against the materialist form of the identity. In fact it is immune to those arguments, and enables us to explain as illusions of contingency the modal premises on which they depend. This is so for reasons that invoke Kripke's own theory of reference.

Kripke argues that I can imagine a headache existing without any brain state, and since this can't be explained as the imagination of something that only feels like a headache but isn't, it provides strong reason for believing that a headache really can exist without a brain state, and therefore that it can't be a brain state.

But the apparent conceivability of a mental event occurring without a brain event may be due to the fact that mental concepts grasp only one aspect of the mind. If I could *know* that I could conceive of the occurrence of my current visual experience without the occurrence of any particular event in my brain, then I could know that the two were not identical. But I cannot know this simply on the basis of my concept of visual experience or on the basis of having the experience. A visual experience is a state whose phenomenological properties enable me to identify it without external observation of myself, but this does not mean that I know its complete nature. If in fact it is an activity—at once phenomenological and physical—of the brain, then I cannot conceive of its occurring without the brain, and the conviction that I can is just the product of a confusion between epistemic and metaphysical possibility.

So far as the ordinary concepts of pain or visual experience are concerned, they might have no essential properties that are not mental. But those concepts may not capture all the essential properties of the phenomena. It may in fact be impossible for a mental event not to have physical properties as well, even though we cannot form a conception of such a necessary link. If this is true, then the illusion that I can imagine my present experiences occurring without a brain does not have to be explained as the imagination of something else which *is* possible (as Kripke suggests would be necessary to block the argument). It may be nothing but an unsuccessful attempt to imagine something I do not know to be *im*possible—an attempt that I therefore don't know is unsuccessful.

Similarly, it is easy to assume that I can conceive that when other people are in exactly the same physical condition as I am in when I feel pain, they feel something entirely different, or nothing at all. But in fact this may not be conceivable, because the physical conditions and the subjective experience may be two aspects of the same thing. My concept and personal experience of pain cannot tell me either that its independence of a brain state is conceivable or that it is not.

In general, Kripke's view about how we must explain away an illusion of conceivability is too restrictive. If something is in fact impossible and yet we seem to be able to conceive of it, this need not mean we are actually conceiving of something else similar to it which *is* possible. We may be conceiving of no real possibility at all, though we fail to realize it because we do not know certain necessary truths about the things we are thinking about.

We have at present no conception of how a single event or thing could have both physical and phenomenological aspects, or how if it did they might be related. But our ideas of pain, of anger, of auditory or visual experience no more guarantee us a complete knowledge of the nature of those things, even when we are undergoing them ourselves, than do our concepts of gold, tiger, or digestion.

There is one important difference, however, between psychological concepts and certain other natural kind concepts. As Kripke points out, the reference of "heat" or "gold" is originally fixed by contingent features of those things—how they feel or look to us, where they are found, etc. But the reference of "pain" is fixed not by a contingent feature of pain, but by its intrinsic phenomenological character, the way it feels. This makes a difference to the process of discovering more about the nature of the thing. If we fix a reference by some contingent feature, what we discover about the essential nature of the referent will be only contingently related to that feature. But if, as in the case of pain, our original concept already picks the thing out by an essential feature, then further discoveries about its nature will have to be of things connected with this feature in a more intimate way.

I am not sure of the exact character of the connection. Let us suppose, as seems unavoidable, that according to dual aspect theory both the mental and the physical properties of a mental event are essential properties of it—properties which it could not lack. Can one thing have two distinct essential properties that are not necessarily connected with each other? This seems possible if the two properties are different aspects of a single essence. For example, a tiger is essentially both a mammal and a carnivore, but those two properties are not always linked. They are linked in the case of the tiger because both are parts of the essential nature of the species—a particular type of mammal that can live only on certain kinds of food, and has other essential characteristics as well. We assume these features are more closely linked than the elements of a peanut butter and jelly sandwich or a string quartet.

Presumably something similar would have to be true if mental processes had physical properties. They couldn't just be *slapped together*. Both must be essential components of a more fundamental essence. As for the connection between them, it seems likely that in a rationally designed world the mental properties would be at least supervenient on the physical—a particular type of physical process being a sufficient but not inevitably a necessary condition of a particular type of mental process. There might also be some necessary connections going in both directions—for example, certain physical processes might be both necessary and sufficient for what I call the taste of chocolate.

Why doesn't this admission of the possibility of necessary connections between the mental and the physical conflict with my a priori claim that the mental cannot be reduced to or analyzed in terms of the physical? (I owe the question to Michael Gebauer.) The answer is that psychophysical reduction requires a more direct necessary connection than the one envisioned here. First, if both mental and physical aspects of a process are manifestations of something more fundamental, the mental need not entail the physical nor vice versa even if both are entailed by this something else. More interesting is the case where the only possible basis of a certain mental process is something which also has specific physical properties—and vice versa. Then there is a necessary identity between the mental and the physical process, but it is not of the right kind to support traditional psychophysical reduction, because it proceeds through the intermediate link of a more basic term, neither mental nor physical, of which we have no conception.

We cannot directly see a necessary connection, if there is one, between phenomenological pain and a physiologically described brain state any more than we can directly see the necessary connection between increase in temperature and pressure of a gas at constant volume. In the latter case the necessity of the connection becomes clear only when we descend to the level of molecular description: till then it appears as a contingent correlation. In the psychophysical case we have no idea whether there is such a deeper level or what it could be; but even if there is, the possibility that pain might be necessarily connected with a brain state at this deeper level does not permit us to conclude that pain might be directly analyzable in physical or even topic-neutral terms.

Even if such a deeper level existed, we might be permanently blocked from a general understanding of it. It would have both subjective and objective aspects, and while the objective physical manifestations would be within our grasp, the subjective manifestations would have to be as various as the variety of possible conscious organisms. No creature of any particular subjective type could hope to grasp them all, and a general understanding would depend on how much could be captured by what I have called a general objective concept of mind.

6. Panpsychism and Mental Unity

I don't wish to pretend that dual aspect theory is perfectly intelligible, and that it is only an empirical question whether it is true or not. Though it has its attractions as a way of unifying the radically disparate elements that give rise to the mind-body problem, it also has the faintly sickening odor of something put together in the metaphysical laboratory.

One unsettling consequence of such a theory is that it appears to lead to a form of panpsychism—since the mental properties of the complex organism must result from some properties of its basic components, suitably combined: and these cannot be merely physical properties, or else in combination they will yield nothing but other physical properties. If any two hundred pound chunk of the universe contains the material needed to construct a person, and if we deny both psychophysical reductionism and a radical form of emergence, then everything, reduced to its elements, must have proto-mental properties.[12]

What could these be, and how could they combine to form the mental states with which we are all familiar? It's hard enough to conceive of an organism having mental states and a point of view. But what kind of properties could atoms have (even when they are part of a rock) that

12. This argument is given more fully in Nagel (4), ch. 13.

could qualify as proto-mental; and how could *any* properties of the chemical constituents of a brain combine to form a mental life?

The combinatorial problem and the apparent outlandishness of ascribing "mental" properties to carbon atoms are aspects of a single conceptual difficulty. We cannot at present understand how a mental event could be composed of myriad smaller proto-mental events on the model of our understanding of how a muscle movement is composed of myriad physico-chemical events at the molecular level. We lack the concept of a mental part-whole relation. The mental may be divisible in time, but we can't in the ordinary sense think of it as divisible in space. Yet if mental events occur in a physically complex, spatially extended organism, they must have parts that in some way correspond to the parts of the organism in which they occur, and to the organic processes on which the different aspects of mental life depend. There must be a mental analogue of spatial volume and spatial complexity.[13]

An individual mind seems unified in a way that makes this difficult to imagine: everything going on in it at a given time seems to be present together—present, as we say, to a single subject. Of course this is something of a myth, as we can see by considering ordinary distraction, and sensations and thoughts at the periphery of consciousness,[14] not to mention the radical deconnection syndromes produced by brain damage, when speech and vision or vision and touch are put out of communication with each other in the same person—or the left half of the sensory field out of contact with the right. But the unity of consciousness, even if it is not complete, poses a problem for the theory that mental states are states of something as complex as a brain. Panpsychism is just a particularly startling manifestation of this problem.

If mental events are radically complex, like muscle contractions, then there will be microscopic processes occurring in arbitrarily small subparts of the brain which, in combination, constitute familiar global mental processes. It is already impossible to understand this for the macroscopic case of the two halves of the brain. When the corpus callosum is severed, the separate operation of each half seems to produce a recognizably mental life. Though what goes on in each half of the intact brain is presumably different from what goes on in the halves when separated, it still must be something quasi-mental. And it must be something which, when added to what goes on in the other half, constitutes a whole mental life! But what on earth can this be? We can ask the same question how-

13. See Stanton, pp. 76–9, for a related discussion.
14. For a complex quasi-spatial theory of the structure of the mind, see O'Shaughnessy, especially ch. 14.

ever we slice up the brain. The problem of understanding the proto-mental properties of more minute components of the central nervous system is essentially the same as this.

We can understand "components" of a mental process or experience at the purely mental level. We can analyze a sound or a flavor or an emotion into phenomenological or psychological aspects. We can analyze the visual field or our bodily sensations in the appropriate *phenomenologically* spatial terms. But all these complexities appear within the framework of subjective unity. We can't base an understanding of objective spatial complexity on such models.

This is one example of the difficulty of ascribing mental states to something that also has physical properties: how can a mental unit have physical parts? Perhaps the question depends on false assumptions about the part-whole relation. But it seems to me, precisely because of its impossibility, one of the most promising questions to concentrate on if we wish to generate new ideas about the mind-body problem.

7. The Possibility of Progress

What is needed is something we do not have: a theory of conscious organisms as physical systems composed of chemical elements and occupying space, which also have an individual perspective on the world, and in some cases a capacity for self-awareness as well. In some way that we do not now understand, our minds as well as our bodies come into being when these materials are suitably combined and organized. The strange truth seems to be that certain complex, biologically generated physical systems, of which each of us is an example, have rich nonphysical properties. An integrated theory of reality must account for this, and I believe that if and when it arrives, probably not for centuries, it will alter our conception of the universe as radically as anything has to date.

I may be thought unduly pessimistic about the capacity of physics to provide a complete understanding of reality. I have often heard it seriously urged that we must expect a physical understanding of the mind on inductive grounds. After all, physics and chemistry have explained so much already—witness their recent successes in biology. And we are undeniably physical organisms; we now have partial biochemical explanations of heredity, growth, metabolism, muscle movement, etc. Why not wait and see what physics and biochemistry will say about the real nature of the mind?

The cited examples of scientific progress are impressive, but they are not the only ones. I believe an example of another kind, more relevant to the present subject, can be found within physics itself, in the shift that had to occur to accommodate electromagnetic phenomena. This was beyond the power of the older concepts and theories of mechanics, including action at a distance. Electricity and magnetism could not be analyzed in terms of mechanical concepts of matter in motion.

The shift from the universe of Newton to the universe of Maxwell required the development of a whole new set of concepts and theories— new types of concepts—specifically devised to describe and explain these newly explored phenomena. This was not merely the complex application, as in molecular biology, of fundamental principles already known independently. Molecular biology does not depend on new ultimate principles or concepts of physics or chemistry, like the concept of field. Electrodynamics did.[15]

Since Maxwell there have been further revolutions, and with Einstein the apparent division between radically different types of physical phenomena has apparently been superseded by a deeper unity. But none of this could have happened if everyone had insisted that it must be possible to account for any physical phenomenon by using the concepts that are adequate to explain the behavior of planets, billiard balls, gases, and liquids. An insistence on identifying the real with the mechanical would have been a hopeless obstacle to progress, since mechanics is only one form of understanding, appropriate to a certain limited though pervasive subject matter.

Similarly, I believe that physics is only one form of understanding, appropriate to a broader but still limited subject matter. To insist on trying to explain the mind in terms of concepts and theories that have been devised exclusively to explain nonmental phenomena is, in view of the radically distinguishing characteristics of the mental, both intellectually backward and scientifically suicidal. The difference between mental and physical is far greater than the difference between electrical and mechanical. We need entirely new intellectual tools, and it is precisely by reflection on what appears impossible—like the generation of mind out of the recombination of matter—that we will be forced to create such tools.

It may be that the eventual result of such exploration will be a new unity that is not reductionist. We and all other creatures with minds seem to be composed of the same materials as everything else in the uni-

15. Maxwell himself, though he developed the theory of the electromagnetic field, seems to have thought it would ultimately be given a mechanical explanation. Acceptance of the electromagnetic field as an irreducible feature of physical reality came only at the end of the nineteenth century, with Lorentz. See P. M. Harman.

verse. So any fundamental discoveries we make about how it is that we have minds, and what they really are, will reveal something fundamental about the constituents of the universe as a whole. In other words, if a psychological Maxwell devises a general theory of mind, he may make it possible for a psychological Einstein to follow with a theory that the mental and the physical are really the same. But this could happen only at the end of a process which began with the recognition that the mental is something completely different from the physical world as we have come to know it through a certain highly successful form of detached objective understanding. Only if the uniqueness of the mental is recognized will concepts and theories be devised especially for the purpose of understanding it. Otherwise there is a danger of futile reliance on concepts designed for other purposes, and indefinite postponement of any possibility of a unified understanding of mind and body.

IV

THE OBJECTIVE SELF

1. Being Someone

One acute problem of subjectivity remains even after points of view and subjective experiences are admitted to the real world—after the world is conceded to be full of people with minds, having thoughts, feelings, and perceptions that cannot be completely subdued by the physical conception of objectivity. This general admission still leaves us with an unsolved problem of particular subjectivity. The world so conceived, though extremely various in the types of things and perspectives it contains, is still centerless. It contains us all, and none of us occupies a metaphysically privileged position. Yet each of us, reflecting on this centerless world, must admit that one very large fact seems to have been omitted from its description: the fact that a particular person in it is himself.

What kind of fact is that? What kind of fact is it—if it is a fact—that I am Thomas Nagel? How *can* I be a particular person?

The question actually has two halves, which correspond to the two directions from which one can approach the relation between subjective and objective standpoints. First: how can a particular person be me? Given a complete description of the world from no particular point of view, including all the people in it, one of whom is Thomas Nagel, it seems on the one hand that something has been left out, something absolutely essential remains to be specified, namely which of them I am. But

54

on the other hand there seems no room in the centerless world for such a further fact: the world as it is from no point of view seems complete in a way that excludes such additions; it is just the world, and everything true of TN is already in it. So the first half of the question is this: how can it be true of a particular person, a particular individual, TN, who is just one of many persons in an objectively centerless world, that he is me?

The second half of the question is perhaps less familiar. It is this: how can I be *merely* a particular person? The problem here is not how it can be the case that I am this one rather than that one, but how I can be anything as specific as a particular person in the world at all—any person. The first question arises from the apparent completeness of a description of TN and the world which does not say whether or not he is me. This second question arises from something about the idea of 'I'. It can seem that as far as what I really am is concerned, any relation I may have to TN or any other objectively specified person must be accidental and arbitrary. I may occupy TN or see the world through the eyes of TN, but I can't *be* TN. *I* can't be a mere *person*. From this point of view it can appear that "I am TN," insofar as it is true, is not an identity but a subject-predicate proposition. Unless you have had this thought yourself it will probably seem obscure, but I hope to make it clearer.

The two halves of the question correspond to two directions in which it can be asked: How can TN be me? How can I be TN? They are not just questions about me and TN, for any of you can ask them about himself. But I shall speak about the subject in the first person, in the Cartesian style which is intended to be understood by others as applying in the first person to themselves.

It isn't easy to absorb the fact that I am contained in the world at all. It seems outlandish that the centerless universe, in all its spatiotemporal immensity, should have produced me, of all people—and produced me by producing TN. There was no such thing as me for ages, but with the formation of a particular physical organism at a particular place and time, suddenly there *is* me, for as long as the organism survives. In the objective flow of the cosmos this subjectively (to me!) stupendous event produces hardly a ripple. How can the existence of one member of one species have this remarkable consequence?

These questions may strike you as ridiculous even if you ask them about yourself, but I am trying to evoke a sharp intuitive puzzle and to convince you that there is something real in it, even if its verbal expression is faulty. There may be cases where a trick of language produces the illusion of a question where none really exists, but this is not one of them. We can feel the question apart from its verbal expression, and the difficulty is to pose it without turning it into something superficial, or inviting answers that may seem adequate to its verbal form but that don't really meet the problem beneath the surface. In philosophy the question is never just what we shall say. We can reach that point only after considerable effort has been made to express and deal with inchoate perplexity. Amazement that the universe should have come to contain a being with the unique property of being me is a very primitive feeling.

Let me begin with what I called the first half of the question—How can TN be me?—for its treatment will lead naturally into the second half.

The conception of the world that seems to leave no room for me is a familiar one that people carry around with them most of the time. It is a conception of the world as simply existing, seen from no particular perspective, no privileged point of view—as simply there, and hence apprehensible from various points of view. This centerless world contains everybody, and it contains not only their bodies but their minds. So it includes TN, an individual born at a certain time to certain parents, with a specific physical and mental history, who is at present thinking about metaphysics.

It includes all the individuals in the world, of every kind, and all their mental and physical properties. In fact it *is* the world, conceived from nowhere within it. But if it is supposed to be this world, there seems to be something about it that cannot be included in such a perspectiveless conception—the fact that one of those persons, TN, is the locus of my consciousness, the point of view from which I observe and act on the world.

This seems undeniably to be a further truth, in addition to the most detailed description of TN's history, experiences, and characteristics. Yet there seems no other way of expressing it than by speaking of me or my consciousness; so it appears to be a truth that can be stated and understood only from my perspective, in the first person. And therefore it seems to be something for which there is no room in the world conceived as simply there, and centerless.

If we suppose 'being me' to be any objective property whatever of the person TN, or any relation of that person to something else, the supposition quickly collapses. We are bound to include that property or that relation in the objective conception of the world that contains TN. But as soon as it has been made an aspect of the objective TN, I can ask again, "Which of these persons am I?" and the answer tells me something further. No further fact expressible without the first person will do the trick: however complete we make the centerless conception of the world, the fact that I am TN will be omitted. There seems to be no room for it in such a conception.

But in that case there seems to be no room for it in the world. For when we conceive of the world as centerless we are conceiving of it as it is. Not being a solipsist, I do not believe that the point of view from which I see the world is *the* perspective of reality. Mine is only one of the many points of view from which the world is seen. The centerless conception of the world must include all the innumerable subjects of consciousness on a roughly equal footing—even if some see the world more clearly than others. So what is left out of the centerless conception—the supposed fact that I am TN—seems to be something for which there is no room in the world, rather than something which cannot be included in a special kind of description or conception of the world. The world cannot contain irreducibly first-person facts. But if that is so, the centerless conception cannot be said to leave something *out*, after all. It includes everying and everyone, and what it does not include is not there to be left out. What is left out must exist, and if the world as a whole really doesn't have a particular point of view, how can one of its inhabitants have the special property of being me? I seem to have on my hands a fact about the world, or about TN, which both must exist (for how things are would be incomplete without it) and cannot exist (for how things are cannot include it).

If this problem has a solution, it must be one which brings the subjective and objective conceptions of the world into harmony. That would require an interpretration of the irreducibly first-person truth that TN is me and some development of the centerless conception of the world to accommodate that interpretation. If it is not a fact about the centerless world that I am TN, then something must be said about what else it is, for it certainly seems not only true but extremely nontrivial. Indeed, it seems to be one of the most fundamental things I can say about the world. I shall argue that it provides a clear example of the ineliminability of indexicals from a complete conception of the world, and that it also reveals something about each of us.[1]

2. A Semantic Diagnosis

The problem is to account for the content of the thought, and its truth, without trivializing it. I think this can be done. But first it is necessary to

1. It is worth mentioning that this problem is similar in form to a problem about the reality of time. There is no room in a fully objective description of the world for the identification of a particular time as the present. The temporal order of events can be described from no point of view within the world, but their presence, pastness, or futurity cannot. Yet the fact that it is *now* the particular time that it is seems to be a fundamental truth which we cannot do without. The tenseless description of the temporal order is essentially incomplete, for it leaves out the passage of time. See Dummett (2).

dispose of an objection. It might be held that the statement that I am TN, when posing as the expression of a philosophical thought, is really devoid of significant content—and that the only thought it can be used to express is trivial or at any rate unremarkable: apart from a simple question of semantics, there is no real problem here. I am going to take up this deflationary claim before offering a positive account, because it will help us to locate what is distinctive about the philosophical self-locating thought, and how it transcends the mundane semantics of the first person.[2]

The objection is this. Only someone who misunderstands the logic of the first person can believe that "I am TN" states an important truth that cannot be stated without the first person. When we look at the actual use of that form of words, we see that although it is a special kind of statement, it states no special kind of truth—for it is governed by truth-conditions that are entirely expressible without indexicals.

The statement "I am TN" is true if and only if uttered by TN. The statement "Today is Tuesday" is true if and only if uttered on Tuesday. To understand the operation of such statements it is necessary only to place them in their context of utterance in an entirely centerless conception of the world; then we see that their significance and truth does not depend on the existence of further "facts," expressible only in the first person (or the present tense), which mysteriously seem to be both essential aspects of the world and completely excluded from it. The sense of these statements requires only that the world contain ordinary people, like TN, who use the first person in the ordinary way. Their sense is not the same as that of the third-person statements that express their truth-conditions, since their truth depends on who makes them. They can't be *replaced* by third-person analyses. But the facts that make them true or false are all expressible by such third-person statements.

On this view the world just is the centerless world, and it can be spoken and thought about from within partly with the help of expressions like "I," which form statements whose truth-conditions depend on the context of utterance, a context which in turn is fully accommodated in the centerless conception of the world. Everything about the use of the first person can be analyzed without using the first person. This completely general point provides a simple answer to our question, what kind of truth is it that one of the people in the world, TN, is me? It is a quite minimal truth: the statement "I am TN" is automatically and uninterestingly true if TN makes it. Once we understand its logic, no further question arises as to what it says.

What makes it appear at first glance to express a mysterious further

2. Here I discuss only one version of the objection. Others are taken up in Nagel (6).

fact about the world is that it can't be translated into any statement which doesn't include "I" or some other indexical. It might be translated approximately as "The person making this statement is TN", but then we are still left with the residual indexical "this statement," and *its* relation to the centerless world. The point is that indexicals in general are untranslatable into objective terms, because they are used to refer to persons, things, places, and times from a particular position within the world, without depending on the user's objective knowledge of that position. It is elementary that one can't translate a statement whose truth depends on its context of utterance into one whose truth does not.

This cannot be used to manufacture a metaphysical mystery. "I am TN" seems to state a further truth about the world only because I don't have to know who I am in order to use "I" to refer to TN. That is an instance of the general rule that a speaker can refer to himself as "I" without knowing who, objectively, he is. Hardly a profound truth about the universe.

My objection to this semantic diagnosis is that it doesn't make the problem go away.

It should be a sign of something wrong with the argument that the corresponding semantic point about "now" would not defuse someone's puzzlement about what kind of fact it is that a particular time is the present. The truth-conditions of tensed statements can be given in tenseless terms, but that does not remove the sense that a tenseless description of the history of the world (including the description of people's tensed statements and their truth values) is fundamentally incomplete, because it cannot tell us which time *is* the present. Similarly, the fact that it is possible to give impersonal truth-conditions for first-person statements does not enable one to make those statements without using the first person. The crucial question is whether the elimination of this particular first-person thought in favor of its impersonal truth-conditions leaves a significant gap in our conception of the world. I think it does.

There is nothing wrong with the semantic account of "I" in itself, as one indexical among others, though there is room for disagreement over the details. It tells you how the first person functions in ordinary communication, as when someone asks, "Who owns the blue Ford with the New Jersey license plates that's parked in my driveway?" and you say, "I do;" or when someone asks, "Which of you is TN?" and I say "I am." There is no inclination to believe that such statements express anything remarkable: ordinary objective facts about the speaker make them true or false. Nor is the existence of any special kind of fact involved in the *making* of such statements. They are just utterances produced by ordinary individuals like TN.

But none of this either explains or exorcises the quite different thought that I have when I say to myself, looking at the world full of people saying "I own that car," or "I am his wife," that of all the people in this centerless world, the one I am is TN: this thinking subject regards the world through the person TN. When TN says to someone he meets at a cocktail party, "Hello, I'm TN," that is not the thought he is communicating. Ordinary first-person statements like "Hello, I'm TN" or "I own that car" convey information that others can express in the third person, though they are not synonymous with the corresponding third-person statements. But even when all that public information about the person TN has been included in an objective conception, the additional thought that TN is *me* seems clearly to have further content. And it is important that the content is startling.

While the semantic objection doesn't diagnose the problem out of existence, it suggests that a solution must be general in some sense. The perception that gives rise to the problem can be expressed in the first person by anyone, and not only by me, so the use of "I" here must be governed by semantic conditions general enough to be applicable to any person who can have the thought: my first understanding of it may be in application to my own case, but in some sense I also understand what someone else would mean by it. We should therefore be able to say something about the content of the first-person thought that is also comprehensible to others. We need an analogue of the informational content of ordinary first-person statements if we are to explain why "I am TN" seems to say more about the world than that the person speaking is called TN. This requires a specific account of how the word "I" refers when it is used to express the philosophical thought.

3. The Centerless View

To explain the special form of reference of "I" in this case we must turn to what I called the second half of the question, the half that asks not how a particular person, TN, can be me, but rather how I can be anything so specific as a particular person at all (TN as it happens).

How can this possibly be puzzling? What else could I be but a particular person?

As a first explanation we could say it is puzzling because my being TN (or whoever I in fact am) seems accidental, and my identity can't be accidental. So far as what I am essentially is concerned, it seems as if I just *happen* to be the publicly identifiable person TN—as if what I really am, this conscious subject, might just as well view the world from the perspective of a different person. The real me occupies TN, so to speak; or the publicly identifiable person TN contains the real me. From a purely objective point of view my connection with TN seems arbitrary.

To arrive at this idea I begin by considering the world as a whole, as if from nowhere, and in those oceans of space and time TN is just one person among countless others. Taking up that impersonal standpoint produces in me a sense of complete detachment from TN, who is reduced to a momentary blip on the cosmic TV screen. How can I, who am thinking about the entire, centerless universe, be anything so specific as *this*: this measly, gratuitous creature existing in a tiny morsel of space-time, with a definite and by no means universal mental and physical organization? How can I be anything so *small* and *concrete* and *specific*?

I know this sounds like metaphysical megalomania of an unusually shameless kind. Merely being TN isn't good enough for me: I have to think of myself as the world soul in humble disguise. In mitigation I can plead only that the same thought is available to any of you. You are all subjects of the centerless universe and mere human or Martian identity should seem to you arbitrary. I am not saying that I individually am the subject of the universe: just that I am *a* subject that can have a conception of the centerless universe in which TN is an insignificant speck, who might easily never have existed at all. The self that seems incapable of being anyone in particular is the self that apprehends the world from without rather than from a standpoint within it. But there need not be only one such self.

The picture is this. Essentially I have no particular point of view at all, but apprehend the world as centerless. As it happens, I ordinarily view the world from a certain vantage point, using the eyes, the person, the daily life of TN as a kind of window. But the experiences and the perspective of TN with which I am directly presented are not the point of view of the true self, for the true self has no point of view and includes in its conception of the centerless world TN and his perspective among the contents of that world. It is this aspect of the self which is in question when I look at the world as a whole and ask, "How can TN be me? How can I be TN?" And it is what gives the self-locating philosophical thought its peculiar content.

This first description of the problem has to be modified, however. To evoke the problem I have spoken loosely of the "true" self and its essence, but in the previous chapter it was argued that we cannot discover our essential nature a priori—that it may include features not contained in our conception of ourselves. The fact that I seem able in imagination to detach this perspectiveless or objective self from TN does not show that it is a distinct thing, or that nothing else about TN belongs to me essentially. It does not show, as may at first appear, that the connection between me and TN is accidental. It does show, however, that something essential about me has nothing to do with my perspective and position in the world. That is what I want to examine.

How do I abstract the objective self from the person TN? By treating the individual experiences of that person as data for the construction of an objective picture. I throw TN into the world as a thing that interacts with the rest of it, and ask what the world must be like from no point of view in order to appear to him as it does from his point of view. For this purpose my special link with TN is irrelevant. Though I receive the information of his point of view directly, I try to deal with it for the purpose of constructing an objective picture just as I would if the information were coming to me indirectly. I do not give it any privileged status by comparison with other points of view.[3]

This naturally is an idealization. Much of my conception of the world comes directly from what TN delivers to me. I have had to rely heavily on TN's experience, language, and education, and I do not constantly subject each of his pretheoretical beliefs to detached assessment. But in a general way, I try to do with his perspective on the world what I could do if information about it were reaching me thousands of miles away, not pumped directly into my sensorium but known from outside.

The objective self should be able to deal with experiences from any point of view. It in fact receives those of TN directly, but it treats on an equal footing those it receives directly and those others it learns about only indirectly. So far as its essential nature is concerned, it could base its view of the world on a different set of experiences from those of TN, or even none at all coming directly from a perspective within the world, for in itself it has no such perspective. It is the perspectiveless subject that constructs a centerless conception of the world by casting all perspectives into the content of that world.

Suppose all the nerves feeding sensory data to my brain were cut but I were somehow kept breathing and nourished and conscious. And suppose auditory and visual experiences could be produced in me not by sound and light but by direct stimulation of the nerves, so that I could be fed information in words and images about what was going on in the

---

3. The idea of the objective self has something in common with the "metaphysical subject" of Wittgenstein's *Tractatus* 5.641, though I stop short of excluding it from the world entirely. The metaphysical subject is the logical limit that we reach if all the contents of the mind, including its objective thoughts, are thrown into the world as properties of TN. The objective self is the last stage of the detaching subject before it shrinks to an extensionless point. It also has a good deal in common with Husserl's transcendental ego, though I do not share the "transcendental idealism" to which his phenomenology is committed (Husserl, sec. 41). Neither do I accept the solipsism of the *Tractatus*.

world, what other people saw and heard, and so forth. Then I would have a conception of the world without having any perspective on it. Even if I pictured it to myself I would not be viewing it from where I was. It might even be said that in the sense in which I am now TN, I would under those circumstances not be anyone.[4]

As things are, the objective self is only part of the point of view of an ordinary person, and its objectivity is developed to different degrees in different persons and at different stages of life and civilization. I have already discussed some aspects of that development. The basic step which brings it to life is not complicated and does not require advanced scientific theories: it is simply the step of conceiving the world as a place that includes the person I am within it, as just another of its contents— conceiving myself from outside, in other words. So I can step away from the unconsidered perspective of the particular person I thought I was. Next comes the step of conceiving from outside all the points of view and experiences of that person and others of his species, and considering the world as a place in which these phenomena are produced by interaction between these beings and other things. That is the beginning of science. And again it is I who have done this stepping back, not only from an individual viewpoint but from a specific type of viewpoint.

Because a centerless view of the world is one on which different persons can converge, there is a close connection between objectivity and intersubjectivity. By placing TN in a world along with everyone else, I pursue a conception of him and his point of view that others may share. At the first stage the intersubjectivity is still entirely human, and the objectivity is correspondingly limited. The conception is one that only other humans can share. But if the general human perspective is then placed in the same position as part of the world, the point of view from which this is done must be far more abstract, so it requires that we find within ourselves the capacity to view the world in some sense as very different creatures also might view it when abstracting from the specifics of their type of perspective. The pursuit of objectivity requires the cultivation of a rather austere universal objective self. While we can't free it entirely of infection with a particular human view and a particular historical stage, it represents a direction of possible development toward a universal conception and away from a parochial one.

The objective self that I find viewing the world through TN is not unique: each of you has one. Or perhaps I should say each of you is one, for the objective self is not a distinct entity. Each of us, then, in addition

---

4. For a similar fantasy see "Where Am I?" in Dennett. But more closely related to what I am saying is the fascinating discussion of self-identification in Evans, pp. 249–55.

to being an ordinary person, is a particular objective self, the subject of a perspectiveless conception of reality.

We can account for the content of the philosophical thought "I am TN" if we understand the "I" as referring to me qua subject of the impersonal conception of the world which contains TN. The reference is still essentially indexical, and cannot be eliminated in favor of an objective description, but the thought avoids triviality because it depends on the fact that this impersonal conception of the world, though it accords no special position to TN, is attached to and developed from the perspective of TN.

This also helps to account for the feeling of amazement that is part of the philosophical thought—a strange sense that I both am and am not the hub of the universe. I see myself as its subject or center when I think of the universe, including TN, in purely objective terms, and identify myself simply as the objective self which is the subject of this conception rather than as anything within its range, such as a physical organism, or the occupant of a particular position in space and time, or the subject of an individual perspective within the world. But I am also TN, and the world is not TN's world: he is not its subject. He is just one of the people in it, and none of them is its center or focal point. So I am both the logical focus of an objective conception of the world and a particular being in that world who occupies no central position whatever.

This explains how the thought "I am TN" can have a content that is nontrivial and indeed almost as remarkable as it seems at first. While it does not translate the thought into one about the world objectively conceived, it does identify an objective fact corresponding to the thought, which explains how it can have a content interesting enough to account for its philosophical "flavor". Because TN possesses or is an objective self, I can state a significant identity by referring to myself indexically under that aspect as "I," and again under the objective aspect of the publicly identifiable person TN—and I can make both references from the single standpoint of the possessor of an objective conception of the world that contains TN. This conception does not itself imply anything about who its subject is, or even that he exists at all inside the world being described. So far as the content of the objective view goes, it might be of a world in which I, its subject, never have existed and never will. But since the objective conception *has* a subject, the possibility of its presence in the world is there, and it allows me to bring the subjective and objective views together. Until they are brought together in this way, the purely objective conception will leave something out which is both true and remarkable.

Other forms of self-reference don't have the same impact. I can locate myself in the world in different ways: for example I can think, "This hangover is TN's hangover." That brings the subjective and objective standpoints together, but it doesn't account for the import and sense of uncanniness that attach to the philosophical realization that I am TN. The "I" must refer in virtue of something larger whose inclusion in the world is not obvious, and the objective self qualifies for the role.

This problem has something in common with others, about informative identity statements that cannot be easily explained in terms of facts about the world. What kind of fact is it, for instance, that Hesperus is Phosphorus, or that water is H_2O? If these are identities, and their terms are not definite descriptions but rigid designators (See Kripke (1)), they seem to correspond only to the "facts" that Venus is identical with itself or that water is the substance that it is. To explain why the statements are nevertheless not trivial it is necessary to give an account of how the terms refer—an account of our different types of relation to the things we talk about which explains the significance of the statements. There are rival theories about these matters, but they all attempt to put us into an objectively comprehensible relation to the things we are talking about.

The thought "I am TN" presents a similar problem, though the task is not to explain my dual relations of reference to something outside myself, but rather my dual relation to the entire world. In a sense there are two forms of reference to TN here, and we must explain the first-person reference in this philosophical context without trivializing the thought. What happens when I consider the world objectively is that an aspect of my identity comes into prominence which was previously concealed and which produces a sense of detachment from the world. It then comes to seem amazing that I am in fact attached to it at any particular point. The content of the thought that I am TN can be understood once the objective conception closes over itself by locating the subject that forms it at a particular point in the world that it encompasses.

The objective self is the only significant aspect under which I can refer to myself subjectively that is supplied by the objective conception of the world alone—because it is the subject of that conception. And it is the only aspect of myself that can seem at first only accidentally connected with TN's perspective—a self that views the world *through* the perspective of TN. I believe the possibility of this self-locating thought reveals something about us all, and not only about those who find it remarkable.

What it reveals is not just a peculiar form of self-reference but an aspect of what we are. The objective self functions independently enough to have a life of its own. It engages in various forms of detachment from and opposition to the rest of us, and is capable of autonomous development. In the following chapters I shall sometimes speak as if it were a distinct part of the mind. While it shouldn't be given a metaphysical interpretation, this way of speaking is not altogether innocent. In some sense I think the same faculty or aspect of us is involved in the various functions of objectivity, and I think it is something real. However we may have come to it, and however incomplete our development of its capacities, it places us both inside and outside the world, and offers us possibilities of transcendence which in turn create problems of reintegration. The reconciliation of these two aspects of ourselves is a primary philosophical task of human life—perhaps of any kind of intelligent life.

The existence of our objective capacity does not seem explicable in terms of something more basic—that is it does not seem reducible to simpler, more reactive, less creative mental operations. It turns out that the human mind is much larger than it needs to be merely to accommodate the perspective of an individual human perceiver and agent within the world. Not only can it form the conception of a more objective reality, but it can fill this out in a progression of objective steps that has already led far beyond the appearances. And it enables different individuals, starting from divergent viewpoints, to converge on conceptions that can be universally shared. In what follows I won't try to account for the existence of the objective self, but will explore its operation in various domains and discuss some of the problems it creates.

V

KNOWLEDGE

1. Skepticism

The objective self is responsible both for the expansion of our under-standing and for doubts about it that cannot be finally laid to rest. The extension of power and the growth of insecurity go hand in hand, once we place ourselves inside the world and try to develop a view that accom-modates this recognition fully.

The most familiar scene of conflict is the pursuit of objective knowl-edge, whose aim is naturally described in terms that, taken literally, are unintelligible: we must get outside of ourselves, and view the world from nowhere within it. Since it is impossible to leave one's own point of view behind entirely without ceasing to exist, the metaphor of getting outside ourselves must have another meaning. We are to rely less and less on certain individual aspects of our point of view, and more and more on something else, less individual, which is also part of us. But if initial appearances are not in themselves reliable guides to reality, why should the products of detached reflection be different? Why aren't they either equally doubtful or else valid only as higher-order impressions? This is an old problem. The same ideas that make the pursuit of objectivity seem necessary for knowledge make both objectivity and knowledge seem, on reflection, unattainable.

Objectivity and skepticism are closely related: both develop from the idea that there is a real world in which we are contained, and that appearances result from our interaction with the rest of it. We cannot accept those appearances uncritically, but must try to understand what our own constitution contributes to them. To do this we try to develop an idea of the world with ourselves in it, an account of both ourselves and the world that includes an explanation of why it initially appears to us as it does. But this idea, since it is we who develop it, is likewise the product of interaction between us and the world, though the interaction is more complicated and more self-conscious than the original one. If the initial appearances cannot be relied upon because they depend on our constitution in ways that we do not fully understand, this more complex idea should be open to the same doubts, for whatever we use to understand certain interactions between ourselves and the world is not itself the object of that understanding. However often we may try to step outside of ourselves, something will have to stay behind the lens, something in us will determine the resulting picture, and this will give grounds for doubt that we are really getting any closer to reality.

The idea of objectivity thus seems to undermine itself. The aim is to form a conception of reality which includes ourselves and our view of things among its objects, but it seems that whatever forms the conception will not be included by it. It seems to follow that the most objective view we can achieve will have to rest on an unexamined subjective base, and that since we can never abandon our own point of view, but can only alter it, the idea that we are coming closer to the reality outside it with each successive step has no foundation.

All theories of knowledge are responses to this problem. They may be divided into three types: *skeptical*, *reductive*, and *heroic*.

Skeptical theories take the contents of our ordinary or scientific beliefs about the world to go beyond their grounds in ways that make it impossible to defend them against doubt. There are ways we might be wrong that we can't rule out. Once we notice this unclosable gap we cannot, except with conscious irrationality, maintain our confidence in those beliefs.

Reductive theories grow out of skeptical arguments. Assuming that we do know certain things, and acknowledging that we could not know them if the gap between content and grounds were as great as the skeptic thinks it is, the reductionist reinterprets the content of our beliefs about the world so that they claim less. He may interpret them as claims about possible experience or the possible ultimate convergence of experience among rational beings, or as efforts to reduce tension and surprise or to increase order in the system of mental states of the knower, or he may even take some of them, in a Kantian vein, to describe the limits of all possible experience: an inside view of the bars of our mental cage. In any case on a reductive view our beliefs are not about the world as it is in itself—if indeed that means anything. They are about the world as it appears to us. Naturally not all reductive theories succeed in escaping skepticism, for it is difficult to construct a reductive analysis of claims about the world which has any plausibility at all, without leaving gaps between grounds and content—even if both are within the realm of experience.

Heroic thories acknowledge the great gap between the grounds of our beliefs about the world and the contents of those beliefs under a realist interpretation, and they try to leap across the gap without narrowing it. The chasm below is littered with epistemological corpses. Examples of heroic theories are Plato's theory of Forms together with the theory of recollection, and Descartes' defense of the general reliability of human knowledge through an a priori proof of the existence of a nondeceiving God.[1]

I believe, first of all, that the truth must lie with one or both of the two realist positions—skepticism and heroism. My terminology reflects a realistic tendency: from the standpoint of a reductionist, heroic epistemology would be better described as quixotic. But I believe that skeptical problems arise not from a misunderstanding of the meaning of standard knowledge claims, but from their actual content and the attempt to transcend ourselves that is involved in the formation of beliefs about the world. The ambitions of knowledge and some of its achievements are heroic, but a pervasive skepticism or at least provisionality of commitment is suitable in light of our evident limitations.

Though a great deal of effort has been expended on them recently, definitions of knowledge cannot help us here. The central problem of epistemology is the first-person problem of what to believe and how to justify one's beliefs—not the impersonal problem of whether, given my beliefs together with some assumptions about their relation to what is actually the case, I can be said to have knowledge. Answering the question of what knowledge is will not help me decide what to believe. We must decide what our relation to the world actually is and how it can be changed.

Since we can't literally escape ourselves, any improvement in our beliefs has to result from some kind of self-transformation. And the thing we can do which comes closest to getting outside of ourselves is to form a detached idea of the world that includes us, and includes our

1. A fourth reaction is to turn one's back on the abyss and announce that one is now on the other side. This was done by G. E. Moore.

possession of that conception as part of what it enables us to understand about ourselves. We are then outside ourselves in the sense that we appear inside a conception of the world that we ourselves possess, but that is not tied to our particular point of view. The pursuit of this goal is the essential task of the objective self. I shall argue that it makes sense only in terms of an epistemology that is significantly rationalist.

The question is how limited beings like ourselves can alter their conception of the world so that it is no longer just the view from where they are but in a sense a view from nowhere, which includes and comprehends the fact that the world contains beings which possess it, explains why the world appears to them as it does prior to the formation of that conception, and explains how they can arrive at the conception itself. This idea of objective knowledge has something in common with the program of Descartes, for he attempted to form a conception of the world in which he was contained, which would account for the validity of that conception and for his capacity to arrive at it. But his method was supposed to depend only on propositions and steps that were absolutely certain, and the method of self-transcendence as I have described it does not necessarily have this feature. In fact, such a conception of the world need not be developed by proofs at all, though it must rely heavily on a priori conjecture.[2]

In discussing the nature of the process and its pitfalls, I want both to defend the possibility of objective ascent and to understand its limits. We should keep in mind how incredible it is that such a thing is possible at all. We are encouraged these days to think of ourselves as contingent organisms arbitrarily thrown up by evolution. There is no reason in advance to expect a finite creature like that to be able to do more than accumulate information at the perceptual and conceptual level it occupies by nature. But apparently that is not how things are. Not only can we form the pure idea of a world that contains us and of which our impressions are a part, but we can give this idea a content which takes us very far from our original impressions.

The pure idea of realism—the idea that there is a world in which we are contained—implies nothing specific about the relation between the appearances and reality, except that we and our inner lives are part of reality. The recognition that this is so creates pressure on the imagination to recast our picture of the world so that it is no longer the view from here. The two possible forms this can take, skepticism and objective

---

2. The idea is much closer to what Bernard Williams calls the absolute conception of reality, which is a more general description of Descartes' idea of knowledge. See Williams (7).

knowledge, are products of one capacity: the capacity to fill out the pure idea of realism with more or less definite conceptions of the world in which we are placed. The two are intimately bound together. The search for objective knowledge, because of its commitment to a realistic picture, is inescapably subject to skepticism and cannot refute it but must proceed under its shadow. Skepticism, in turn, is a problem only because of the realist claims of objectivity.

Skeptical possibilities are those according to which the world is completely different from how it appears to us, and there is no way to detect this. The most familiar from the literature are those in which error is the product of deliberate deception by an evil demon working on the mind, or by a scientist stimulating our brain in vitro to produce hallucinations. Another is the possibility that we are dreaming. In the latter two examples the world is not totally different from what we think, for it contains brains and perhaps persons who sleep, dream, and hallucinate. But this is not essential: we can conceive of the possibility that the world is different from how we believe it to be in ways that we cannot imagine, that our thoughts and impressions are produced in ways that we cannot conceive, and that there is no way of moving from where we are to beliefs about the world that are substantially correct. This is the most abstract form of skeptical possibility, and it remains an option on a realist view no matter what other hypotheses we may construct and embrace.

2. Antiskepticism

Not everyone would concede either this skepticism or the realism on which it depends. Recently there has been a revival of arguments against the possibility of skepticism, reminiscent of the ordinary language arguments of the fifties which claimed that the meanings of statements about the world are revealed by the circumstances in which they are typically used, so that it couldn't be the case that most of what we ordinarily take to be true about the world is in fact false.

In their current versions these arguments are put in terms of reference rather than meaning.[3] What we refer to by the terms in our statements about the external world, for example—what we are really talking about—is said to be whatever *actually* bears the appropriate relation to the generally accepted use of those terms in our language. (This relation is left undefined, but it is supposed to be exemplified in the ordinary world by the relation between my use of the word 'tree' and actual trees, if there are such things.)

3. See for example Putnam (2), ch. 1.

The argument against the possibility of skepticism is a *reductio*. Suppose that I am a brain in a vat being stimulated by a mischievous scientist to think I have seen trees, though I never have. Then my word "tree" refers not to what we now call trees but to whatever the scientist usually uses to produce the stimulus which causes me to think, "There's a tree." So when I think that, I am usually thinking something true. I cannot use the word "tree" to form the thought that the scientist would express by saying I have never seen a tree, or the words "material object" to form the thought that perhaps I have never seen a material object, or the word "vat" to form the thought that perhaps I am a brain in a vat. If I were a brain in a vat, then my word "vat" would not refer to vats, and my thought, "Perhaps I am a brain in a vat," would not be true. The original skeptical supposition is shown to be impossible by the fact that if it were true, it would be false. The conditions of reference permit us to think that there are no trees, or that we are brains in a vat, only if this is not true.

This argument is no better than its predecessors. First, I can use a term which fails to refer, provided I have a conception of the conditions under which it would refer—as when I say there are no ghosts. To show that I couldn't think there were no trees if there were none, it would have to be shown that this thought could not be accounted for in more basic terms which would be available to me even if all my impressions of trees had been artificially produced. (Such an analysis need not describe my *conscious* thoughts about trees.) The same goes for "physical object". The skeptic may not be able to produce on request an account of these terms which is independent of the existence of their referents, but he is not refuted unless reason has been given to believe such an account impossible. This has not been attempted and seems on the face of it a hopeless enterprise.

A skeptic does not hold that all his terms fail to refer; he assumes, like the rest of us, that those that do not refer can be explained at some level in terms of those that do. When he says, "Perhaps I have never seen a physical object," he doesn't mean (holding up his hand), "Perhaps *this*, whatever it is, doesn't exist!" He means, "Perhaps I have never seen anything with the spatiotemporal and mind-independent characteristics necessary to be a physical object—nothing of the kind that I take physical objects to be." It has to be shown that he couldn't have *that* thought if it were true. Clearly we will be pushed back to the conditions for the possession of very general concepts. Nothing here is obvious, but it seems clear at least that a few undeveloped assumptions about reference will not enable one to prove that a brain in a vat or a disembodied spirit couldn't have the concept of mind-independence, for example. The main issue simply hasn't been addressed.

Second, although the argument doesn't work it wouldn't refute skepticism if it did. If I accept the argument, I must conclude that a brain in a vat can't think truly that it is a brain in a vat, even though others can think this about it. What follows? Only that I can't express my skepticism by saying, "Perhaps I'm a brain in a vat." Instead I must say, "Perhaps I can't even *think* the truth about what I am, because I lack the necessary concepts and my circumstances make it impossible for me to acquire them!" If this doesn't qualify as skepticism, I don't know what does.

The possibility of skepticism is built into our ordinary thoughts, in virtue of the realism that they automatically assume and their pretensions to go beyond experience. Some of what we believe must be true in order for us to be able to think at all, but this does not mean we couldn't be wrong about vast tracts of it. Thought and language have to latch onto the world, but they don't have to latch onto it directly at every point, and a being in one of the skeptic's nightmare situations should be able to latch onto enough of it to meet the conditions for formulating his questions.[4]

Critics of skepticism bring against it various theories of how the language works—theories of verifiability, causal theories of reference, principles of charity. I believe the argument goes in the opposite direction.[5] Such theories are refuted by the evident possibility and intelligibility of skepticism, which reveals that by "tree" I don't mean just anything that is causally responsible for my impressions of trees, or anything that looks and feels like a tree, or even anything of the sort that I and others have traditionally called trees. Since those things could conceivably not be trees, any theory that says they have to be is wrong.

The traditional skeptical possibilities that we can imagine stand for limitless possibilities that we can't imagine. In recognizing them we recognize that our ideas of the world, however sophisticated, are the products of one piece of the world interacting with part of the rest of it in ways that we do not understand very well. So anything we come to believe must remain suspended in a great cavern of skeptical darkness.

---

4. There is perhaps one form of radical skepticism which could be ruled out as unthinkable, by an argument analogous to the *cogito*: skepticism about whether I am the kind of being who can have thoughts *at all*. If there were possible beings whose nature and relation to the world was such that nothing they did could constitute thinking, whatever went on inside them, then I could not wonder whether I was such a being, because if I were, I wouldn't be thinking, and even to consider the possibility that I may not be thinking is to think. But most forms of skepticism are not this extreme.

5. This is a theme of Clarke's and Stroud's work on skepticism. See Stroud, pp. 205–6. Stroud's book is a highly illuminating discussion of skepticism and the inadequacy of most responses to it. He is nevertheless slightly more optimistic than I am about the possibility of finding something wrong with skepticism—and with the desire for an objective or external understanding of our position in the world that leads to it.

Once the door is open, it can't be shut again. We can only try to make our conception of our place in the world more complete—essentially developing the objective standpoint. The limit to which such development must tend is presumably unreachable: a conception that closes over itself completely, by describing a world that contains a being that has precisely that conception, and explaining how the being was able to reach that conception from its starting point within the world. Even if we did arrive at such a self-transcendent idea, that wouldn't guarantee its correctness. It would recommend itself as a possibility, but the skeptical possibilities would also remain open. The best we can do is to construct a picture that might be correct. Skepticism is really a way of recognizing our situation, though it will not prevent us from continuing to pursue something like knowledge, for our natural realism makes it impossible for us to be content with a purely subjective view.

3. Self-transcendence

To provide an alternative to the imaginable and unimaginable skeptical possibilities, a self-transcendent conception should ideally explain the following four things: (1) what the world is like; (2) what we are like; (3) why the world appears to beings like us in certain respects as it is and in certain respects as it isn't; (4) how beings like us can arrive at such a conception. In practice, the last condition is rarely met. We tend to use our rational capacities to construct theories, without at the same time constructing epistemological accounts of how those capacities work. Nevertheless, this is an important part of objectivity. What we want is to reach a position as independent as possible of who we are and where we started, but a position that can also explain how we got there.

In a sense, these conditions could also be satisfied by a conception of the world and our place in it that was developed by other beings, different from us; but in that case the fourth element would not involve self-referential understanding, as it does in the understanding of ourselves. The closest we can come to an external understanding of our relation to the world is to develop the self-referential analogue of an external understanding. This leaves us in no worse position than an external observer, for any being who viewed us from outside would have to face the problem of self-understanding in its own case, to be reasonably secure in its pretensions to understand us or anything else. The aim of objectivity would be to reach a conception of the world, including oneself, which involved one's own point of view not essentially, but only instrumentally, so to speak: so that the form of our understanding would be specific to ourselves, but its content would not be.

The vast majority of additions to what we know do not require any advance in objectivity: they merely add further information at a level that already exists. When someone discovers a previously undetected planet, or the chemical composition of a hormone, or the cause of a disease, or the early influences on a historical figure, he is essentially filling in a framework of understanding that is already given. Even something as fruitful as the discovery of the structure of DNA is in this category. It merely extended the methods of chemistry into genetics. Discoveries like this may be difficult to make, but they do not involve fundamental alterations in the idea of our epistemic relation to the world. They add knowledge without objective advance.

An advance in objectivity requires that already existing forms of understanding should themselves become the object of a new form of understanding, which also takes in the objects of the original forms. This is true of any objective step, even if it does not reach the more ambitious goal of explaining itself. All advances in objectivity subsume our former understanding under a new account of our mental relation to the world.

Consider for example the distinction between primary and secondary qualities, the precondition for the development of modern physics and chemistry. This is a particularly clear example of how we can place ourselves in a new world picture. We realize that our perceptions of external objects depend both on their properties and on ours, and that to explain both their effects on us and their interactions with each other we need to attribute to them fewer types of properties than they may initially appear to have.

Colin McGinn has argued convincingly that this is in the first instance an a priori philosophical discovery, not an empirical scientific one. Things have colors, tastes, and smells in virtue of the way they appear to us: to be red simply *is* to be the sort of thing that looks or would look red to normal human observers in the perceptual circumstances that normally obtain in the actual world. To be square, on the other hand, is an independent property which can be used to explain many things about an object, including how it looks and feels. (McGinn, ch. 7)

Once this is recognized and we consider how the various perceptible properties of objects are to be explained, it becomes clear that the best account of the appearance of colors will not involve the ascription to things of intrinsic color properties that play an ineliminable role in the explanation of the appearances: the way in which the appearances vary with both physical and psychological conditions makes this very implausible. Objective shape and size, on the other hand, enter naturally into an account of variable appearance of shape and size. So much is evident even if we have only a very rough idea of how as perceivers we are acted upon by the external world—an idea having to do primarily with the type of peripheral impact involved. It is then a short step to the conjecture that the appearances of secondary qualities are caused by other primary qualities of objects, which we can then try to discover.

The pressure to make an objective advance comes, here as elsewhere, from the incapacity of the earlier view of the world to include and explain itself—that is, to explain why things appear to us as they do. This makes us seek a new conception that can explain both the former appearances and the new impression that it itself is true. The hypothesis that objects have intrinsic colors in addition to their primary qualities would conspicuously fail this test, for it provides a poorer explanation of why they appear to have colors, and why those appearances change under internal and external circumstances, than the hypothesis that the primary qualities of objects and their effects on us are responsible for all the appearances.

Consider another example. Not all objective advances have been so widely internalized as this, and some, like general relativity and quantum mechanics, are advances beyond already advanced theories that are not generally accessible. But one huge step beyond common appearance was taken by Einstein with the special theory of relativity. He replaced the familiar idea of unqualified temporal and spatial relations between events, things, and processes by a relativistic conception according to which events are not without qualification simultaneous or successive, objects are not without qualification equal or unequal in size, but only with respect to a frame of reference. What formerly seemed to be an objective conception of absolute space and time was revealed to be a mere appearance, from the perspective of one frame of reference, of a world whose objective description from no frame of reference is not given in a four-dimensional coordinate system of independent spatial and temporal dimensions at all. Instead, events are objectively located in relativistic space-time, whose division into separate spatial and temporal dimensions depends on one's point of view. In this case it was reflection on electrodynamic phenomena rather than ordinary perception that revealed that the appearances had to be transcended. There was also, as with the primary-secondary quality distinction, an important philosophical element in the discovery that absolute simultaneity of spatially separated events was not a well-defined notion, in our ordinary system of concepts.

These examples illustrate the human capacity to escape the limits of the original human situation, not merely by traveling around and seeing the world from different perspectives, but by ascending to new levels from which we can understand and criticize the general forms of previous perspectives. The step to a new perspective is the product of epistemological insight in each case.

Of course it is also the product in some cases of new observations that can't be accommodated in the old picture. But the satisfactoriness of a new external perspective depends on whether it can place the internal perspective within the world in a way that enables one to occupy both of them simultaneously, with a sense that the external perspective gives access to an objective reality that one's subjective impressions are impressions of. Experience is not the sole foundation of our knowledge of the world, but a place must be found for it as part of the world, however different that world may be from the way it is depicted in experience.

Only objectivity can give meaning to the idea of intellectual progress. We can see this by considering any well-established objective advance, like the examples discussed already, and asking whether it could be reversed. Could a theory which ascribed intrinsic colors, tastes, smells, feels, and sounds to things account for the appearance that these are to be explained as the effects on our senses of primary qualities? Could a theory of absolute space and time explain the appearance that we occupy relativistic space-time? In both cases the answer is no. An objective advance may be superseded by a further objective advance, which reduces it in turn to an appearance. But it is not on the same level as its predecessors, and may well have been essential as a step on the route to its successors.

Still, the fact that objective reality is our goal does not guarantee that our pursuit of it succeeds in being anything more than an exploration and reorganization of the insides of our own minds. On a realist view this always remains a possibility, at least in the abstract, even if one isn't thinking of a specific way in which one might be deceived. A less radical point is that whatever we may have achieved we are only at a passing stage of intellectual development, and much of what we now believe will be overthrown by later discoveries and later theories.

A certain expectation of further advance and occasional retreat is rational: there have been enough cases in which what was once thought a maximally objective conception of reality has been included as appearance in a still more objective conception so that we would be foolish not to expect it to go on. Indeed we should want it to go on, for we are evidently just at the beginning of our trip outward, and what has so far been achieved in the way of self-understanding is minimal.

4. Evolutionary Epistemology

Because self-understanding is at the heart of objectivity, the enterprise faces serious obstacles. The pursuit of objective knowledge requires a much more developed conception of the mind in the world than we now possess: a conception which will explain the possibility of objectivity. It requires that we come to understand the operations of our minds from a point of view that is not just our own. This would not be the kind of self-understanding that Kant aimed for, that is, an understanding from within of the forms and limits of all our possible experience and thought (though that would be amazing enough, and there is no reason to suppose that it could be arrived at a priori). What is needed is something even stronger: an explanation of the possibility of objective knowledge of the real world which is itself an instance of objective knowledge of that world and our relation to it. Can there be creatures capable of this sort of self-transcendence? We at least seem to have taken some steps in this direction, though it is not clear how far we can go. But how is even this much possible? In fact, the objective capacity is a complete mystery. While it obviously exists and we can use it, there is no credible explanation of it in terms of anything more basic, and so long as we don't understand it, its results will remain under a cloud.

Some may be tempted to offer or at least to imagine an evolutionary explanation, as is customary these days for everything under the sun. Evolutionary hand waving is an example of the tendency to take a theory which has been successful in one domain and apply it to anything else you can't understand—not even to apply it, but vaguely to imagine such an application. It is also an example of the pervasive and reductive naturalism of our culture. 'Survival value' is now invoked to account for everything from ethics to language. I realize that it is dangerous to enter into discussion of a topic on which one is not an expert, but since these speculations can't be ignored, and since even when they come from professional biologists they are in the nature of obiter dicta, let me try to say something about them.

The Darwinian theory of natural selection, assuming the truth of its historical claims about how organisms develop, is a very partial explanation of why we are as we are. It explains the selection among those organic possibilities that have been generated, but it does not explain the possibilities themselves. It is a diachronic theory which tries to account for the particular path evolution will take through a set of possibilities under given conditions. It may explain why creatures with vision or reason will survive, but it does not explain how vision or reasoning are possible.

These require not diachronic but timeless explanations. The range of biological options over which natural selection can operate is extraordinarily rich but also severely constrained. Even if randomness is a factor in determining which mutation will appear when (and the extent of the randomness is apparently in dispute), the range of genetic possibilities is not itself a random occurrence but a necessary consequence of the natural order. The possibility of minds capable of forming progressively more objective conceptions of reality is not something the theory of natural selection can attempt to explain, since it doesn't explain possibilities at all, but only selection among them.[6]

But even if we take as given the unexplained possibility of objective minds, natural selection doesn't offer a very plausible explanation of their actual existence. In themselves, the advanced intellectual capacities of human beings, unlike many of their anatomical, physiological, perceptual, and more basic cognitive features, are extremely poor candidates for evolutionary explanation, and would in fact be rendered highly suspect by such an explanation. I am not suggesting, as Kant once did (Kant (2), pp. 395–6), that reason has negative survival value and could from that point of view be replaced by instinct. But the capacity to form cosmological and subatomic theories takes us so far from the circumstances in which our ability to think would have had to pass its evolutionary tests that there would be no reason whatever, stemming from the theory of evolution, to rely on it in extension to those subjects. In fact if, per impossibile, we came to believe that our capacity for objective theory were the product of natural selection, that would warrant serious skepticism about its results beyond a very limited and familiar range. An evolutionary explanation of our theorizing faculty would provide absolutely no confirmation of its capacity to get at the truth. Something else must be going on if the process is really taking us toward a truer and more detached understanding of the world.

There is a standard reply to skepticism about evolutionary explanation of the intellect, namely that Darwinian theory doesn't require every feature of an organism to be separately selected for its adaptive value. Some features may be the side effects of others, singly or in combination, that have been so selected, and if they are not harmful they will survive. In the case of the intellect, a common speculation is that rapid enlargement of the human brain occurred through natural selection after the development of an erect posture and the capacity to use tools made brain size

6. Stephen Jay Gould reports that Francis Crick once said to him, "The trouble with you evolutionary biologists is that you are always asking 'why' before you understand 'how' " (Gould (2), p.10).

an advantage. This permitted the acquisition of language and the capacity to reason, which in turn conferred survival value on still larger brains. Then, like an adaptable computer, this complex brain turned out to be able to do all kinds of things it wasn't specifically "selected" to do: study astronomy, compose poetry and music, invent the internal combustion engine and the long-playing record, and prove Gödel's theorem. The great rapidity of civilized cultural evolution requires that the brains which took part in it have been developed to full capacity from its beginning.

Since this is pure speculation, not much can be said about its consistency with the empirical evidence. We know nothing about how the brain performs the functions that permitted our hunter-gatherer ancestors to survive, nor do we know anything about how it performs the functions that have permitted the development and understanding of the mathematics and physics of the past few centuries. So we have no basis for evaluating the suggestion that the properties which were necessary to fit the brain for the first of these purposes turned out to be sufficient for the second as well, and for all the cultural developments that have led to it.

Spinoza gives this description of the process of intellectual evolution:

> As men at first made use of the instruments supplied by nature to accomplish very easy pieces of workmanship, laboriously and imperfectly, and then, when these were finished, wrought other things more difficult with less labour and greater perfection; and so gradually mounted from the simplest operations to the making of tools, and from the making of tools to the making of more complex tools, and fresh feats of workmanship, till they arrived at making, with small expenditure of labour, the vast number of complicated mechanisms which they now possess. So, in like manner, the intellect, by its native strength, makes for itself intellectual instruments, whereby it acquires strength for performing other intellectual operations, and from these operations gets again fresh instruments, or the power of pushing its investigations further, and thus gradually proceeds till it reaches the summit of wisdom. (Spinoza (1), p. 12)

The question is whether not only the physical but the mental capacity needed to make a stone axe automatically brings with it the capacity to take each of the steps that have led from there to the construction of the hydrogen bomb, or whether an enormous excess mental capacity, not explainable by natural selection, was responsible for the generation and spread of the sequence of intellectual instruments that has emerged over the last thirty thousand years. This question is unforgettably posed by the stunning transformation of bone into spaceship in Stanley Kubrick's *2001*.

I see absolutely no reason to believe that the truth lies with the first alternative. The only reason so many people do believe it is that advanced intellectual capacities clearly exist, and this is the only available candidate for a Darwinian explanation of their existence. So it all rests on the assumption that every noteworthy characteristic of human beings, or of any other organism, must have a Darwinian explanation. But what is the reason to believe that? Even if natural selection explains all adaptive evolution, there may be developments in the history of species that are not specifically adaptive and can't be explained in terms of natural selection.[7] Why not take the development of the human intellect as a probable counterexample to the law that natural selection explains everything, instead of forcing it under the law with improbable speculations unsupported by evidence? We have here one of those powerful reductionist dogmas which seem to be part of the intellectual atmosphere we breathe.

What, I will be asked, is my alternative? Creationism? The answer is that I don't have one, and I don't need one in order to reject all existing proposals as improbable. One should not assume that the truth about this matter has already been conceived of—or hold onto a view just because no one can come up with a better alternative. Belief isn't like action. One doesn't have to believe anything, and to believe nothing is not to believe something.

I don't know what an explanation might be like either of the possibility of objective theorizing or of the actual biological development of creatures capable of it. My sense is that it is antecedently so improbable that the only possible explanation must be that it is in some way necessary. It is not the kind of thing that could be either a brute fact or an accident, any more than the identity of inertial and gravitational mass could be; the universe must have fundamental properties that inevitably give rise through physical and biological evolution to complex organisms capable of generating theories about themselves and it. This is not itself an explanation; it merely expresses a view about one condition which an acceptable explanation should meet: it should show why this had to happen, given the relatively short time since the Big Bang, and not merely that it could have happened—as is attempted by Darwinian proposals. (I think an explanation of the original development of organic life should meet

7. See Gould (1) for details.

the same condition.) There is no reason to expect that we shall ever come up with such an explanation, but we are at such a primitive stage of biological understanding that there is no point in making any predictions.[8]

5. Rationalism

One image of self-reconstruction that has appealed to philosophers is Neurath's: that we are like sailors trying to rebuild our ship plank by plank on the high seas. This can be interpreted in more than one way. We might think of ourselves as simply rearranging and perhaps reshaping the planks, making small alterations one at a time, and using the materials we find ready to hand.[9] Such an image may fit the mundane case where knowledge is accumulated gradually and piecemeal, at a given objective level. But if we wish to depict the great objective advances on which real progress depends, we need a different image. Though we may incorporate parts of the original ship in the new one we are about to create, we call up out of ourselves most of the materials from which we will construct it. The place which we occupy for this purpose may be one we could not have reached except on the old ship, but it is really in a new world, and in some sense, I believe, what we find in it is already there. Each of us is a microcosm, and in detaching progressively from our point of view and forming a succession of higher views of ourselves

8. It might be argued that the observation that the universe contains intelligent beings does not have to be explained in terms of fundamental principles which show it to be inevitable, because it has a much simpler explanation: if there were no such beings, there would be no observers and hence no observations. No general inferences can therefore be drawn from their existence. I am not persuaded by this argument. The fact that an observation can be predicted on this sort of ground does not mean that it needn't be explained by other, more fundamental principles as well.

It may be worth mentioning an analogy, the application of the anthropic principle in cosmology. The anthropic principle states that "what we can expect to observe must be restricted by the conditions necessary for our presence as observers" (Carter, p. 291). A special case of this is the strong anthropic principle: "the Universe (and hence the fundamental parameters on which it depends) must be such as to admit the creation of observers within it at some stage" (p. 294). About this Carter says that "even an entirely rigorous prediction based on the *strong* principle will not be completely satisfying from the physicist's point of view since the possibility will remain of finding a deeper underlying theory explaining the relationships that have been predicted" (p. 295). In other words, predictability does not always eliminate the need for explanation.

9. As Neurath puts it, we are "never able to dismantle it in dry-dock and to reconstruct it there out of the best materials" (Neurath, p. 201).

in the world, we are occupying a territory that already exists: taking possession of a latent objective realm, so to speak.

I said earlier that the position to which I am drawn is a form of rationalism. This does not mean that we have innate knowledge of the truth about the world, but it does mean that we have the capacity, not based on experience, to generate hypotheses about what in general the world might possibly be like, and to reject those possibilities that we see could not include ourselves and our experiences. Just as important, we must be able to reject hypotheses which appear initially to be possibilities but are not. The conditions of objectivity that I have been defending lead to the conclusion that the basis of most real knowledge must be a priori and drawn from within ourselves. The role played by particular experience and by the action of the world on us through our individual perspectives can be only selective—though this is a very important factor, which makes the acquisition of such knowledge as we may have importantly subject to luck: the luck of the obervations and data to which we are exposed and the age in which we live. Also important, for possession of the a priori component, are the possibilities and questions that are suggested to us and that we might not have formulated for ourselves— like the boy in Plato's *Meno*.

If the possibilities, or at least some of them, are available a priori to any mind of sufficient complexity, and if the general properties of reality are fairly uniform throughout, then the pursuit of objective knowledge can be expected to lead to gradual convergence from different starting points. But this limit of convergence is not the definition of truth, as Peirce suggests: it is a consequence of the relation between reality and the mind, which in turn must be explained in terms of the kind of part of reality the mind is. Obviously the capacities of different minds, and of different species of mind, differ. But in our case the capacities go far beyond the merely adaptive. A reasonably intelligent human being is capable of grasping, even if it cannot generate on its own, an extraordinary and rich range of conceptual possibilities, as we know from what has been learned already. There is no reason to think our mental capacities mirror reality completely, but I assume we all carry potentially in our heads the possibilities that will be revealed by scientific and other developments over the next few thousand years at least: we just aren't going to be around for the trip—perhaps it should be called the awakening.

This conception of knowledge is in the rationalist tradition, though without the claim that reason provides an indubitable foundation for belief. Even empirical knowledge, or empirical belief, must rest on an a priori base, and if large conclusions are derived from limited empirical evidence a large burden must be carried by direct a priori formulation and selection of hypotheses if knowledge is to be possible at all.[10]

This accounts for the extremely high ratio of rational to empirical grounds for great theoretical advances like Newton's theory of gravitation or the special and general theories of relativity: even though the empirical predictions of those theories are enormous, they were arrived at on the basis of relatively limited observational data, from which they could not be deduced. And I would maintain that even induction, that staple of empiricism, makes sense only with a rationalist basis. Observed regularities provide reason to believe that they will be repeated only to the extent that they provide evidence of hidden *necessary* connections, which hold timelessly. It is not a matter of assuming that the contingent future will be like the contingent past.

The capacity to imagine new forms of hidden order, and to understand new conceptions created by others, seems to be innate. Just as matter can be arranged to embody a conscious, thinking organism, so some of these organisms can rearrange themselves to embody more and more thorough and objective mental representations of the world that contains them, and this possibility too must exist in advance. Although the procedures of thought by which we progress are not self-guaranteeing, they make sense only if we have a natural capacity for achieving harmony with the world far beyond the range of our particular experiences and surroundings. When we use our minds to think about reality, we are not, I assume, performing an impossible leap from inside ourselves to the world outside. We are developing a relation to the world that is implicit in our mental and physical makeup, and we can do this only if there are facts we do not know which account for the possibility. Our position is problematic so long as we have not even a candidate for such an account.

Descartes tried to provide one, together with grounds for certainty that it was true, by proving the existence of the right sort of God. While he was not successful, the problem remains. To go on unambivalently

10. Both Chomsky and Popper have in very different ways rejected empiricist theories of knowledge and emphasized the incomprehensibility, at present, of our capacities to understand and think about the world. Chomsky in particular has argued that our innate capacity to learn languages is contrary to the empiricist conception of how the mind works. This is one aspect of his general attack on reductionism with respect to the mind. I believe that the scientific gaps between data and conclusions are of much greater importance to the theory of knowledge than the gap between the fragmentary linguistic data of early childhood and the grammar of the language that is learned from it, remarkable as that is. Somehow we call up whole worlds out of our heads, not just languages whose form has presumably evolved in part to suit our ability to learn them.

holding our beliefs once this has been recognized requires that we believe that something—we know not what—is true that plays the role in our relation to the world that Descartes thought was played by God. (Perhaps it would be more accurate to say that Descartes' God is a personification of the fit between ourselves and the world for which we have no explanation but which is necessary for thought to yield knowledge.)

I have no idea what unheard-of property of the natural order this might be. But without something fairly remarkable, human knowledge is unintelligible. My view is rationalist and antiempiricist, not because I believe a firm foundation for our beliefs can be discovered a priori, but because I believe that unless we suppose that they have a basis in something global (rather than just human) of which we are not aware, they make no sense—and they do make sense. A serious rationalist epistemology would have to complete this picture—but our beliefs may rest on such a basis even if we cannot discover it. There is no reason to assume that even if we are so organized as to be capable of partly understanding the world, we can also gain access to these facts about ourselves in a way that will fill the blanks in our understanding.[11]

A theory of reality with pretensions to completeness would have to include a theory of the mind. But this too would be a hypothesis generated by the mind, and would not be self-guaranteeing. The point is made by Stroud with reference to Quine's proposal of naturalized epistemology, which is essentially an empiricist psychological theory of the formation of empirical theories (Stroud, ch. 6). It applies equally to a possible rationalist theory of the mind's capacity for a priori theorizing. But of course we have neither of these theories: we don't even have a hypothesis about our capacity to transcend the phenomena. The idea of a full conception of reality that explains our ability to arrive at it is just a dream.

Nevertheless, it's what we aim toward: a gradual liberation of the dormant objective self, trapped initially behind an individual perspective of

---

11. It may be that those areas of knowledge that are entirely a priori permit greater access to their sources in us than do other types of knowledge—that we can develop a better understanding of how our thoughts can lead us to the truths of arithmetic than of how they can lead us to the truths of chemistry. It is possible to make discoveries about something a priori if our representation of the thing has so intimate a relation with the thing itself that the properties to be discovered are already buried in the representation. Thus we can think about mathematics because we are able to operate with a system of symbols whose formal properties make it capable of representing the numbers and all their relations. This system can itself be mathematically investigated. To that extent mathematics gives us a partial answer to the question of how the world that it describes can contain beings who will be able to arrive at some of its truths.

human experience. The hope is to develop a detached perspective that can coexist with and comprehend the individual one.

6. Double Vision

To summarize, what we can hope to accomplish along these lines is bound to be limited in several ways. First, we are finite beings, and even if each of us possesses a large dormant capacity for objective self-transcendence, our knowledge of the world will always be fragmentary, however much we extend it. Second, since the objective self, though it can escape the human perspective, is still as short-lived as we are, we must assume that its best efforts will soon be superseded. Third, the understanding of the world of which we are intrinsically capable—leaving aside limitations of time and technology—is also likely to be limited. As I shall argue in the next chapter, reality probably extends beyond what we can conceive of. Finally, the development of richer and more powerful objective hypotheses does nothing to rule out the known and unknown skeptical possibilities which are the other aspect of any realist view.

None of this will deter us from the effort to make objective progress so far as our minds, our culture, and our epoch may permit. But there are other dangers in the pursuit of that goal, dangers not of failure but of ambition. These dangers are of three kinds: excessive impersonality, false objectification, and insoluble conflict between subjective and objective conceptions of the same thing.

The first comes from taking too literally the image of the true self trapped in the individual human perspective. This is a compelling image, and many have succumbed to its attractions. If the real me views the world from nowhere, and includes the empirical perspective and particular concerns of TN as merely one of myriad sentient flickers in the world so viewed, then it may seem that I should take as little interest in TN's life and perspective as possible, and perhaps even try to insulate myself from it. But the discovery and awakening of the objective self with its universal character doesn't imply that one is not also a creature with an empirical perspective and individual life. Objective advance produces a split in the self, and as it gradually widens, the problems of integration between the two standpoints become severe, particularly in regard to ethics and personal life. One must arrange somehow to see the world both from nowhere and from here, and to live accordingly.

The second danger, that of false objectification, is one I have already discussed in connection with the philosophy of mind—though it arises also in other areas. The success of a particular form of objectivity in expanding our grasp of some aspects of reality may tempt us to apply the same methods in areas where they will not work, either because those areas require a new kind of objectivity or because they are in some respect irreducibly subjective. The failure to recognize these limits produces various kinds of objective obstinacy—most notably reductive analyses of one type of thing in terms that are taken from the objective understanding of another. But as I have said, reality is not just objective reality, and objectivity itself is not one thing. The kinds of objective concepts and theories that we have developed so far, mostly to understand the physical world, can be expected to yield only a fragment of the objective understanding that is possible. And the detachment that objectivity requires is bound to leave something behind.

The third problem, that of insoluble subjective-objective conflict, arises when we succeed in constructing an objective conception of something and then don't know what to do with it because it can't be harmoniously combined with the subjective conception we still have of the same thing. Sometimes an internal conception can't acknowledge its own subjectivity and survive, nor can it simply disappear.

Often an objective advance will involve the recognition that some aspects of our previous understanding belong to the realm of appearance. Instead of conceiving the world as full of colored objects, we conceive it as full of objects with primary qualities that affect human vision in certain subjectively understandable ways. The distinction between appearance and objective reality becomes the object of a new, mixed understanding that combines subjective and objective elements and that is based on recognition of the limits of objectivity. Here there is no conflict.[12]

But it may happen that the object of understanding cannot be so cleanly divided. It may happen that something appears to require subjective and objective conceptions that cover the same territory, and that cannot be combined into a single complex but consistent view. This is particularly likely with respect to our understanding of ourselves, and it is at the source of some of the most difficult problems of philosophy, including the problems of personal identity, free will, and the meaning of life. It is also present in the theory of knowledge, where it takes the form of an inability to hold in one's mind simultaneously and in a consistent form the possibility of skepticism and the ordinary beliefs that life is full of.

12. This is McGinn's point; the scientific image doesn't on reflection conflict with the manifest image over secondary qualities.

What should be the relation between the beliefs we form about the world, with their aspirations to objectivity, and the admission that the world might be completely different from the way we think it is, in unimaginable ways? I believe we have no satisfactory way of combining these outlooks. The objective standpoint here produces a split in the self which will not go away, and we either alternate between views or develop a form of double vision.

Double vision is the fate of creatures with a glimpse of the view *sub specie aeternitatis*. When we view ourselves from outside, a naturalistic picture of how we work seems unavoidable. It is clear that our beliefs arise from certain dispositions and experiences which, so far as we know, don't guarantee their truth and are compatible with radical error. The trouble is that we can't fully take on the skepticism that this entails, because we can't cure our appetite for belief, and we can't take on this attitude toward our own beliefs while we're having them. Beliefs are about how things probably are, not just about how they might possibly be, and there is no way of bracketing our ordinary beliefs about the world so that they dovetail neatly with the possibility of skepticism. The thought "I'm a professor at New York University, unless of course I'm a brain in a vat" is not one that can represent my general integrated state of mind.[13]

The problems of free will and personal identity yield similarly unharmonious conclusions. In some respects what we do and what happens to us fits very naturally into an objective picture of the world, on a footing with what other objects and organisms do. Our actions seem to be events with causes and conditions many of which are not our actions. We seem to persist and change through time much as other complex organisms do. But when we take these objective ideas seriously, they appear to threaten and undermine certain fundamental self-conceptions that we find it very difficult to give up.

Earlier I said it was impossible fully to internalize a conception of one's own personal identity that depended on the organic continuity of one's brain. Ordinarily, an objective view of something with a subjective aspect does not require us simply to give up the subjective view, for it

13. There is a further problem. In the course of arriving at a skeptical conclusion, we pass through thoughts to which we do not simultaneously take up a skeptical stance—thoughts about the relation of the brain to experience, for example. These appear in the skeptic's reasoning in unqualified form. In order to draw skeptical conclusions from the objective standpoint, we have to engage in the kind of direct thought about the world that skepticism undermines. This is like the Cartesian circle in reverse: Descartes tried to prove the existence of God by the use of reasoning on which we can rely only if God exists; the skeptic reaches skepticism through thoughts that skepticism makes unthinkable.

can be reduced to the status of an appearance, and can then coexist with the objective view. But in these cases that option seems not to be available. We cannot come to regard our ideas of our own agency or of the purity of our self-identity through time as mere appearances or impressions. That would be equivalent to giving them up. Though our intuitive convictions about these things emerge very much from our own point of view, they have pretensions to describe not just how we appear to ourselves but how we are, in some as yet unspecified sense which appears to conflict with the objective picture of what we are. This problem arises even if the objective picture does not claim to take in everything—for what it willingly omits is only subjective appearance, and that is not good enough. The claims of both the objective and the subjective self seem to be too strong to allow them to live together in harmony.

This problem will reappear in later chapters, but let me mention one further example: Wittgenstein's unacknowledged skepticism about deduction. I believe his view is rightly regarded by Kripke as a form of skepticism because the external account it gives of what is really going on when we apply a formula or a concept to indefinitely many cases— what the apparently infinite reach of meaning really rests on—is not an account we can take on internally. For example we can't think of the correct application of 'plus 2' as being determined by nothing more than the fact that a certain application is natural to those who share our language and form of life, or by anything else of the sort. In employing the concept we must think of it as determining a unique function over infinitely many cases, beyond all our applications and those of our community and independent of them, or else it would not be the concept it is. *Even if Wittgenstein is right,* we can't think of our thoughts this way while we have them. And even in the philosophical act of thinking naturalistically about how language and logic work, we can't take the Wittgensteinian stance toward *those* thoughts, but must think them straight.

I think a view deserves to be called skeptical if it offers an account of ordinary thoughts which cannot be incorporated into those thoughts without destroying them. One may be a skeptic about x no matter how sincerely one protests that one is not denying the existence of x but merely explaining what x really amounts to.[14]

14. See Kripke (2), p. 65.

VI

THOUGHT AND REALITY

1. Realism

I have at various points expressed commitment to a form of realism, and must now say more about it. In simple terms it is the view that the world is independent of our minds, but the problem is to explain this claim in a nontrivial way which cannot be easily admitted by everyone, and thereby to show how it conflicts with a form of idealism that is held by many contemporary philosophers.

Realism makes skepticism intelligible. In the last chapter we discussed skepticism with regard to knowledge. Here I want to introduce another form of skepticism—not about what we know but about how far our thoughts can reach. I shall defend a form of realism according to which our grasp on the world is limited not only in respect of what we can know but also in respect of what we can conceive. In a very strong sense, the world extends beyond the reach of our minds.[1]

The idealism to which this is opposed holds that what there is is what we can think about or conceive of, or what we or our descendants could come to be able to think about or conceive of—and that this is necessarily true because the idea of something that we could not think about or conceive of makes no sense. The "we" is important. I leave aside

1. This thesis is also defended by Fodor (pp. 120–6).

views, also called idealist, that hold reality to be correlative with mind in a much wider sense—including infinite minds, if there are such things. Perhaps, given any type of world, there could be a mind capable of conceiving it adequately; I have no idea of the limits on possible minds. The realism I am defending says the world may be inconceivable to *our* minds, and the idealism I am opposing says it could not be.

There are more radical forms of idealism than this, such as the view that to exist is to be perceived, or that what exists must be an object of possible experience for us, or that what exists or is the case must be an object of possible knowledge for us, or must be verifiable by us, or that it must be something about which we could have evidence. These views have all found adherents, but I believe that they depend finally on the more general form of idealism I have described, together with different specific views about the conditions of human thought. The common element is a broadly epistemological test of reality—which has never lost its popularity despite the supposed death of logical positivism.

I want to oppose to this general position a different view of the relation of our thoughts to reality, particularly those thoughts that attempt to represent the world objectively. In pursuing objectivity we alter our relation to the world, increasing the correctness of certain of our representations of it by compensating for the peculiarities of our point of view. But the world is in a strong sense independent of our possible representations, and may well extend beyond them. This has implications both for what objectivity achieves when it is successful and for the possible limits of what it can achieve. Its aim and sole rationale is to increase our grasp of reality, but this makes no sense unless the idea of reality is not merely the idea of what can be grasped by those methods. In other words, I want to resist the natural tendency to identify the idea of the world as it really is with the idea of what can be revealed, at the limit, by an indefinite increase in objectivity of standpoint.

It has already been argued that in various respects the pursuit of objectivity can be carried to excess, that it can lead away from the truth if carried out in the wrong way or with respect to the wrong subject matter. That is one way in which objectivity does not correspond to reality: it is not always the best mode of understanding. But human objectivity may fail to exhaust reality for another reason: there may be aspects of reality beyond its reach because they are altogether beyond our capacity to form conceptions of the world. What there is and what we, in virtue of our nature, can think about are different things, and the latter may be smaller than the former. Certainly *we* are smaller, so this should not be surprising. Human objectivity may be able to grasp only part of the world, but when it is successful it should provide us with an understanding of aspects of reality whose existence is completely independent of our capacity to think about them—as independent as the existence of things we can't conceive.

The idea that the contents of the universe are limited by our capacity for thought is easily recognized as a philosophical view, which at first sight seems crazily self-important given what small and contingent pieces of the universe we are. It is a view that no one would hold except for philosophical reasons that seem to rule out the natural picture.

That picture is that the universe and most of what goes on in it are completely independent of our thoughts, but that since our ancestors appeared on Earth we have gradually developed the capacity to think about, know about, and represent more and more aspects of reality. There are some things that we cannot now conceive but may yet come to understand; and there are probably still others that we lack the capacity to conceive not merely because we are at too early a stage of historical development, but because of the kind of beings we are. About some of what we cannot conceive we are able to speak vaguely—this may include the mental lives of alien creatures, or what went on before the Big Bang—but about some of it we may be unable to say anything at all, except that there might be such things. The only sense in which we can conceive of them is under that description—that is, as things of which we can form no conception—or under the all-encompassing thought "Everything," or the Parmenidean thought "What is."

I am not claiming that much of what we find *positively inconceivable*— what we can see to be *im*possible, like round squares—may nevertheless be possible. Though there may be cases where our strong convictions of positive inconceivability cannot be relied on as evidence of impossibility, I assume they are rare. I am concerned here rather with the admission of possibilities and actualities which are *negatively* inconceivable to us in the sense that we have and can have no conception of them. (This is different from seeing positively that no such conception could be coherent, because, for example, it would involve a contradiction.)

Not everything about the universe must lie in the path of our possible cognitive development or that of our descendants—even if beings like us should exist forever. It is a philosophical problem how we are able to think about those aspects of reality that we can think about. There is also the question of whether we can think about those things 'as they are in themselves' or only 'as they appear to us'. But what there is, or what is the case, does not coincide necessarily with what is a possible object of thought for us. Even if through some miracle we are capable in principle of conceiving of everything there is, that is not what makes it real.

2. Idealism

The philosophical argument against this natural view is simple. It parallels one of Berkeley's arguments for the view that for unthinking things, to exist is to be perceived. Berkeley claimed that this became evident if we tried to form the idea of an unperceived object. It turns out to be impossible, he said, because as soon as we try to think, for example, of an unperceived tree, we find that all we can do is to call up a perceptual image of a tree, and that is not unperceived.[2]

It would be generally recognized now that this argument involves the mistake of confusing perceptual imagination as the vehicle of thought with a perceptual experience as part of the object of thought. Even if I employ a visual image to think about the tree, that does not mean I am thinking about a visual impression of the tree, any more than if I draw a tree, I am drawing a drawing of a tree (cf. Williams (1)).

A similar mistake would be to argue that we cannot form the thought of something that no one is actually thinking about or the conception of something that no one is conceiving of. Clearly we can think and talk about the possible state of affairs in which no one is thinking or talking about Bishop Berkeley. The fact that we must talk about Berkeley to talk about the situation in which he is not being talked about doesn't make that situation either inexpressible or impossible.

But the form of idealism with which I am concerned isn't based on this mistake: it is not the view that what there is must be actually conceived or even currently conceivable. Rather it is the position that what there is must be possibly conceivable by us, or possibly something for which we could have evidence. An argument for this general form of idealism must show that the notion of what *cannot* be thought about by us or those like us makes no sense.

The argument is this. If we try to make sense of the notion of what we could never conceive, we must use general ideas like that of something existing, or some circumstance obtaining, or something being the case, or something being true. We must suppose that there are aspects of reality to which these concepts that we *do* possess apply, but to which no other concepts that we *could* possess apply. To conceive simply that such things may exist is not to conceive of them adequately; and the realist would maintain that everything else about them might be inconceivable to us. The idealist reply is that our completely general ideas of what

2. Berkeley, secs. 22–3. This is not Berkeley's only argument for idealism, but he says he is "content to put the whole upon this issue."

exists, or is the case, or is true, cannot reach any further than our more specific ideas of kinds of things that can exist, or be the case, or be true. We do not, in other words, possess a completely general concept of reality that reaches beyond any possible filling in of its content that we could in principle understand.

Or to put the same point in terms of language, as Davidson does, we do not possess a general concept of truth that goes beyond the truth of all possible sentences in any language that we could understand, or that could be translated into a language that we or others like us could understand. Our general idea of what is the case does not transcend the sum of what we could truly assert to be the case. Here is Davidson rejecting the idea of a conceptual scheme that meets the conditions for applying to the world but is different from our own: "The criterion of a conceptual scheme different from our own now becomes: largely true but not translatable. The question whether this is a useful criterion is just the question how well we understand the notion of truth, as applied to a language, independent of the notion of translation. The answer is, I think, that we do not understand it independently at all."[3]

So the argument that parallels Berkeley's is that if we try to form the notion of something we could never conceive, or think about, or talk about, we find ourselves having to use ideas which imply that we could in principle think about it after all (even if we cannot do so now): because even the most general ideas of truth or existence we have carry that implication. We cannot use language to reach beyond the possible range of its specific application. If we attempt to do so, we are either misusing the language or using it to refer to what is conceivable after all.

This argument is not guilty of Berkeley's error. It does not ascribe to the object of thought something which is only an aspect of the vehicle of thought. It does not claim that to exist is to be thought about, or to have been or to be going to be thought about. Nevertheless, it works in a similar way, for it claims that certain attempts to form significant thoughts fail because they run up against boundaries set by the conditions of the possibility of thought. In Berkeley's argument the hypothesis of existence without the mind is said to conflict with the conditions of thought, and the same is said here about the hypothesis of inconceivability. Realists are deluded, in other words, if they think they have the idea of a reality beyond the reach of any possible human thought except

---

3. Davidson (3), p. 194; note that some realists might wish to accept the "largely true" condition for a different conceptual scheme, provided it could be shown not to conflict with the "not translatable" condition.

that one. If we examine carefully what they take to be that idea, we will discover that it is either the idea of something more fully within our reach, or no idea at all.

To answer this objection it is necessary to dispute the view of thought on which it depends—as with Berkeley's argument. But first let me try to make clear how paradoxical the conclusion of the idealist argument is. An examination of what is wrong with the conclusion may shed some light on what is wrong with the argument. I must say at the outset that I do not have an alternative theory of thought to offer in place of those that support idealism. My argument will be essentially negative. I believe that the statement of a realist position can be rejected as unintelligible only on grounds which would also require the abandonment of other, much less controversial claims. My position is that realism makes as much sense as many other unverifiable statements, even though all of them, and all thought, may present fundamental philosophical mysteries to which there is at present no solution.

It certainly seems that I can believe that reality extends beyond the reach of possible human thought, since this would be closely analogous to something which is not only possibly but actually the case. There are plenty of ordinary human beings who constitutionally lack the capacity to conceive of some of the things that others know about. People blind or deaf from birth cannot understand colors or sounds. People with a permanent mental age of nine cannot come to understand Maxwell's equations or the general theory of relativity or Gödel's theorem. These are all humans, but we could equally well imagine a species for whom these characteristics were normal, able to think and know about the world in certain respects, but not in all. Such people could have a language, and might be similar enough to us so that their language was translatable into part of ours.

If there could be people like that coexisting with us, there could also be such people if we did not exist—that is, if there were no one capable of conceiving of these things that they cannot understand. Then their position in the world would be analogous to the one which I have claimed we are probably in.

We can elaborate the analogy by imagining first that there are higher beings, related to us as we are related to the nine-year-olds, and capable of understanding aspects of the world that are beyond our comprehension. Then they would be able to say of us, as we can say of the others, that there are certain things about the world that we cannot even conceive. And now we need only imagine that the world is just the same, except that these higher beings do not exist. Then what they could say

if they did exist remains true. So it appears that the existence of unreachable aspects of reality is independent of their conceivability by any actual
mind.

Does this analogy work? Or is there some asymmetry between our situation and that of the hypothetical nine-year-olds?

An objection might be that in thinking about them I have all along
been conceiving of the world—even the world from which we are
absent—in terms of what we actually know about it. The features they
can't conceive are fully specifiable in our language. It might be held illegitimate to try to explain simply by analogy with this the idea of our own
situation in a world that in some respects we can't think about. We cannot talk sense simply by saying that these people are related to the laws
of general relativity as we are to some other features of the world—
unless independent significance has been given in this statement to the
general expression "features of the world." How can an analogy give
sense to something that has no sense on its own, apart from the analogy?

In response, let me extend the analogy to make room for this general
concept, by an addition to the story about the congenital nine-year-olds.
Suppose that, in the world in which we do not exist, one of them, call
him Realist junior, develops philosophical leanings (why not?) and won-
ders whether there may be things about the world that he and others like
him are incapable of ever finding out about or understanding. Is this
impossible? That is, if he were to utter these words (supposing in other
respects his language were like part of ours), would it be a mistake to
take them as expressing a hypothesis which would in fact be true in that
situation? Would he simply be talking nonsense without realizing it?
Would he be incapable of thinking in general terms what we know to be
true about his situation (what we have stipulated to be true)? Here the
analogy goes in the other direction. If we would be talking nonsense by
engaging in such speculation, so would he.

The question is whether we can attribute to Realist junior a general
concept of reality which applies, though he can never know it, to the laws
of general relativity and all the other features of the universe that
humans may be capable of comprehending. Can he have, on the basis of
the examples of reality with which he is acquainted, a general concept
which applies beyond everything with which he and his like could conceivably become acquainted? If he can, then we ourselves can have the
same concept, which will apply to features of the universe that we are
incapable of comprehending.

Suppose Realist junior expands on the idea by speculating that there
might be other beings, with capacities that the nine-year-olds lack, who
could understand aspects of reality that are inaccessible to them, though

intellectual distance would make it impossible for the higher beings to communicate their understanding to the lower. (I assume an intellectual distance great enough so that the lower beings couldn't form a vicarious conception of something by relying to some extent on the judgments of the higher beings. Much of our ordinary conception of the world is vicarious in this sense—depending on the greater expertise or intelligence of other humans. But merely believing there might be something others could understand is not yet a conception of it, not even a vicarious one.)

Admittedly the idea of a higher form of understanding depends for its significance on the idea of something to be understood, and it is in dispute whether they have the latter idea. But it seems very artificial to deny that someone in this position could believe something we know to be not only significant but true: that there are concepts usable by other types of minds, which apply to the world and can be used to formulate truths about it, but which cannot be translated into his language or any language that he can understand. Wouldn't a nine-year-old Davidson who arose among them be wrong?

In fact, wouldn't Davidson himself have to say that this lesser Davidson was wrong in denying the intelligibility of realism? How would Davidson's principle of charity be applied to the dispute between Davidson junior and Realist junior? Wouldn't it imply that Realist junior was right, because what he said could be translated into something we would assert, whereas what Davidson junior said couldn't be translated into something we would assert? I'm not sure. The problem is that Davidson's notion of translation seems to be asymmetrical. I might be able to translate a sentence of someone else's language into a sentence of my language, even though he cannot translate my sentence into his. According to Davidson (so far as I can see) I could say that Realist junior was right and Davidson junior wrong, but Realist junior would be wrong to agree with me—as Davidson junior would no doubt point out to him. This doesn't make the doctrine any less paradoxical. And if these consequences are unacceptable with regard to the nine-year-olds, they are unacceptable with regard to us.

This issue recalls the one discussed in chapter 5, section 2, about the intelligibility of skepticism. In both cases the question is how far we can go in forming the idea of a world with which our minds cannot make contact. The general point I wish to make against restrictive theories of what is thinkable is this. Every concept that we have contains potentially the idea of its own complement—the idea of what the concept doesn't apply to. Unless it has been shown positively that there cannot be such things—that the idea involves some kind of contradiction (like the idea of things that are not self-identical)—we are entitled to assume that it makes sense even if we can say nothing more about the members of the class, and have never met one.

To be the value of a variable in our universal or existential quantifications it is not necessary to be the referent of a specific name or description in our language, because we already have the general concept of *everything*, which includes both the things we can name or describe and those we can't. Against that background we can speak of the complement of any concept whatever, unless it has been shown to be positively inconceivable. We can speak of 'all the things we can't describe', 'all the things we can't imagine', 'all the things humans can't conceive of', and finally, 'all the things humans are constitutionally incapable of ever conceiving'. The universal quantifier does not have a built-in limitation to what can be designated in some other way. It could even be used to form the idea, 'all the things *no* finite mind could ever form a conception of'. Naturally the possibility of forming these ideas does not guarantee that anything corresponds to them. But in the nature of the case it is unlikely that we could ever have reason to believe that nothing does.

Creatures who recognize their limited nature and their containment in the world must recognize both that reality may extend beyond our conceptual reach and that there may be concepts that we could not understand. The condition is met by a general concept of reality under which one's actual conception, as well as all possible extensions of that conception, falls as an instance. This concept seems to me adequately explained through the idea of a hierarchical set of conceptions, extending from those much more limited than one's own but contained in it to those larger than one's own but containing it—of which some are reachable by discoveries one might make but others, larger still, are not. (The hierarchy could also include parallel conceptions, not intersecting our own but joined with it only in a larger one.) We could ascribe this concept to the philosophical nine-year-olds in our example, and I maintain that it is the same as our general concept of what there is. It seems to me so clear that we have this concept that any theory of thought or reference which implies that we can't have it is for that reason deeply suspect.

The pursuit of a more objective view, by which we place ourselves in the world and try to understand our relation to it, is the primary method of extending and filling out our particular conception of this reality. But the general concept implies that there is no guarantee that the whole of what there is coincides with what we or beings like us could arrive at if we carried the pursuit of objectivity to the limit—to the convergence of views that would come at that mythical point of stupefaction, "the end of inquiry."

There are limits of objectivity as a form of understanding that follow from the fact that it leaves the subjective behind. These are inner limits. There are also outer limits of objectivity that fall at different points for different types of beings, and that depend not on the nature of objectivity but on how far it can be pursued by a given individual. Objectivity is only a way of extending one's grasp of the world, and besides leaving certain aspects of reality behind, it may fail to reach others, even if more powerful forms of objectivity could encompass them.

3. Kant and Strawson

As with the topic of knowledge, so with the topic of thought, I believe there is a middle ground between skepticism and reductionism. In the case of knowledge, skepticism arises when we reflect that our beliefs inevitably claim to go beyond their grounds. The effort to avoid skepticism by eliminating this gap can lead to reductionism, a reinterpretation of the content of our beliefs in terms of their grounds.

With thought, the problem is the relation between our conceptions and what is possible. Thought purports to represent facts and possibilities beyond itself, and skepticism is the view that our thoughts themselves give us no way of telling whether they correspond enough to the nature of actual and possible reality to be able to make contact with it at all— even to the extent of permitting false beliefs about it. To escape from such skepticism the reductionist reinterprets the domain of possibilities as the domain of what is or could become conceivable to us—thus guaranteeing (finally) that our thoughts can make contact with it.

To explain the intermediate position let me try to locate it in relation to two opposed views: Kant's skepticism and Strawson's reductionism. (Needless to say, this is not a term Strawson would use to describe his own view.) They are related to one another in that Strawson's view is offered as an empiricist criticism of Kant. Since Strawson's reductionism is quite generous, admitting a great deal into the universe of possibilities, it is important to explain what I think it leaves out.

Kant's position is that we can conceive of things only as they appear to us and never as they are in themselves: how things are in themselves remains forever and entirely out of the reach of our thought. "Doubtless, indeed, there are intelligible entities corresponding to the sensible entities; there may also be intelligible entities to which our sensible faculty of intuition has no relation whatsoever; but our concepts of understanding, being mere forms of thought for our sensible intuition, could not in the least apply to them" (Kant (1), pp. B308–9).

Strawson wishes to remove the Kantian opposition between thinking

of things as they appear to us and thinking of them as they are in themselves by declaring the latter idea (in its Kantian version) nonsensical. He
believes there is an appearance-reality distinction *within* what Kant
regards as the world of appearance, but it is basically the distinction
between how things appear to us at any particular time or from a particular vantage point, and how they would come to appear as the result of
an improved view or further investigation. Application of the distinction
depends, he says, on identity of reference plus a corrected view: the
world that now appears to me in one way might come, as a result of
procedures of corrective revision, to appear to me or others like me in
another way—a way that could be seen as a correction of the first. No
idea of reality is left standing by this account which could have application to anything outside the range of possible human conception, evidence, or discovery.

Strawson does not claim that the real is coextensive with what we can
actually form a conception of. Here is what he says:

> In rejecting the senseless dogma that our conceptual scheme corresponds
> at no point with Reality, we must not embrace the restrictive dogma that
> Reality is completely comprehended by that scheme as it actually is. We
> admit readily that there are facts we do not know. We must admit also that
> there may be *kinds* of fact of which we have, at present, no more concep-
> tion than our human predecessors had of some kinds of fact admitted in
> our conceptual schemes but not in theirs. We learn not only how to answer
> old questions, but how to ask new ones. The idea of the aspects of Reality
> which would be described in the answers to the questions we do not yet
> know how to ask is one which, like the idea of the realm of the noumenal,
> though not in the same drastic style, limits the claim of actual human
> knowledge and experience to be "co-extensive with the real".
>
> This seems to be the necessary, and not very advanced, limit of sympathy
> with the metaphysics of transcendental idealism.[4]

This is, as I have said, a broad interpretation of the range of possibilities. But the extension of reality beyond what we can now conceive is
here still thought of as what *we* might come to if we developed new experiences or ways of thinking, and therefore conceptions of new types of
individual, property, and relation that would have application on the
basis of possible experience. The implied reference to ourselves and our
world remains, even if the series of discoveries is thought of as incom-

4. Strawson (3), p.42. See also Strawson (4), where he explicitly endorses the position that
scientific realism is acceptable so long as we recognize its relativity to a particular intellectual standpoint.

pletable. That is the basis for Strawson's claim that we cannot be said to know things only as they appear or might appear to us, because the contrasting idea of what never could appear to us is meaningless.

I want to agree with Strawson in denying that we know things *only* as they appear to us, but agree with Kant in holding that how things are in themselves transcends all possible appearances or human conceptions. Our knowledge of the phenomenal world is partial knowledge of the world as it is in itself; but the entire world can't be identified with the world as it appears to us because it probably includes things of which we cannot and never could conceive, no matter how far the human understanding is expanded, as Strawson suggests, in directions we cannot now imagine. The difficulty is to state this in a way that defies idealist reinterpretation; realists always find it hard to say anything with which idealists cannot arrange to agree by giving it their own meaning.

Let me first explain my disagreement with Kant.[5] I hold the familiar view that secondary qualities describe the world as it appears to us but primary qualities do not. To be red simply is to be something which would appear red to us in normal conditions—it is a property whose definition is essentially relative. But to be square is not simply to be such as to appear square, even though what is square does appear square. Here the appearance of squareness is significantly explained in terms of the effect on us of squareness in objects, which is not in turn analyzed in terms of the appearance of squareness. The red appearance of red things, on the other hand, cannot be noncircularly explained in terms of their redness, because the latter is analyzed in terms of the former. To explain why things appear red we have to go outside the circle of color qualities.

The Kantian view that primary qualities, too, describe the world only as it appears to us depends on taking the entire system of scientific explanations of observable phenomena as itself an appearance, whose ultimate explanation cannot without circularity refer to primary qualities since they on the contrary have to be explained in terms of it. Primary qualities are nothing more on this view than an aspect of our world picture, and if that picture has an explanation, it must be in terms of the effect on us of something outside it, which will be for that reason unimaginable to us—the noumenal world.

The view that this must be how things are results from a refusal to distinguish between two ways in which the human point of view enters into our thoughts—as form and as content. The content of a thought

5. I am indebted here to Colin McGinn, though he does not explicitly consider the possibility of things we could never conceive of. See McGinn, chs. 6 and 7.

may be quite independent of its particular form—independent, for example, of the particular language in which it is expressed. All of our thoughts must have a form which makes them accessible from a human perspective. But that doesn't mean they are all about our point of view or the world's relation to it. What they are about depends not on their subjective form but on what has to be referred to in any explanation of what makes them true.

The content of some thoughts transcends every form they can take in the human mind. If primary qualities were conceivable only from a human point of view, then the ultimate explanation of why the world appears to us in that way could not refer to primary qualities of things in themselves. But if primary qualities can equally well be grasped from a point of view that has nothing subjectively in common with ours, then the description of the world in terms of them is not relative to our point of view; they are not merely aspects of the phenomenal world but can on the contrary be used, by us or by others, to explain the appearance of that world.

The question is whether every possible explanation of our awareness of primary qualities, either perceptual or theoretical, must refer to the primary qualities of things outside us, or whether they disappear from the final explanation by being entirely included, as appearances, in what is to be explained. Unless the latter is true, the analogy with secondary qualities is meaningless. The mere fact that any thoughts we have about primary qualities must be formulated in language and images that we understand does not settle the matter, nor does the fact that any explanation we accept will be ours. It has to be claimed that at the limit, whether or not we are able to reach it, primary qualities *drop out* of the explanation of their appearance.

But there is no reason to believe that reference to primary qualities will disappear from the explanation of the appearance of primary qualities, no matter how complicated we make the "appearance" to be explained. We can't explain the fact that things look spatially extended except in terms of their being extended. And we can't explain the fact that *that* explanation seems true except again in terms of things being extended, their extension affecting us perceptually in certain ways, and the existence of that relation affecting the results of our investigation into the causes of our perceptual impressions of extension. And so on. If each explanation of the appearance of spatial extension in terms of extension in the world is counted as a new, higher-level appearance of extension, then that too has to be explained in terms of extension in the world. However far up we escalate in the series of "appearances" of extension, the extension of things in themselves will keep one step ahead and recur in the explanation of those appearances.[6]

The only thing that can refute this view is a better alternative. There might be one—at some level the explanation of the fact that so far all our theories of the physical world involve spatial extension might conceivably be explained in terms of something entirely different, something which we might or might not be able to grasp. But Kant's nonexplanation in terms of the inconceivable noumenal world is not that better alternative. It is just a placeholder for something beyond our comprehension, and there is no reason to accept it unless the available realist position, ascribing extension to things in themselves, is ruled out as impossible.

But what reason could there be to hold that, granting the intelligibility of the notion of things in themselves, they couldn't be spatially extended? There is no good reason—only a bad Berkeleyan reason: the move from subjectivity of form to subjectivity of content. In other words, it would have to be claimed that because *we have* the conception of primary qualities, detect them through observation, and use them in explanations, they are essentially relative to our point of view, though in a more complex way than secondary qualities are: relative not just to our perceptual point of view, but to our entire cognitive point of view. I believe there is no defense of this position which does not beg the question.

But it is necessary to mention one Kantian argument for doubting that things in themselves have primary qualities, even though it does not show this to be impossible. The argument is this. Suppose Kant is right to claim that the primary qualities are essential features of our world picture, so that we cannot conceive of a world without them. This doesn't imply that they can't also be features of the world as it is in itself. But it does mean that we could not understand any explanation of the appearance of primary qualities which did not involve the ascription of primary qualities to things in the world. And if any such alternative would be inconceivable to us, the fact that every explanation we come up with involves primary qualities is not very good evidence that no better explanation of some other kind exists.

That is true. On the other hand, whatever may be the limits of our world picture (whether or not it has to include primary qualities), there

6. By contrast, the colors of things drop out of explanations very early. We can explain something's looking red to *me* in terms of its being red, but we can't nonvacuously explain the fact that red things generally look red to human beings in terms of their being red.

is no guarantee that we will be able to find credible explanations of the appearances within those limits at all. To the extent that we do, there is some reason to think that the picture does describe things in themselves, as far as it goes. At any rate it may. Moreover, there is remarkable flexibility in our conception of the kinds of primary qualities there are—far beyond anything Kant would have imagined to be conceivable—and it has enabled us to formulate theories of the physical world further and further removed from immediate experience. If we agree with Kant that the idea of the world as it is in itself makes sense, then there is no reason to deny that we know anything about it.

Let me now turn to the other aspect of the view I am trying to defend—the claim that there are probably things about the world that we (humans) cannot conceive. This follows naturally from what has already been said. If our conception of primary qualities is a partial conception of things as they are in themselves, its existence is a side-effect of the existence of those things: it results from their effects on each other and on us, together with our mental activity. What we are able to understand about the world depends on the relation between us and the rest of it. It appears to us naturally in certain ways, and with the help of reason and controlled observation we can form hypotheses about the objective reality underlying those appearances. But how much of what there is we can in principle reach by these methods is contingent on our mental makeup and the hypotheses it enables us to understand. Our capacity for understanding what there is may be only partial, because where it exists it depends not only on how things are but on our constitution, and the former is independent of the latter. In this global picture we are contained in the world and able to conceive some of it objectively, but much of it may remain constitutionally beyond our reach. This too, of course, is *our* conception, but that doesn't mean it is only a higher-order description of the world as it appears to us. To insist otherwise is to assume that if any conception has a possessor, it must be about the possessor's point of view—a slide from subjective form to subjective content. If there are other intelligent beings whose point of view is incommensurate with ours, there is no reason why they should not also see us as contained in the world in this way.

My disagreement with Strawson, then, is with the way he interprets the idea that we are embedded in a world larger than we can conceive. What lies beyond our current understanding is not adequately captured in the idea of answers to questions we do not yet know how to ask. It may include things that we or creatures like us could never formulate questions about.

Whether such things are possible is absolutely central, for if they are,

they set a standard of reality independent of the mind, which more familiar things may also meet. We may then say that the reality of the features
of things in themselves that we have discovered is just as independent of
our capacity to discover them as is the reality of whatever may lie outside
our conceptual reach, actual or possible. In that case what we know or
think about when we think about the structure of matter or the physical
nature of light or sound is something whose appearance to us in any
form is incidental, and whose existence is not merely that of a character
in our best theories.

4. Wittgenstein

Let me turn finally to one of the most important sources of contemporary idealism: Wittgenstein.[7] His later views on the conditions of meaning
seem to imply that nothing can make sense which purports to reach
beyond the outer bounds of human experience and life, for it is only
within a community of actual or possible users of the language that there
can exist that possibility of agreement in its application which is a condition of the existence of rules, and of the distinction between getting it
right and getting it wrong. This appears to rule out not only languages
which could be understood by only one person, but also the use of language—even the general language of existence and states of affairs—to
talk about what we cannot in principle make any judgments about.

Wittgenstein doesn't propose sociological truth-conditions for propositions about rules and meaning any more than he proposes behavioral
truth-conditions for propositions about the mind. The criterial conditions he describes are assertability-conditions—truth-conditions having
been abandoned as a tool of analysis in the *Philosophical Investigations*.[8]
Still, if Wittgenstein is right, it makes sense to say that someone is or is
not using a concept correctly only against the background of the possibility of agreement and identifiable disagreement in judgments employing the concept. What implications does this have for my claim that the
concepts of existence and reality can be significantly applied in the
thought that there may be things that we could never conceive of?

As a desperate measure one might argue that Wittgenstein's claim
about rules, if true, does not have such restrictive consequences as it is
often thought to have. The possibility of agreement in judgments is a
very broad condition that can be met in many ways. It need not imply,

7. See Williams (5).
8. See Dummett (1), and Kripke (2), pp. 73 ff.

and was not thought by Wittgenstein to imply, that we could understand only what we could verify or confirm. That would be true only if the judgments in which there had to be agreement were specific judgments of fact. But that need not be so. In regard to the possibility that there are things about the world that we couldn't conceive and that what there is very likely extends beyond the range of possible human thought, it might be suggested that Wittgensteinian conditions of publicity and possible agreement could be met in another way. Agreement about what we do not know and cannot conceive, and about what is possible, are as important as agreement about what we do know and what is true. That too is agreement in judgments.

The defense of my position would then be this: if it is a natural consequence of things that human beings are generally willing to admit, that what there is and what is true may extend beyond what they or their human successors could ever discover or conceive of or describe in some extension of human language, then that casts doubt on philosophical arguments purporting to show that such words transgress the rules of our language. Such arguments must appeal to truth-conditions for meaning that are stronger than Wittgensteinian assertability-conditions. It might even be suggested that Wittgenstein's occasional evocation of possible forms of life incomprehensibly different from our own was a gesture in the direction of admitting the reality of what we cannot conceive.

What convinces me of the hopelessness of this attempt to reconcile my realism with Wittgenstein's picture of language is that the interpretation supports a similar argument against some, though by no means all of the conclusions Wittgenstein himself draws concerning linguistic illegitimacy. I claimed in the last chapter that certain kinds of skepticism, for example, cannot be ruled out as violations of the language because they are part of the data about how people are naturally inclined to use the language, the judgments—of ignorance, of possibility, of doubt—which they naturally agree to in certain circumstances. If these are errors, they are not linguistic errors, and the disposition to make them must be taken as important evidence of how the language works: what factual judgments and claims to knowledge mean—specifically, how ambitious they are to reach beyond their grounds.

The position I am trying to defend is not really compatible with Wittgenstein's picture of the relation of language to the world, even if some of what he says about rules can be interpreted in a way which seems to allow it. His view of how thought is possible clearly implies that any thoughts we can have of a mind-independent reality must remain within the boundaries set by our human form of life, and that we can't appeal to a completely general idea of what there is to defend the existence of kinds of facts which are in principle beyond the possibility of human confirmation or agreement. We fall into nonsense, he thinks, if we try to take language too far from these conditions. We can't think of our world as part of a larger universe that also contains things revealed only to forms of life inaccessible to us; we can't apply the concepts of belief or truth to a point of view totally unreachable from our own.

The radical problem to which Wittgenstein's position is a response—how finite beings can grasp concepts and rules with infinite applications—has been forcefully expounded by Kripke, and I have no idea how to deal with it. If Wittgenstein is right, then my claim to have formed a significant thought about what is entirely beyond the reach of our minds clearly won't stand up. The assertion that there are such transcendent "facts" can have no foothold in human life. But though I have no alternative, I find it completely impossible to believe Wittgenstein's view—psychologically impossible. For example, it is a clear sign of something wrong that Wittgenstein is led to doubt that there must be an answer to the question whether the sequence 7777 occurs in the decimal expansion of π (Wittgenstein (2), sec. 516). If he is right, *nothing* in my mind determines the infinite application of any of my concepts. We simply do apply them, unhesitatingly, in certain ways, and correct others who do not.

It seems to me that to accept this as the final story is to acknowledge that all thought is an illusion. If our thoughts do not have infinite reach in a much stronger sense than this, then even the most mundane of them is not what it pretends to be. It is as if a natural Platonism makes the attempt to view the world in any other way look phony. In sum, the Wittgensteinian attack on transcendent thoughts depends on a position so radical that it also undermines the weaker transcendent pretensions of even the least philosophical of thoughts. I can't imagine what it would be like to believe it, as opposed to subscribing to it verbally.

I don't know how thought is possible. But assuming it is, I continue to believe that the general concept of reality, reaching beyond anything we could do to fill it out, involves no mistake, linguistic or otherwise. Like the unrecoverable details of the past, which cannot be given verificationist or even evidential significance, or the truth value of undecidable propositions in mathematics, it is part of our common system of concepts. Whether or not we will ever be able to conceive, let alone know, what things were like before the Big Bang, for example, the idea of what was the case then stands without the support of such elaboration, or even the remote possibility of it. The general idea of what we can never conceive is just another form of this kind of extension.

Realism is most compelling when we are forced to recognize the existence of something which we cannot describe or know fully, because it lies beyond the reach of language, proof, evidence, or empirical understanding. *Something* must be true with respect to the 7s in the expansion of π, even if we can't establish it; there must be something it is like to be a bat, even if we can never conceive it adequately. But once it is accepted in these cases, realism becomes a possible position with regard to what we *can* understand as well.

The idea of objectivity always points beyond mere intersubjective agreement, even though such agreement, criticism, and justification are essential methods of reaching an objective view. The language that we can have because of our agreement in responses enables us to reach beyond the responses to talk about the world itself. As almost everyone would concede, it enables us to say, truly or falsely, that rain was falling on Gibraltar exactly fifty thousand years ago, even if there is no way of reaching agreement in the application of the term to such a case. My position is simply a radical extension of this straight antiverificationism, and I do not see on what grounds Wittgenstein can draw the line between legitimate and illegitimate extensions beyond the range of actual agreement in judgments. Language reaches beyond itself, whether in the concept of rain or in the concept of what there is, though what it reaches can only be designated by using language or some other form of representation.

Any conception of the world must include some acknowledgment of its own incompleteness: at a minimum it will admit the existence of things or events we don't know about now. The issue is only how far beyond our actual conception of the world we should admit that the world may extend. I claim that it may contain not only what we don't know and can't yet conceive, but also what we never could conceive— and that this acknowledgment of the likelihood of its own limits should be built into our conception of reality. This amounts to a strong form of antihumanism: the world is not our world, even potentially. It may be partly or largely incomprehensible to us not just because we lack the time or technical capacity to acquire a full understanding of it, but because of our nature.

This may strike some as an extreme example of objective overreach. For it gives priority over the view from within our lives and our language to a view so far outside that we cannot even take it up directly, but must form a secondary conception of it, as something closed off to us, though perhaps accessible to other beings who could observe us from outside. But in fact the reference to an external view is inessential: it is just a device to make vivid the idea of the world in which we are contained. That world is not dependent on our view of it, or any other view: the direction of dependence is the reverse. Even though we must use language to talk about the world and our relation to it, and even though certain conditions of agreement enable us to have this language, the areas of such possible agreement are a limited part of the world.

There may be some portions of discourse where rock bottom is the language game and the shared responses on which it depends, with no real reference in the world outside of our responses and no objectivity except what comes from agreement. There is a real issue about this with respect to ethics and aesthetics, and room for disagreement about where to draw the line between realism and mere intersubjectivity without external reference. But there seems to me still much of language and thought that must be interpreted in a strong sense "realistically."

As Wittgenstein points out (Wittgenstein (2), secs. 241–2), there is a parallel between conditions of meaning and conditions of measurement. We cannot measure temperature with a thermometer unless there is a certain constancy in the results of such measurement. But that doesn't mean that temperature is nothing but a phenomenon of agreement among thermometer readings. It would exist even if there were no thermometers, and we can explain the actual agreement among thermometers by the uniform effect on them of temperature. In giving this explanation we use the concept of temperature, and a condition of our having the concept of temperature we have is that we can measure it. But that doesn't make the explanation circular, any more than a lecture on the operation of the larynx is circular. To use something that one is trying to explain is not to explain it in terms of itself.

In the employment of language we are ourselves a bit like measuring instruments, able to respond consistently to certain aspects of the world, and therefore able to talk about them. We can then explain these responses without circularity in terms of the things that produce them, using the concepts that the responses enable us to have. My contention is that just as our concepts allow us to recognize that these things would exist even if we lacked the responses that enable us to talk about them, so they allow us to recognize that there are other things we haven't been able to connect with yet, and that there may be still others (I should say there almost certainly are) with which creatures like us could never make such a connection, because we couldn't develop the necessary responses or the necessary concepts. I do not see how this supposition violates the conditions of significant thought.

In fact, to deny it shows a lack of humility, even if the denial is defended by reference to a theory of the concepts of existence and truth. Idealism—the view that what exists in the widest sense must be identified with what is thinkable by us in the widest sense—is an attempt to cut the universe down to size.

VII

FREEDOM

1. Two Problems

I turn next to the relation between objectivity and action. This will lead eventually to the subject of ethics, but I shall start by talking about freedom.

Something peculiar happens when we view action from an objective or external standpoint. Some of its most important features seem to vanish under the objective gaze. Actions seem no longer assignable to individual agents as sources, but become instead components of the flux of events in the world of which the agent is a part. The easiest way to produce this effect is to think of the possibility that all actions are causally determined, but it is not the only way. The essential source of the problem is a view of persons and their actions as part of the order of nature, causally determined or not. That conception, if pressed, leads to the feeling that we are not agents at all, that we are helpless and not responsible for what we do. Against this judgment the inner view of the agent rebels. The question is whether it can stand up to the debilitating effects of a naturalistic view.

Actually the objective standpoint generates three problems about action, only two of which I shall take up. Those two both have to do with freedom. The first problem, which I shall simply describe and put aside, is the general metaphysical problem of the nature of agency. It belongs to the philosophy of mind.

The question "What is action?" is much broader than the problem of free will, for it applies even to the activity of spiders and to the peripheral, unconscious or subintentional movements of human beings in the course of more deliberate activity (see Frankfurt (2)). It applies to any movement that is not involuntary. The question is connected with our theme because *my doing* of an act—or the doing of an act by someone else—seems to disappear when we think of the world objectively. There seems no room for agency in a world of neural impulses, chemical reactions, and bone and muscle movements. Even if we add sensations, perceptions, and feelings we don't get action, or doing—there is only what happens.

In line with what was said earlier about the philosophy of mind, I think the only solution is to regard action as a basic mental or more accurately psychophysical category—reducible neither to physical nor to other mental terms. I cannot improve on Brian O'Shaughnessy's exhaustive defense of this position. Action has its own irreducibly internal aspect as do other psychological phenomena—there is a characteristic mental asymmetry between awareness of one's own actions and awareness of the actions of others—but action isn't anything else, alone or in combination with a physical movement: not a sensation, not a feeling, not a belief, not an intention or desire. If we restrict our palette to such things plus physical events, agency will be omitted from our picture of the world.

But even if we add it as an irreducible feature, making subjects of experience also (and as O'Shaughnessy argues, inevitably) subjects of action, the problem of free action remains. We may act without being free, and we may doubt the freedom of others without doubting that they act. What undermines the sense of freedom doesn't automatically undermine agency.[1] I shall leave the general problem of agency aside in what follows, and simply assume that there is such a thing.

What I shall discuss are two aspects of the problem of free will, corresponding to the two ways in which objectivity threatens ordinary assumptions about human freedom. I call one the problem of autonomy and the other the problem of responsibility; the first presents itself initially as a problem about our own freedom and the second as a problem about the freedom of others.[2] An objective view of actions as events in

1. Here I agree with Taylor, p. 140.
2. Jonathan Bennett makes this distinction, calling them the problems of agency and accountability, respectively (Bennett, ch. 10).

the natural order (determined or not) produces a sense of impotence and futility with respect to what we do ourselves. It also undermines certain basic attitudes toward all agents—those reactive attitudes (see Strawson (2)) that are conditional on the attribution of responsibility. It is the second of these effects that is usually referred to as the problem of free will. But the threat to our conception of our own actions—the sense that we are being carried along by the universe like small pieces of flotsam—is equally important and equally deserving of the title. The two are connected. The same external view that poses a threat to my own autonomy also threatens my sense of the autonomy of others, and this in turn makes them come to seem inappropriate objects of admiration and contempt, resentment and gratitude, blame and praise.

Like other basic philosophical problems, the problem of free will is not in the first instance verbal. It is not a problem about what we are to *say* about action, responsibility, what someone could or could not have done, and so forth. It is rather a bafflement of our feelings and attitudes—a loss of confidence, conviction or equilibrium. Just as the basic problem of epistemology is not whether we can be *said to know* things, but lies rather in the loss of belief and the invasion of doubt, so the problem of free will lies in the erosion of interpersonal attitudes and of the sense of autonomy. Questions about what we are to say about action and responsibility merely attempt after the fact to express those feelings—feelings of impotence, of imbalance, and of affective detachment from other people.

These forms of unease are familiar once we have encountered the problem of free will through the hypothesis of determinism. We are undermined but at the same time ambivalent, because the unstrung attitudes don't disappear: they keep forcing themselves into consciousness despite their loss of support. A philosophical treatment of the problem must deal with such disturbances of the spirit, and not just with their verbal expression.

I change my mind about the problem of free will every time I think about it, and therefore cannot offer any view with even moderate confidence; but my present opinion is that nothing that might be a solution has yet been described. This is not a case where there are several possible candidate solutions and we don't know which is correct. It is a case where nothing believable has (to my knowledge) been proposed by anyone in the extensive public discussion of the subject.

The difficulty, as I shall try to explain, is that while we can easily evoke disturbing effects by taking up an external view of our own actions and the actions of others, it is impossible to give a coherent account of the internal view of action which is under threat. When we try to explain what we believe which seems to be undermined by a conception of actions as events in the world—determined or not—we end up with something that is either incomprehensible or clearly inadequate.

This naturally suggests that the threat is unreal, and that an account of freedom can be given which is compatible with the objective view, and perhaps even with determinism. But I believe this is not the case. All such accounts fail to allay the feeling that, looked at from far enough outside, agents are helpless and not responsible. Compatibilist accounts of freedom tend to be even less plausible than libertarian ones. Nor is it possible simply to dissolve our unanalyzed sense of autonomy and responsibility. It is something we can't get rid of, either in relation to ourselves or in relation to others. We are apparently condemned to want something impossible.

2. Autonomy

The first problem is that of autonomy. How does it arise?

In acting we occupy the internal perspective, and we can occupy it sympathetically with regard to the actions of others. But when we move away from our individual point of view, and consider our own actions and those of others simply as part of the course of events in a world that contains us among other creatures and things, it begins to look as though we never really contribute anything.

From the inside, when we act, alternative possibilities seem to lie open before us: to turn right or left, to order this dish or that, to vote for one candidate or the other—and one of the possibilities is made actual by what we do. The same applies to our internal consideration of the actions of others. But from an external perspective, things look different. That perspective takes in not only the circumstances of action as they present themselves to the agent, but also the conditions and influences lying behind the action, including the complete nature of the agent himself. While we cannot fully occupy this perspective toward ourselves while acting, it seems possible that many of the alternatives that appear to lie open when viewed from an internal perspective would seem closed from this outer point of view, if we could take it up. And even if some of them are left open, given a complete specification of the condition of the agent and the circumstances of action, it is not clear how this would leave anything further for the agent to contribute to the outcome—anything that he could contribute as source, rather than merely as the scene of the outcome—the person whose act it is. If they are left open given everything about him, what does he have to do with the result?

From an external perspective, then, the agent and everything about him seems to be swallowed up by the circumstances of action; nothing of him is left to intervene in those circumstances. This happens whether or not the relation between action and its antecedent conditions is conceived as deterministic. In either case we cease to face the world and instead become parts of it; we and our lives are seen as products and manifestations of the world as a whole. Everything I do or that anyone else does is part of a larger course of events that no one "does," but that happens, with or without explanation. Everything I do is part of something I don't do, because I am a part of the world. We may elaborate this external picture by reference to biological, psychological, and social factors in the formation of ourselves and other agents. But the picture doesn't have to be complete in order to be threatening. It is enough to form the idea of the possibility of a picture of this kind. Even if we can't attain it, an observer literally outside us might.

Why is this threatening, and what does it threaten? Why are we not content to regard the internal perspective of agency as a form of clouded subjective appearance, based as it inevitably must be on an incomplete view of the circumstances? The alternatives are alternatives only relative to what we know, and our choices result from influences of which we are only partly aware. The external perspective would then provide a more complete view, superior to the internal. We accept a parallel subordination of subjective appearance to objective reality in other areas.

The reason we cannot accept it here, at least not as a general solution, is that action is too ambitious. We aspire in some of our actions to a kind of autonomy that is not a mere subjective appearance—not merely ignorance of their sources—and we have the same view of others like us. The sense that we are the authors of our own actions is not just a feeling but a belief, and we can't come to regard it as a pure appearance without giving it up altogether. But what belief is it?

I have already said that I suspect it is no intelligible belief at all; but that has to be shown. What I am about to say is highly controversial, but let me just describe what I take to be our ordinary conception of autonomy. It presents itself initially as the belief that antecedent circumstances, including the condition of the agent, leave some of the things we will do undetermined: they are determined only by our choices, which are motivationally explicable but not themselves causally determined. Although many of the external and internal conditions of choice are inevitably fixed by the world and not under my control, some range of open possibilities is generally presented to me on an occasion of action—and when by acting I make one of those possibilities actual, the final explanation of this (once the background which defines the possibilities has been taken into account) is given by the intentional explanation of my action, which is comprehensible only through my point of view. My reason for doing it is the *whole* reason why it happened, and no further explanation is either necessary or possible. (My doing it for no particular reason is a limiting case of this kind of explanation.)

The objective view seems to wipe out such autonomy because it admits only one kind of explanation of why something happened—causal explanation—and equates its absence with the absence of any explanation at all. It may be able to admit causal explanations that are probabilistic, but the basic idea which it finds congenial is that the explanation of an occurrence must show how that occurrence, or a range of possibilities within which it falls, was necessitated by prior conditions and events. (I shall not say anything about the large question of how this notion of necessity is to be interpreted.) To the extent that no such necessity exists, the occurrence is unexplained. There is no room in an objective picture of the world for a type of explanation of action that is not causal. The defense of freedom requires the acknowledgment of a different kind of explanation essentially connected to the agent's point of view.

Though it would be contested, I believe we have such an idea of autonomy. Many philosophers have defended some version of this position as the truth about freedom: for example Farrer, Anscombe, and Wiggins. (The metaphysical theories of agent-causation espoused by Chisholm and Taylor are different, because they try to force autonomy into the objective causal order—giving a name to a mystery.) But whatever version one picks, the trouble is that while it may give a correct surface description of our prereflective sense of our own autonomy, when we look at the idea closely, it collapses. The alternative form of explanation doesn't really explain the action at all.

The intuitive idea of autonomy includes conflicting elements, which imply that it both is and is not a way of explaining why an action was done. A free action should not be determined by antecedent conditions, and should be fully explained only intentionally, in terms of justifying reasons and purposes. When someone makes an autonomous choice such as whether to accept a job, and there are reasons on both sides of the issue, we are supposed to be able to explain what he did by pointing to his reasons for accepting it. But we could equally have explained his refusing the job, if he had refused, by referring to the reasons on the other side—and he could have refused for those other reasons: that is

the essential claim of autonomy. It applies even if one choice is significantly more reasonable than the other. Bad reasons are reasons too.[3]

Intentional explanation, if there is such a thing, can explain either
choice in terms of the appropriate reasons, since either choice would be
intelligible if it occurred. But for this very reason it cannot explain why
the person accepted the job for the reasons in favor instead of refusing
it for the reasons against. It cannot explain on grounds of intelligibility
why one of two intelligible courses of action, both of which were possible, occurred. And even where it can account for this in terms of further
reasons, there will be a point at which the explanation gives out. We say
that someone's character and values are revealed by the choices he
makes in such circumstances, but if these are indeed independent conditions, they too must either have or lack an explanation.

If autonomy requires that the central element of choice be explained
in a way that does not take us outside the point of view of the agent
(leaving aside the explanation of what faces him with the choice), then
intentional explanations must simply come to an end when all available
reasons have been given, and nothing else can take over where they leave
off. But this seems to mean that an autonomous intentional explanation
cannot explain precisely what it is supposed to explain, namely *why I did
what I did rather than the alternative that was causally open to me.* It says I
did it for certain reasons, but does not explain why I didn't decide not
to do it for other reasons. It may render the action subjectively intelligible, but it does not explain why this rather than another equally possible and comparably intelligible action was done. That seems to be
something for which there is no explanation, either intentional or causal.

Of course there is a trivial intentional explanation: my reasons for

3. Some would hold that we have all the autonomy we should want if our choice is determined by compelling reasons. Hampshire, for example, attributes to Spinoza the position
that "a man is most free, . . . and also feels himself to be most free, when he cannot help
drawing a certain conclusion, and cannot help embarking on a certain course of action
in view of the evidently compelling reasons in favor of it . . . The issue is decided for him
when the arguments in support of a theoretical conclusion are conclusive arguments"
(Hampshire (1), p. 198). And Wolf proposes as the condition of freedom that the agent
"could have done otherwise if there had been good and sufficient reason" (Wolf (1), p.
159)—which means that if there wasn't a good reason to act differently, the free agent
needn't have been able to act differently.

Something like this has more plausibility with respect to thought, I believe, than it has
with respect to action. In forming beliefs we may hope for nothing more than to be determined by the truth (see Wiggins (1), pp. 145–8; see also Wefald, ch. 15), but in action
our initial assumption is different. Even when we feel rationally compelled to act, this does
not mean we are causally determined. When Luther says he *can* do nothing else, he is
referring to the normative irresistibility of his reasons, not to their causal power, and I
believe that even in such a case causal determination is not compatible with autonomy.

doing it are also my reasons against not doing it for other reasons. But since the same could be said if I had done the opposite, this amounts to explaining what happened by saying it happened. It does not stave off the question why these reasons rather than the others were the ones that motivated me. At some point this question will either have no answer or it will have an answer that takes us outside of the domain of subjective normative reasons and into the domain of formative causes of my character or personality.[4]

So I am at a loss to account for what we believe in believing that we are autonomous—what intelligible belief is undermined by the external view. That is, I cannot say what would, if it were true, support our sense that our free actions originate with us. Yet the sense of an internal explanation persists—an explanation insulated from the external view which is complete in itself and renders illegitimate all further requests for explanation of my action as an event in the world.

As a last resort the libertarian might claim that anyone who does not accept an account of what I was up to as a basic explanation of action is the victim of a very limited conception of what an explanation is—a conception locked into the objective standpoint which therefore begs the question against the concept of autonomy. But he needs a better reply than this. Why aren't these autonomous subjective explanations really just descriptions of how it seemed to the agent—before, during, and after—to do what he did; why are they something more than impressions? Of course they are at least impressions, but we take them to be impressions *of* something, something whose reality is not guaranteed by the impression. Not being able to say what that something is, and at the same time finding the possibility of its absence very disturbing, I am at a dead end.

I have to conclude that what we want is something impossible, and that the desire for it is evoked precisely by the objective view of ourselves that reveals it to be impossible. At the moment when we see ourselves from outside as bits of the world, two things happen: we are no longer satisfied in action with anything less than intervention in the world from outside; and we see clearly that this makes no sense. The very capacity that is the source of the trouble—our capacity to view ourselves from outside—encourages our aspirations of autonomy by giving us the sense that we

4. Lucas notices this but is not, I think, sufficiently discouraged by it: "There remains a tension between the programme of complete explicability and the requirements of freedom. If men have free will, then no complete explanation of their actions can be given, except by reference to themselves. We can give their reasons. But we cannot explain why their reasons were reasons for them. . . . Asked why I acted, I give my reasons: asked why I chose to accept them as reasons, I can only say 'I just did'" (Lucas, pp. 171–2).

ought to be able to encompass ourselves completely, and thus become the absolute source of what we do. At any rate we become dissatisfied with anything less.

When we act we are not cut off from the knowledge of ourselves that is revealed from the external standpoint, so far as we can occupy it. It is, after all, *our* standpoint as much as the internal one is, and if we take it up, we can't help trying to include anything it reveals to us in a new, expanded basis of action. We act, if possible, on the basis of the most complete view of the circumstances of action that we can attain, and this includes as complete a view as we can attain of ourselves. Not that we want to be paralyzed by self-consciousness. But we can't regard ourselves, in action, as subordinate to an external view of ourselves, because we automatically subordinate the external view to the purposes of our actions. We feel that in acting we ought to be able to determine not only our choices but the inner conditions of those choices, provided we step far enough outside ourselves.

So the external standpoint at once holds out the hope of genuine autonomy, and snatches it away. By increasing our objectivity and self-awareness, we seem to acquire increased control over what will influence our actions, and thus to take our lives into our own hands. Yet the logical goal of these ambitions is incoherent, for to be really free we would have to act from a standpoint completely outside ourselves, choosing everything about ourselves, including all our principles of choice—creating ourselves from nothing, so to speak.

This is self-contradictory: in order to do anything we must already be something. However much material we incorporate from the external view into the grounds of action and choice, this same external view assures us that we remain parts of the world and products, determined or not, of its history. Here as elsewhere the objective standpoint creates an appetite which it shows to be insatiable.

The problem of freedom and the problem of epistemological skepticism are alike in this respect. In belief, as in action, rational beings aspire to autonomy. They wish to form their beliefs on the basis of principles and methods of reasoning and confirmation that they themselves can judge to be correct, rather than on the basis of influences that they do not understand, of which they are unaware, or which they cannot assess. That is the aim of knowledge. But taken to its logical limit, the aim is incoherent. We cannot assess and revise or confirm our entire system of thought and judgment from outside, for we would have nothing to do it with. We remain, as pursuers of knowledge, creatures inside the world who have not created ourselves, and some of whose processes of thought have simply been given to us.

In the formation of belief, as in action, we belong to a world we have not created and of which we are the products; it is the external view which both reveals this and makes us wish for more. However objective a standpoint we succeed in making part of the basis of our actions and beliefs, we continue to be threatened by the idea of a still more external and comprehensive view of ourselves that we cannot incorporate, but that would reveal the unchosen sources of our most autonomous efforts. The objectivity that seems to offer greater control also reveals the ultimate givenness of the self.

Can we proceed part way along the inviting path of objectivity without ending up in the abyss, where the pursuit of objectivity undermines itelf and everything else? In practice, outside of philosophy we find certain natural stopping places along the route, and do not worry about how things would look if we went further. In this respect too the situation resembles that in epistemology, where justification and criticism come fairly peacefully to an end in everyday life. The trouble is that our complacency seems unwarranted as soon as we reflect on what would be revealed to a still more external view, and it is not clear how we can reestablish these natural stopping places on a new footing once they are put in doubt.

It would require some alternative to the literally unintelligible ambition of intervening in the world from outside (an ambition expressed by Kant in the unintelligible idea of the noumenal self which is outside time and causality). This ambition arises by a natural extension or continuation of the pursuit of freedom in everyday life. I wish to act not only in light of the external circumstances facing me and the possibilities that they leave open, but in light of the internal circumstances as well: my desires, beliefs, feelings, and impulses. I wish to be able to subject my motives, principles, and habits to critical examination, so that nothing moves me to action without my agreeing to it. In this way, the setting against which I act is gradually enlarged and extended inward, till it includes more and more of myself, considered as one of the contents of the world.

In its earlier stages the process does genuinely seem to increase freedom, by making self-knowledge and objectivity part of the basis of action. But the danger is obvious. The more completely the self is swallowed up in the circumstances of action, the less I have to act with. I cannot get completely outside myself. The process that starts as a means to the enlargement of freedom seems to lead to its destruction. When I contemplate the world as a whole I see my actions, even at their empirically most "free," as part of the course of nature, and this is not my doing or anyone else's. The objective self is not in a position to pull the strings of my life from outside any more than TN is.

At the end of the path that seems to lead to freedom and knowledge lie skepticism and helplessness. We can act only from inside the world, but when we see ourselves from outside, the autonomy we experience from inside appears as an illusion, and we who are looking from outside cannot act at all.

3. Responsibility

It seems to me that the problem of responsibility is insoluble, or at least unsolved, for similar reasons. We hold ourselves and others morally responsible for at least some actions when we view them from the inside; but we cannot give an account of what would have to be true to justify such judgments. Once people are seen as parts of the world, determined or not, there seems no way to assign responsibility to them for what they do. Everything about them, including finally their actions themselves, seems to blend in with the surroundings over which they have no control. And when we then go back to consider actions from the internal point of view, we cannot on close scrutiny make sense of the idea that what people do depends ultimately on them. Yet we continue to compare what they do with the alternatives they reject, and to praise or condemn them for it. (My examples will generally involve negative judgments, but everything I say is meant to apply to praise as well as to condemnation.)

What is going on here? Let me begin with a prephilosophical account of what a judgment of responsibility is. It always involves two parties, whom I shall call the *judge* and the *defendant*. These may be the same person, as when someone holds himself responsible for doing or having done something. But it will be easier to examine the complexities of the phenomenon if we concentrate first on the interpersonal case, and how it ultimately breaks down.

The defendant is an agent, and in a judgment of responsibility the judge doesn't just decide that what has been done is a good or a bad thing, but tries to enter into the defendant's point of view as an agent. He is not, however, concerned merely with how it felt: rather, he tries to assess the action in light of the alternatives presenting themselves to the defendant—among which he chose or failed to choose, and in light of the considerations and temptations bearing on the choice—which he considered or failed to consider. To praise or blame is not to judge merely that what has happened is a good or a bad thing, but to judge the person for having done it, in view of the circumstances under which it was done. The difficulty is to explain how this is possible—how we can do more than welcome or regret the event, or perhaps the psychology of the agent.

The main thing we do is to compare the act or motivation with alternatives, better or worse, which were deliberately or implicitly rejected
though their acceptance in the circumstances would have been motivationally comprehensible. That is the setting into which one projects both
an internal understanding of the action and a judgment of what should
have been done. It is the sense of the act in contrast with alternatives
not taken, together with a normative assessment of those alternatives—
also projected into the point of view of the defendant—that yields an
internal judgment of responsibility. What was done is seen as a selection
by the defendant from the array of possibilities with which he was faced,
and is defined by contrast with those possibilities.

When we hold the defendant responsible, the result is not merely a
description of his character, but a vicarious occupation of his point of
view and evaluation of his action from within it. While this process need
not be accompanied by strong feelings, it often is, and their character
will depend on the makeup of the judge. Condemnatory judgments, for
example, may be accompanied by impulses of retribution and punishment. These are most likely to appear in their full ferocity when the
psychic configuration of the judge subjects him to strong conflicts with
respect to the defendant's situation of choice. A judgment of responsibility involves a double projection: into the actual choice and into the
possible alternatives, better or worse. If the judge identifies strongly with
the bad act done or avoided, his contempt or admiration will be correspondingly strong. It is a familiar fact that we hate most the sins that
tempt us most, and admire most the virtues we find most difficult.

The kinds of things we judge others for vary. We condemn a rattlesnake for nothing, and a cat for nothing or practically nothing. Our
understanding of their actions and even of their point of view puts us
too far outside them to permit any judgments about what they should
have done. All we can do is to understand why they have done what they
did, and to be happy or unhappy about it. With regard to small children
the possibilities of moral judgment are somewhat greater, but we still
cannot project ourselves fully into their point of view in order to think
about what they should do, as opposed to what would be required of an
adult in corresponding circumstances. Similar limits apply to judgments
of other people's intelligence or stupidity. Someone has not made a stu-
pid mistake if he completely lacks the capacity of thought needed to draw
the correct conclusion from the evidence available to him. The larger his
intellectual capacities, the greater his opportunities for stupidity, as well
as for intelligence. It is the same with good and evil. A five-year-old can
be blamed for throwing the cat out the window, but not for a gross failure of tact.

Two kinds of thing may undermine a judgment of responsibility, and familiar excusing conditions fall into one or other of these classes. First, it may emerge that the character of the choice or the circumstances of action facing the defendant are different from what they at first appeared to be. He may not have full knowledge of the consequences of what he is doing; he may be acting under severe coercion or duress; certain alternatives which seemed available may not be, or he may be unaware of them. Such discoveries alter the character of the action to be assessed, but do not block a judgment of responsibility altogether.

Second, something may prevent the judge from projecting his standards into the point of view of the defendant—the initial move needed for any judgment of responsibility. Certain discoveries render the judge's projection into the defendant's perspective irrelevant to the assessment of what the defendant has done, because he is quite different from the defendant in crucial ways. For example, the defendant may have been acting under hypnotic suggestion, or under the influence of a powerful drug, or even, in the vein of science fiction, under the direct control of a mad scientist manipulating his brain. Or he may turn out not to be a rational being at all. In these cases the judge will not regard the vantage point of the defendant as the correct one to take up for purposes of assessment. He will not project himself into the defendant's point of view, but will stay outside him—so that the contemplation of alternative possibilities will not support praise or blame but only relief or regret.

The philosophical disappearance of all responsibility is an extension of this second type of disengagement. The essence of a judgment of responsibility is an *internal* comparison with alternatives—choices the agent did not make which we contrast with what he did, for better or for worse. In ordinary judgments of responsibility an objective view of the agent may lead us to alter our assumption about which alternatives are eligible for such comparison. Even alternatives that seemed to the agent to be available at the time may seem to us out of the running, once our external view of him becomes more complete.

The radically external standpoint that produces the philosophical problem of responsibility seems to make every alternative ineligible. We see the agent as a phenomenon generated by the world of which he is a part. One aspect of the phenomenon is his sense of choosing among alternatives, for good or bad reasons. But this makes no difference. Whether we think of his practical reasoning and his choices as causally determined or not, we cannot project ourselves into his point of view for the purpose of comparing alternatives once we have ascended to that extreme objective standpoint which sees him merely as a bit of the world.

The alternatives that he may think of as available to him are from this point of view just alternative courses that the world might have taken. The fact that what didn't happen would have been better or worse than what did doesn't support an internal judgment of responsibility about a human being any more than it does about a rattlesnake.

Furthermore, as is true with respect to autonomy, there is nothing we can imagine being true of the agent, even taking into account his own point of view, which would support such a judgment. Once we are in this external position, nothing about the intentional explanation of action will help. Either something other than the agent's reasons explains why he acted for the reasons he did, or nothing does. In either case the external standpoint sees the alternatives not as alternatives for the agent, but as alternatives for the *world*, which *involve* the agent. And the world, of course, is not an agent and cannot be held responsible.

The real problem is the external vantage point. In ordinary judgments of responsibility we do not go that far outside, but stay inside our natural human point of view and project it into that of other, similar beings, stopping only where it will not fit. But judgments so based are vulnerable to the more external view, which can take in both the defendant and the judge. Then the whole complex—the defendant's choice and the judge's projection into it and resulting judgment—is seen as a phenomenon also. The judge's sense of the defendant's alternatives is revealed as an illusion which derives from the judge's projection of his own illusory—indeed unintelligible—sense of autonomy into the defendant.

I can no more help holding myself and others responsible in ordinary life than I can help feeling that my actions originate with me. But this is just another way in which, from some distance outside, I seem to myself to be trapped.

As usual, a radically external view presents me with an unfulfillable demand. It gives me the idea that to be truly autonomous I would have to be able to act in light of everything about myself—from outside myself and indeed from outside the world. And it makes any projection into the point of view of an ordinary agent seem unreal. What he sees as alternatives among which he can decide are really, from this point of view, alternative courses the world might take, within which his actions fall. While I can compare the course of events which includes his actual conduct with an alternative which includes his doing something else, my evaluation of these alternatives will not yield a judgment of his action from within. Alternatives for the world are not alternatives *for* him just because they include him. In a sense, the radically external standpoint is not a standpoint of choice at all. It is only when I forget about it and return to my status as fellow creature that I can project myself into the point of view of another agent in the way required for a judgment of responsibility. Only then can I evaluate the alternatives facing *him*, and thereby judge him for what he did.

The bafflement of moral judgments by objective detachment is unstable. We may be able temporarily to view William Calley, for example, as a phenomenon—a repulsive and dangerous bit of the zoosphere—without condemning him on the basis of a projection into his standpoint of our own sense of genuine alternatives in action. But it is next to impossible to remain in the attitude of inability to condemn Lieutenant Calley for the murders at My Lai: our feelings return before the ink of the argument is dry. That is because we don't stay in the rarefied objective atmosphere but drop back into our point of view as agents, which then allows us to see Calley's point of view, as he entered the village to encounter only peasants eating breakfast, and no resistance, as the point of view within which evaluation must proceed.[5] We cannot stay outside Lieutenant Calley because we cannot stay outside ourselves. Nevertheless, the external standpoint is always there as a possibility, and once having occupied it we can no longer regard our internal judgments of responsibility in the same way. From a point of view that is available to us, they can suddenly seem to depend on an illusion—a forgetting of the fact that we are just parts of the world and our lives just parts of its history.

4. Strawson on Freedom

Let me contrast my view of the problem, specifically of its genuineness, with Strawson's. In his classic essay "Freedom and Resentment" he argues that though we can on occasion adopt the objective attitude toward other persons, it is not possible for the reactive attitudes to be philosophically undermined *in general* by any belief about the universe or human action, including the belief in determinism. The essence of his view, expressed toward the end of the essay, is this:

> Inside the general structure or web of human attitudes and feelings of which I have been speaking, there is endless room for modification, redirection, criticism, and justification. But questions of justification are internal to it. The existence of the general framework of attitudes itself is something we are given with the fact of human society. As a whole, it neither calls for, nor permits, an external 'rational' justification. (Strawson (2), p. 23)

5. See Hirsch for the details.

His view here is the same as his view about knowledge (and in a footnote to the passage, he draws an explicit parallel with the problem of induction). Justification and criticism make sense only within the system: justification of the system from outside is unnecessary, and therefore criticism from outside is impossible.

I believe this position is incorrect because there is no way of preventing the slide from *internal* to *external* criticism once we are capable of an external view. It needs nothing more than the ordinary idea of responsibility. The problem of free will, like the problem of skepticism, does not arise because of a philosophically imposed demand for external justification of the entire system of ordinary judgments and attitudes. It arises because there is a continuity between familiar "internal" criticism of the reactive attitudes on the basis of specific facts, and philosophical criticisms on the basis of supposed general facts. When we first consider the possibility that all human actions may be determined by heredity and environment, it threatens to defuse our reactive attitudes as effectively as does the information that a particular action was caused by the effects of a drug—despite all the differences between the two suppositions. It blocks the projection into the point of view of the agent on which the reactive attitudes depend. The same is true when we expand the point to cover every way in which our lives can be seen as part of the course of nature, whether determined or not. No new standards come into it; in fact no demand for justification comes into it, since the challenge depends only on generalizing familiar standards of criticism. We cease to resent what someone has done if we cease to see the alternatives as alternatives for him.

The parallel with skepticism in epistemology is again clear. The extremely general possibilities of error that the skeptic imagines undermine confidence in all our beliefs in just the way that a more mundane particular possibility of error undermines confidence in a particular belief. The possibility of complete erosion by skeptical possibilities is built into our ordinary beliefs from the start: it is not created by the philosophical imposition of new standards of justification or certainty. On the contrary, new justifications seem to be required only in response to the threat of erosion from ordinary criticisms, sufficiently generalized.

Similarly with action. Some of the externally imposed limitations and constraints on our actions are evident to us. When we discover others, internal and less evident, our reactive attitudes toward the affected action tend to be defused, for it seems no longer attributable in the required way to the person who must be the target of those attitudes. The philosophical challenges to free will are nothing but radical extensions of this encroachment. As the unchosen conditions of action are extended into the agent's makeup and psychological state by an expanded objectivity, they seem to engulf everything, and the area of freedom left to him shrinks to zero. Since this seems to happen whether determinism is true or not, we are threatened with the conclusion that the idea of free agency with which we began is really unintelligible. It only seemed to mean something when we located it in the space left open by those familiar limits on action imposed by the external world—and only because we did not think enough about what would have to occupy that blank space. Nothing, it seems, could.

This is a genuine challenge to our freedom and the attitudes that presuppose it, and it cannot be met by the claim that only internal criticisms are legitimate, unless that claim is established on independent grounds. The push to objectivity is after all a part of the framework of human life. It could only be stopped from leading to these skeptical results if the radically external view of human life could be shown to be illegitimate—so that our questions had to stop before we got there.[6]

5. The Blind Spot

I am now going to change the subject. I have said this problem has no available solution and will not contradict myself by proposing one. But I want to do something else, and that is to describe a kind of reconciliation between the objective standpoint and the inner perspective of agency which reduces the radical detachment produced by initial contemplation of ourselves as creatures in the world. This does not meet the central problem of free will. But it does reduce the degree to which the objective self must think of itself as an impotent spectator, and to that extent it confers a kind of freedom. It is a bit like the relation between the ordinary pursuit of objective knowledge and philosophical skepticism—to explain the obscure by the equally obscure: a limited harmony between external and internal, in the shadow of an even more external view.

We cannot act from outside ourselves, nor create ourselves *ex nihilo*. But the impulse to this logically impossible goal also pushes us toward something else, which is not logically impossible and which may assuage

---

6. See Stroud, ch. 7, for the analogous point that skepticism is unavoidable unless we can somehow show the demand for an 'external' account of knowledge to be illegitimate. Once the question has been raised, it can't be answered. This makes it tempting to look for a way of showing that it can't be raised—but I am skeptical about the prospects of such a strategy.

the original impulse somewhat to the extent that we can attain it. We want to bring the external view of ourselves back into connection with our actions, as far as we can. We must learn to act from an objective standpoint as well as to view ourselves from an objective standpoint.

The problem here is continuous with the prephilosophical problem of seeking freedom from inner bondage in ordinary life. We all want external freedom, of course: the absence of obstacles to doing what we want. We don't want to be locked or tied up, or closed off from opportunities, or too poor or weak to do what we would like. But reflective human beings want something more. They want to be able to stand back from the motives and reasons and values that influence their choices, and submit to them only if they are acceptable. Since we can't act in light of *everything* about ourselves, the best we can do is to try to live in a way that wouldn't have to be revised in light of anything more that could be known about us. This is a practical analogue of the epistemological hope for harmony with the world.

Let me repeat that this is not autonomy, not a solution to the problem of free will, but a substitute—one which falls short of the impossible aspiration to act from outside ourselves, but which nevertheless has value in its own right. I want to discuss some of the ways in which we can reduce the detachment from our own actions that initially results from taking up the objective standpoint, by coming to act from that standpoint.

We might try, first, to develop as complete an objective view of ourselves as we can, and include it in the basis of our actions, wherever it is relevant. This would mean consistently looking over our own shoulders at what we are doing and why (though often it will be a mere formality). But this objective self-surveillance will inevitably be incomplete, since some knower must remain behind the lens if anything is to be known. Moreover, each of us knows this—knows that some of the sources of his actions are not objects of his attention and choice. The objective view of ourselves includes both what we know and can use, and what we know that we do not know, and therefore know that we cannot use.

Let me call this the *essentially incomplete objective view*, or *incomplete view* for short. The incomplete view of ourselves in the world includes a large blind spot, behind our eyes, so to speak, that hides something we cannot take into account in acting, because it is what acts. Yet this blind spot is part of our objective picture of the world, and to act from as far out as possible we must to some extent include a recognition of it in the basis of our actions.

We may discover our freedom to be limited if the objective view turns up an irrational impulse or fear whose influence on our conduct we can't

prevent, but which we know to be irrational and cannot accept as justified. But we can also reflect that our actions may be constrained by an
influence we know nothing about. This might be either something we
could successfully resist if we did know about it, or something we
wouldn't be able to resist even then, but which we also couldn't accept
as a legitimate ground for action.

The incomplete view faces us with the possibility that we are constrained in one of these ways without knowing it, by factors operating in
the blind spot. It also faces us with the certainty that however much we
expand our objective view of ourselves, something will remain beyond
the possibility of explicit acceptance or rejection, because we cannot get
entirely outside ourselves, even though we know that there is an outside.

We hope we aren't under influences that we would see grounds for
resisting if we became aware of them—various forms of prejudice, irrationality, and narrow-mindedness. This is a fairly ordinary limitation on
freedom, which we can take measures to avoid. Some of these measures
involve widening the range of our self-awareness, and some require
rather an attunement to the selective need for seeking it. The real difficulty, though, is to say what it is reasonable to hope for with respect to
the core of the self that lies at the center of the blind spot.

It is clear that we can't decisively and irrevocably endorse our actions,
any more than we can endorse our beliefs, from the most objective
standpoint we can take toward ourselves, since what we see from that
standpoint is the incomplete view. All we can do to avoid the disengagement of that standpoint from action is to try to satisfy a negative condition: the absence of positive reasons to detach. The best we can hope
for is to act in a way that permits some confidence that it would not
prove unacceptable no matter how much more completely we developed
the objective view—no matter how many more steps we took outside
ourselves, even beyond all real possibility.

This involves the idea of an unlimited hypothetical development on
the path of self-knowledge and self-criticism, only a small part of which
we will actually traverse. We assume that our own advances in objectivity
are steps along a path that extends beyond them and beyond all our
capacities. But even allowing unlimited time, or an unlimited number of
generations, to take as many successive steps as we like, the process of
enlarging objectivity can never be completed, short of omniscience.
First, every objective view will contain a blind spot, and cannot comprehend everything about the viewer himself. But second, there will not
even be a limiting point beyond which it is impossible to go. This is
because each step to a new objective vantage point, while it brings more
of the self under observation, also adds to the dimensions of the

observer something further which is not itself immediately observed. And this becomes possible material for observation and assessment from a still later objective standpoint. The mind's work is never done.

So the creation of an objective will is not a completable task. What is wanted is some way of making the most objective standpoint the basis of action: subordinating it to my agency instead of allowing it, and therefore me, to stay outside of my actions as a helpless observer. Given that I cannot do this by acting from outside the world, on the basis of a complete objective view of myself and it, the next best thing is to act from within the world on the basis of the most objective view of which I am capable—the incomplete view—in such a way as to guard against rejection by its successors in the objective sequence, both those that I can achieve and those that I can't. The attempt to achieve immunity from later objective revision (independently of whether I will actually reach the later objective stages) is the only way to make the incomplete objective view a continuing part of the basis of my actions. That is the closest I can come to acting on the world from outside myself while being part of it.

This form of integration between the standpoints must be distinguished from the position of a creature that doesn't suffer from the sense of helplessness because it can't take up the external view toward itself. When a cat stalks a bird, no element of the cat's self can remain outside as a detached observer of the scene, so there is no sense in which the cat can feel that *he* is not doing it. But because there is more to me than there is to a cat, I am threatened by the feeling that I do not really act when I act only on the basis of that internal view which suffices for a cat.

The cat's immunity to the problem of autonomy does not mean that it is free. We can consider the cat from outside and it may be that we will see it as trapped, in certain respects, by ignorance, fear, or instinct. Its nature is given and cannot be subjected by the cat to endorsement, criticism, or revision. It cannot increase its own rationality.

We would not be in much better shape than the cat if, though we remained engaged in our actions however objective a standpoint we achieved, nevertheless there was a standpoint more objective than any open to us, from which we would appear to an outside observer as the cat appears to us. But in fact, unlike the cat, we can form the idea of views of ourselves more objective than any we can reach, and can make our own detachment or engagement parasitic on what we suppose those views would reveal. We wish to believe that the possibility of engagement is not limited to the maximum level that we can actually attain, and we would like to be able to regard this level as a link to unlimited objectivity—so that there is no view of us, no matter how external, that permits complete detachment. This is to extend the ambition of rationalism to practical reason.

Descartes tried to recapture knowledge by imagining his relation to the world from the point of view of God. Finding one's feet within the world in a way that will withstand criticism from more objective standpoints than one can take up is a Cartesian enterprise, and like Descartes' it can hope at best for only partial success. But with this qualification, there are several strategies for increasing objective engagement with one's actions—or at least decreasing objective disengagement from them.

6. Objective Engagement

The most ambitious strategy would be to seek positive grounds for choice that commanded the assent of the objective will no matter how far removed it was from my particular perspective. This, if it were possible, would amount to acting *sub specie aeternitatis*. It would be analogous to the epistemological strategy of grounding belief in a priori certainties: mathematical or logical truths or methods of reasoning of whose falsehood one cannot conceive—of which one can't even conceive that a far wiser being might see that they were false, though it was beyond one's own powers.

Since such absolute objective grounds are even harder to come by in practical than in theoretical reason, a less ambitious strategy seems called for. One such strategy—a strategy of objective tolerance as opposed to objective affirmation—is to find grounds for acting within my personal perspective that will not be *rejected* from a larger point of view: grounds which the objective self can tolerate because of their limited pretensions to objectivity. Such latitude would be acceptable within the constraints imposed by any more positive results of the objective view.

The epistemological analogue would be the identification of certain beliefs as limited in the objectivity of their claims. These would be about the world of appearance, and an objective view could admit them as such. The danger with this strategy is that it can be misused as a general escape from skepticism by reducing all apparently objective judgments to subjective claims about the appearances. But if we avoid this kind of escapist reductionism, there certainly remain some beliefs which are just about the appearances. Beliefs about the subjective character of my sensory experiences, for example, are not threatened by the prospect that they might be overthrown from a much more objective standpoint.

With respect to decision and action, the strategy of objective tolerance is appropriate in areas where I do not aspire to the highest degree of self-command. When I choose from a menu I am interested only in opening myself to the play of inclinations and appetites, in order to see what I most feel like having (providing it's a cheap restaurant and I'm not on a diet). I am content here to be guided by my strongest appetite, without fear that from a more detached perspective it might appear that one of the weaker ones should really be preferred.

In fact I don't know what it would mean to wonder whether, *sub specie aeternitatis*, wanting a chicken salad sandwich was perhaps really preferable as a ground for action to wanting a salami sandwich. Nothing happens when I put myself outside of these desires and contemplate the choice: it can be made only from an internal perspective, for the preferences are neither undermined nor endorsed from an external one. Perhaps there could be some objective endorsement of the satisfaction of the preferences without endorsement of the preferences themselves. But even this principle of prima facie hedonism seems superfluous until I am faced with the problem of weighing these preferences against other motives and values.

In these kinds of cases, then, I do not feel trapped or impotent when I consider my situation objectively, because I do not aspire to more control than I have if my choice is dictated by my immediate inclinations. I am content with the freedom of a cat choosing which armchair to curl up in. External assessment can add nothing to this, nor does it detract.

The strategy of finding areas for objective tolerance rather than objective endorsement may have application at higher levels than that of choosing from a menu. It may be that from a standpoint sufficiently external to that of ordinary human life, not only chicken salad and salami but much of what is important to human beings—their hopes, projects, ambitions, and very survival—cannot be seen positively to matter. Insofar as I can regard that standpoint as part of my own, I may be able to endorse objectively almost nothing that I do. Whether this makes me the helpless victim of most of the motives and values that govern my life depends on whether from this most objective standpoint such values would be rejected as erroneous, or whether, like a taste for pecan pie, they could be tolerated as limited in their objective pretensions, and therefore subjectively legitimate as grounds for action. If in the sequence of more and more external perspectives they would be endorsed up to a certain point and thereafter tolerated, then I need not fear radical objective separation from acts that depend on them—though there will be a certain detachment.

This form of "reentry" leaves us in a different position with respect to our impulses from the one we are in prereflectively. The belief that they do not make strongly objective claims, and therefore are not liable to being overthrown or discredited from a more objective standpoint, is now in the background of our motives. As with sensory impressions, they have a different status in our picture of the world once we have distinguished between appearance and reality. When we act on such impulses we need not feel objectively dissociated, because if we consider the possibility that they would be rejected from a higher standpoint, we can conclude that because of their limited pretensions they would not.

But while many choices have this uncomplicated character, more difficult questions arise in connection with the characteristically human capacity to move to a higher vantage point and a higher order of desires—particularly where there is conflict among different types of first-order desires. Then practical judgment originates with the objective standpoint, and we look for some assurance that it will not be overthrown by a still more objective or detached view.

An important method of objective integration is ordinary practical rationality, which is roughly analogous to the process of forming a coherent set of beliefs out of one's prereflective personal impressions. This involves not mere tolerance, but actual endorsement of some motives, suppression or revision of others, and adoption of still others, from a standpoint outside that within which primary impulses, appetites, and aversions arise. When these conflict we can step outside and choose among them. Although such rationality can be exercised purely with respect to present desires, it is naturally extended to prudential rationality, which is exercised from an objective standpoint detached from the present, and decides on the weight to be accorded to all one's interests, present and future.

Prudence may itself conflict with other motives, and then it becomes itself subject to assessment from outside. But if it is just one's own present and future desires that are in question, prudence consists in taking up a standpoint outside the present—and perhaps refusing to permit one's choices to be dictated by the strongest present desire. Most simply, preference may be given to the satisfaction of stronger or longer-term expected desires; but other interests may also count.

The conflict between prudence and impulse is not like the conflict between chicken salad and salami, for it is a conflict between levels: the immediate perspective of the present moment and the (partly) transcendent perspective of temporal neutrality among the foreseeable moments of one's life. It is an example of the pursuit of freedom because through prudence we try to stand back from the impulses that press on us immediately, and to act in a temporal sense from outside of ourselves. If we could not do this, we would as agents be trapped in the present moment, with temporal neutrality reduced to a vantage point of observation.[7] And we would be even more trapped if we couldn't exercise practical rationality by harmonizing our desires even in the present: we would just have to watch ourselves being pushed around by them.

Prudence itself does not hold comparable dangers unless it is viewed from a larger perspective in competition with motives of a quite different kind. One must be careful here: prudence itself can be a kind of slavery, if carried too far. The dominance of a timeless view of one's life may be objectively unwise. And compulsiveness or neurotic avoidance based on repressed desires can easily be disguised as rational self-control. But in its normal form, prudence increases one's freedom by increasing one's control over the operation of first-order motives, through a kind of objective will.

The objective stance here is not merely permissive, but active. The prudential motives do not exist prior to the adoption of an objective standpoint, but are produced by it. Even the direct motivation of present desires is replaced by the objective weight they are given in a timeless prudential assessment, when they are thrown into a class with future ones. (I shall not try to discuss the difficult problems that arise about past desires in relation to the analysis of prudence—problems vividly exposed and thoroughly explored in Parfit (2), ch. 8.)

Although prudence is only the first stage in the development of an objective will, it is selective in its endorsement of more immediate motives and preferences. From outside of the present moment, not all the impulses and goals of each present moment can be equally endorsed, especially if they conflict with one another. Certain basic and persistent desires and needs will be natural candidates for prudential endorsement, but passing whims won't be, as such—although the general capacities and liberties that enable one to indulge such whims may be objectively valued. (Parfit has suggested to me that this same division may also show up in ethics, for the desires that provide the material for prudence may be the ones we have to consider in according objective weight to the interests of other people.) This does not mean that motives which cannot be endorsed from a timeless standpoint must be crushed completely. Their immediate operation is objectively tolerable, but they do have to compete with prudential reasons in whose formation they do not have a significant voice, so to speak.

Even when I choose not to submit entirely to prudential considerations as against present impulse, this depends on squaring my acts with

7. I've said more about this in Nagel (1).

the objective view. For I must objectively tolerate those impulses and their success, even if I do not endorse them with their full weight. Otherwise it is not freedom that I display but weakness of will.

The timeless standpoint may to some extent take a hands-off attitude toward the motives of the present moment. This restrained manifestation of objectivity is an example of something more general and very important in the relation between subjective and objective: there are limits to the degree to which the objective standpoint can simply take over and replace the original perspectives which it transcends.

Nevertheless, we are led outside the standpoint of the present, to a position from which we can at least subject our immediate impulses to objective scrutiny. And this first step into objective time is taken with the hope that its results would not be overthrown by more advanced steps not yet taken, or perhaps not even takable by us. The essential activity of the objective will, in assessing, endorsing, rejecting, and tolerating immediate impulses, is to recognize or form values, as opposed to mere preferences.[8]

7. Morality as Freedom

More external than the standpoint of temporal neutrality is the standpoint from which one sees oneself as just an individual among others, viewing one's interests and concerns entirely from outside. In some respects, the appropriate attitude from this standpoint may be tolerance rather than endorsement. But we are not in general content to regard our lives in this way once we have taken up an external view, nor are we content to act without a more positive endorsement from the objective self.

Moreover, tolerance runs into difficulty when the interests of different individuals conflict. I can't continue to regard my impulses and desires as making no objective claims if I wish to pursue them in opposition to the desires of others—unless I am prepared to regard the outcome of all such conflicts with objective indifference, like the choice between chicken salad and salami. But if I'm going to take a dim view, from an external standpoint, of the situation in which I don't get any lunch at all because a greedy fellow picnicker has eaten all the sandwiches, then I must move beyond objective tolerance to objective endorsement.

8. See Watson for a discussion of the relation between freedom and values. The present discussion of objective will is an attempt to say more about what values are and how they provide an alternative to the autonomy we cannot have.

This is a different connection between the objective standpoint and action: engagement not just from outside the present moment, but from outside one's life.[9] Thus in a sense I come to act on the world from outside my particular personal place in it—to control the behavior of TN from a standpoint that is not mine qua TN. The objective self for whom the problem of free will arises is co-opted into agency.

All this manifests itself in the formation of impersonal values, and the modification of conduct and motivation in accordance with them. It imposes serious constraints. Values are judgments from a standpoint external to ourselves about how to be and how to live. Because they are accepted from an impersonal standpoint, they apply not only to the point of view of the particular person I happen to be, but generally. They tell me how I should live because they tell me how anyone should live.

A proper discussion of this form of inner-outer integration belongs to ethics, and I shall undertake it later. In a sense, I am agreeing with Kant's view that there is an internal connection between ethics and freedom: subjection to morality expresses the hope of autonomy, even though it is a hope that cannot be realized in its original form. We cannot act on the world from outside, but we can in a sense act from both inside and outside our particular position in it. Ethics increases the range of what it is about ourselves that we can will—extending it from our actions to the motives and character traits and dispositions from which they arise. We want to be able to will the sources of our actions down to the very bottom, reducing the gap between explanation and justification. To put it another way, we want to reduce the size of the range of determinants of our actions that are not willable but merely observable—that from outside we can only *watch*.

Naturally there are many determinants of action to which the will cannot extend. Ethics cannot make us omnipotent: if we wished to close the gap between explanation and justification completely, it would mean willing the entire history of the world that produced us and faced us with the circumstances in which we must live, act, and choose. Such *amor fati* is beyond the aspiration of most of us.

There is a way of extending the will beyond ourselves to the circumstances of action, but it is through the extension of ethics into politics. Objective engagement is increased not only if we can will the sources of

9. See Parfit (2), ch. 7, for an argument that if one accepts the first, one has to accept the second. Prudence, he argues, cannot be identified with practical rationality, because it is unreasonable to hold that reasons cannot be relative to time but must be relative to persons.

our actions relative to the circumstances, but also if the circumstances of life are such that we can will from an objective standpoint that the conditions in which we must act should be as they are. Then in a sense the harmony between observation and will, or between explanation and justification, is extended into the world. (The epistemological analogue would be objective endorsement of the intellectual environment and process of education that led to the formation of one's capacity for reasoning, assessing evidence, and forming beliefs.)

What we hope for is not only to do what we want given the circumstances, but also to be as we want to be, to as deep a level as possible, and to find ourselves faced with the choices we want to be faced with, in a world that we can want to live in. If we were interested only in eliminating the external barriers to freedom, we would not be led into ethics, but only into the attempt to increase control over our environment. This would involve politics too, but only a politics based on our interests, like that of Hobbes, not an ethical politics. It is the attack on inner barriers that leads to the development of ethics, for it means that we hope to be able to will that our character and motives should be as they are, and not feel simply stuck with them when viewing ourselves objectively.

Values express the objective will. Ethical values in particular result from the combination of many lives and sets of interests in a single set of judgments. The demands of balancing, coordination, and integration that this imposes have consequences for what can be objectively willed for each individual, and therefore for oneself. Ethics is one route to objective engagement because it supplies an alternative to pure observation of ourselves from outside. It permits the will to expand at least some of the way along the path of transcendence possible for the understanding. How far we can travel on this path is partly a matter of luck. We may be so constituted that our objective judgments cannot keep pace with our capacity for doubt. And of course we can always raise the purely abstract doubt that even the strongest sense of harmony between internal and external views might be an illusion, identifiable as such only from a superior vantage point that we cannot reach.

None of this, as I have said, solves the traditional problem of free will. However much harmony with an objective view we may achieve in action, we can always undermine the sense of our own autonomy by reflecting that the chain of explanation or absence of explanation for this harmony can be pursued till it leads outside our lives.

When it comes to moral responsibility and the internal comparison of action with the alternatives, nothing is changed by the possibilities of objective engagement I have discussed. If there is such a thing as responsibility, it would have to be found in bad actions as well as good ones—

that is, in actions which one could not endorse from an objective standpoint. This means that any attempt to locate freedom in the development of rational and moral self-command will run into the problem Sidgwick posed as an objection to Kant. The problem is that if freedom can be pursued and approached only through the achievement of objective and ultimately ethical values of some kind, then it is not clear how someone can be both free and bad, hence not clear how someone can be morally responsible for doing wrong, if freedom is a condition of responsibility.[10]

In practice we project ourselves for purposes of judgment into the standpoint of anyone whose actions we can interpret subjectively as a manifestation of his values.[11] This is perfectly natural, but it cannot defuse the problem of responsibility, which can always be raised again, both about us and about the people we feel able to understand and evaluate from inside.

I can see no way to bring judgments of responsibility back into line with the external view—no way to reengage it with such judgments as it can be partially reengaged with action. Judgments of responsibility depend on a kind of projection into the standpoint of the defendant which we cannot carry out unless we forget the external view to a certain extent. I can't simultaneously think of Lieutenant Calley as a natural phenomenon from outside and assess his actions from inside by contrasting them with the alternatives that appeared subjectively available to him at the time. Nothing analogous to partial objective engagement is available here. Unless there is a way to block the ascent to the external view, we cannot find a place to stand inside the world which will permit us to make such judgments without the threat that they will seem senseless from farther out. But we seem locked into a practice of projection in which we take the sense of our own autonomy, intelligible or not, as our measure for the judgment of others.

As I have said, it seems to me that nothing approaching the truth has yet been said on this subject.

---

10. Sidgwick, bk. 1, ch. 5, sec. 1. Kant grapples with this problem in Kant (4), bk. 1, which deals explicitly with responsibility for evil.
11. This includes actions which go against the values he holds explicitly—as when someone out of fear fails to decide to do what he thinks he should, or fails to do what he has decided to do. The failure to act on one's values shows something about their strength, as well as about the strength of one's will.

VIII

VALUE

1. Realism and Objectivity

Objectivity is the central problem of ethics. Not just in theory, but in life. The problem is to decide in what way, if at all, the idea of objectivity can be applied to practical questions, questions of what to do or want. To what extent can they be dealt with from a detached point of view toward ourselves and the world? I have already indicated, in the discussion of free will, a connection between ethics and the objective standpoint. I want now to defend the objectivity of ethics by showing how that standpoint alters and constrains our motives. The possibility of ethics and many of its problems can be best understood in terms of the impact of objectivity on the will. If we can make judgments about how we should live even after stepping outside of ourselves, they will provide the material for moral theory.

In theoretical reasoning objectivity is advanced when we form a new conception of reality that includes ourselves as components. This involves an alteration or at least an extension of our beliefs. In the sphere of values or practical reasoning, the problem is different. As in the theoretical case, we must take up a new, comprehensive viewpoint after stepping back and including our former perspective in what is to be understood. But here the new viewpoint will be not a new set of beliefs, but a new or extended set of values. We try to arrive at normative judgments, with motivational content, from an impersonal standpoint. We cannot use a nonnormative criterion of objectivity, for if values are objective, they must be so in their own right and not through reducibility to some other kind of objective fact. They have to be objective *values*, not objective anything else.

Here as elsewhere there is a connection between objectivity and realism, though realism about values is different from realism about empirical facts. Normative realism is the view that propositions about what gives us reasons for action can be true or false independently of how things appear to us, and that we can hope to discover the truth by transcending the appearances and subjecting them to critical assessment. What we aim to discover by this method is not a new aspect of the external world, called value, but rather just the truth about what we and others should do and want.

It is important not to associate this form of realism with an inappropriate metaphysical picture: it is not a form of Platonism. The claim is that there are reasons for action, that we have to discover them instead of deriving them from our preexisting motives—and that in this way we can acquire new motives superior to the old. We simply aim to reorder our motives in a direction that will make them more acceptable from an external standpoint. Instead of bringing our thoughts into accord with an external reality, we try to bring an external view into the determination of our conduct.

The connection between objectivity and truth is therefore closer in ethics than it is in science. I do not believe that the truth about how we should live could extend radically beyond any capacity we might have to discover it (apart from its dependence on nonevaluative facts we might be unable to discover). The subject matter of ethics *is* how to engage in practical reasoning and the justification of action once we expand our consciousness by occupying the objective standpoint—not something else about action which the objective standpoint enables us to understand better. Ethical thought is the process of bringing objectivity to bear on the will, and the only thing I can think of to say about ethical truth in general is that it must be a possible result of this process, correctly carried out. I recognize that this is empty. If we wish to be more specific, all we can do is to refer to the arguments that persuade us of the objective validity of a reason or the correctness of a normative principle (and a given principle may be established in more than one way—got at from different starting points and by different argumentative routes).

Perhaps a richer metaphysic of morals could be devised, but I don't know what it would be. The picture I associate with normative realism is not that of an extra set of properties of things and events in the world, but of a series of possible steps in the development of human motivation which would improve the way we lead our lives, whether or not we will actually take them. We begin with a partial and inaccurate view, but by stepping outside of ourselves and constructing and comparing alternatives we can reach a new motivational condition at a higher level of objectivity. Though the aim is normative rather than descriptive, the method of investigation is analogous in certain respects to that of seeking an objective conception of what there is. We first form a conception of the world as centerless—as containing ourselves and other beings with particular points of view. But the question we then try to answer is not "What can we see that the world contains, considered from this impersonal standpoint?" but "What is there reason to do or want, considered from this impersonal standpoint?"

The answer will be complex. As in metaphysics, so in the realm of practical reason the truth is sometimes best understood from a detached standpoint; but sometimes it will be fully comprehensible only from a particular perspective within the world. If there are such subjective values, then an objective conception of what people have reasons to do must leave room for them. (I said something about this in the last chapter, under the heading of objective tolerance.) But once the objective step is taken, the possibility is also open for the recognition of values and reasons that are independent of one's personal perspective and have force for anyone who can view the world impersonally, as a place that contains him. If objectivity means anything here, it will mean that when we detach from our individual perspective and the values and reasons that seem acceptable from within it, we can sometimes arrive at a new conception which may endorse some of the original reasons but will reject some as false subjective appearances and add others.

So without prejudging the outcome—that is, how much of the domain of practical reasons can be objectively understood—we can see what the objectifying impulse depends on. The most basic idea of practical objectivity is arrived at by a practical analogue of the rejection of solipsism in the theoretical domain. Realism about the facts leads us to seek a detached point of view from which reality can be discerned and appearance corrected, and realism about values leads us to seek a detached point of view from which it will be possible to correct inclination and to discern what we really should do. Practical objectivity means that practical reason can be understood and even engaged in by the objective self.

This assumption, though powerful, is not yet an ethical position. It merely marks the place which an ethical position will occupy if we can make sense of the subject. It says that the world of reasons, including my reasons, does not exist only from my own point of view. I am in a world whose character is to a certain extent independent of what I think, and if I have reasons to act it is because the person who I am has those reasons, in virtue of his condition and circumstances. The basic question of practical reason from which ethics begins is not "What shall I do?" but "What should this person do?"

This sets a problem and indicates a method of attacking it. The problem is to discover the form which reasons for action take, and whether it can be described from no particular point of view. The method is to begin with the reasons that appear to obtain from my own point of view and those of other individuals; and ask what the best perspectiveless account of those reasons is. As in other domains, we begin from our position inside the world and try to transcend it by regarding what we find here as a sample of the whole.

That is the hope. But the claim that there are objective values is permanently controversial, because of the ease with which values and reasons seem to disappear when we transcend the subjective standpoint of our own desires. It can seem, when one looks at life from outside, that there is no room for values in the world at all. So to say: "There are just people with various motives and inclinations, some of which they may express in evaluative language; but when we regard all this from outside, all we see are psychological facts. The ascent to an objective view, far from revealing new values that modify the subjective appearances, reveals that appearances are all there is: it enables us to observe and describe our subjective motives but does not produce any new ones. Objectivity has no place in this domain except what is inherited from the objectivity of theoretical and factual elements that play a role in practical reasoning. Beyond that it applies here with a nihilistic result: nothing is objectively right or wrong because objectively nothing matters; if there are such things as right and wrong, they must rest on a subjective foundation."

I believe this conclusion is the result of a mistake comparable to the one that leads to physicalism, with its attendant reductionist elaborations. An epistemological criterion of reality is being assumed which pretends to be comprehensive but which in fact excludes large domains in advance without argument.

The assumption is surreptitious, but natural. Values can seem really to disappear when we step outside of our skins, so that it strikes us as a philosophical *perception* that they are illusory. This is a characteristic Humean step: we observe the phenomenon of people acting for what they take to be reasons, and *all we see* (compare Hume's treatment of causality) are certain natural facts: that people are influenced by certain motives, or would be if they knew certain things.

We are continually tempted to reoccupy Hume's position by the difficulties we encounter when we try to leave it. Skepticism, Platonism, reductionism, and other familiar philosophical excesses all make their appearance in ethical theory. Particularly attractive is the reaction to skepticism which reinterprets the whole field, ethics included, in completely subjective terms. Like phenomenalism in epistemology, this conceals the retreat from realism by substituting a set of judgments that in some way resemble the originals.

The only way to resist Humean subjectivism about desires and reasons for action is to seek a form of objectivity appropriate to the subject. This will not be the objectivity of naturalistic psychology. It must be argued that an objective view limited to such observations is not correct. Or rather, not necessarily correct, for the point is that an objective view of ourselves should leave room for the apprehension of reasons—should not exclude them in advance.

They seem to be excluded in advance if the objective standpoint is assumed to be one of pure observation and description.[1] When we direct this sort of attention to what appears subjectively as a case of acting for reasons and responding to good and evil, we get a naturalistic account that seems to give the complete objective description of what is going on. Instead of normative reasons, we see only a psychological explanation.

But I believe it is a mistake to give these phenomena a purely psychological reading when we look at them from outside. What we see, unless we are artificially blind, is not just people being moved to act by their desires, but people acting and forming intentions and desires for reasons, good or bad. That is, we recognize their reasons *as reasons*—or perhaps we think they are bad reasons—but in any case we do not drop out of the evaluative mode as soon as we leave the subjective standpoint. The recognition of reasons as reasons is to be contrasted with their use purely as a form of psychological explanation (see Davidson (1)). The latter merely connects action with the agent's desires and beliefs, without touching the normative question whether he *had* an adequate reason for acting—whether he should have acted as he did. If this is all that can be said once we leave the point of view of the agent behind, then I think it would follow that we don't really act for reasons at all. Rather, we are caused to act by desires and beliefs, and the terminology of reasons can be used only in a diminished, nonnormative sense to express this kind of explanation.

---

1. Cf. Anscombe (1), p. 137: "This often happens in philosophy; it is argued that 'all we find' is such-and-such, and it turns out that the arguer has excluded from his idea of 'finding' the sort of thing he says we don't 'find.'"

   The substitution of an account in which values or normative reasons play no part is not something that simply falls out of the objective view. It depends on a particular objective claim that can be accepted only if it is more plausible than its denial: the claim that our sense that the world presents us with reasons for action is a subjective illusion, produced by the projection of our preexisting motives onto the world, and that there aren't objectively any reasons for us to do anything—though of course there are motives, some of which mimic normative reasons in form.

   But this would have to be established: it does not follow from the idea of objectivity alone. When we take the objective step, we don't leave the evaluative capacity behind automatically, since that capacity does not depend on antecedently present desires. We may find that it continues to operate from an external standpoint, and we may conclude that this is not just a case of subjective desires popping up again in objective disguise. I acknowledge the dangers of false objectification, which elevates personal tastes and prejudices into cosmic values. But it isn't the only possibility.

2. Antirealism

Where does the burden of proof lie with respect to the possibility of objective values? Does their possibility have to be demonstrated before we can begin to think more specifically about which values are revealed or obliterated by the objective standpoint? Or is such an inquiry legitimate so long as objective values haven't been shown to be *im*possible?

   I think the burden of proof has been often misplaced in this debate, and that a defeasible presumption that values need not be illusory is entirely reasonable until it is shown not to be. Like the presumption that things exist in an external world, the presumption that there are real values and reasons can be defeated in individual cases, if a purely subjective account of the appearances is more plausible. And like the presumption of an external world, its complete falsity is not self-contradictory. The reality of values, impersonal or otherwise, is not entailed by the totality of appearances any more than the reality of a physical universe is. But if either of them is recognized as a possibility, then its reality in detail can be confirmed by appearances, at least to the extent of being rendered more plausible than the alternatives. So a lot depends on whether the possibility of realism is admitted in the first place.

   It is very difficult to argue for such a possibility, except by refuting arguments against it. (Berkeley's argument against the conceivability of a world independent of experience is an impossibility argument in the domain of metaphysics.) What is the result when such an argument is refuted? Is the contrary possibility in a stronger position? I believe so: in general, there is no way to prove the possibility of realism; one can only refute impossibility arguments, and the more often one does this the more confidence one may have in the realist alternative. So to consider the merits of an admission of realism about value, we have to consider the reasons against it—against its possibility or against its truth. I shall discuss three. They have been picked for their apparent capacity to convince.

The first type of argument depends on the unwarranted assumption that if values are real, they must be real objects of some other kind. John Mackie, in his book *Ethics*, denies the objectivity of values by saying that they are "not part of the fabric of the world," and that if they were, they would have to be "entities or qualities or relations of a very strange sort, utterly different from anything else in the universe" (Mackie (2), p. 38). He clearly has a definite picture of what the universe is like, and assumes that realism about value would require crowding it with extra entities, qualities, or relations, things like Platonic Forms or Moore's nonnatural qualities. But this assumption is not correct. The objective badness of pain, for example, is not some mysterious further property that all pains have, but just the fact that there is reason for anyone capable of viewing the world objectively to want it to stop. The view that values are real is not the view that they are real occult entities or properties, but that they are real values: that our claims about value and about what people have reason to do may be true or false independently of our beliefs and inclinations. No other kinds of truths are involved. Indeed, no other kinds of truths *could* imply the reality of values. This applies not only to moral values but also to prudential ones, and even to the simple reasons people have to do what will achieve their present aims.

In discussion, Mackie objected that his disbelief in the reality of values and reasons did not depend on the assumption that to be real they must be strange entities or properties. As he says in his book, the point applies directly to reasons themselves. For whatever they are they are not needed to explain anything that happens, and there is consequently no reason to believe in their existence.

But this raises the same issue. Mackie meant that reasons play no role in causal explanations. But it begs the question to assume that this sort of explanatory necessity is the test of reality for values. The claim that certain reasons exist is a normative claim, not a claim about the best causal explanation of anything. To assume that only what has to be included in the best causal theory of the world is real is to assume that there are no irreducibly normative truths.

However, there is another difficulty here which I'm not sure how to deal with. If there are normative truths, they enter into normative rather than causal explanations of the existence of particular reasons or the rightness or wrongness of particular actions. But our apprehension of these truths also explains our acquisition of new motives, and ultimately it can influence our conduct. Even if we set aside the issues about free will and the intentional explanation of action discussed in the previous chapter, there is a problem here about the relation between normative and causal explanation. It is not clear whether normative realism is compatible with the hypothesis that all our normative beliefs can be accounted for by some kind of naturalistic psychology.

Gilbert Harman formulates the problem thus:

> Observation plays a role in science that it does not seem to play in ethics. The difference is that you need to make assumptions about certain physical facts to explain the occurrence of the observations that support a scientific theory, but you do not seem to need to make assumptions about any moral facts to explain the occurrence of . . . so-called moral observations . . . In the moral case, it would seem that you need only make assumptions about the psychology or moral sensibility of the person making the moral observation.[2]

Any defender of realism about values must claim that the purely psychological account is incomplete, either because normative explanations are an additional element or because they are somehow present in certain types of psychological explanations—perhaps in a way like that in which explanations of belief by logical reasoning can be simultaneously causal and justificatory (if in fact they can be). So when, for example, we become convinced by argument that a distinction is morally relevant, the explanation of our conviction can be given by the content and validity of the argument.

While we cannot prove the purely psychological, antirealist account to be false—so that it remains literally true that you don't *need* to explain normative judgments in terms of normative truths—I believe the most plausible account will refer to such truths, even at the most elementary level. To dispense with them is too radical a denial of the appearances. If I have a severe headache, the headache seems to me to be not merely unpleasant, but a bad thing. Not only do I dislike it, but I think I have a reason to try to get rid of it. It is barely conceivable that this might be an illusion, but if the idea of a bad thing makes sense at all, it need not be an illusion, and the true explanation of my impression may be the

---

2. G. Harman, p. 6; this is his formulation of the problem, not his proposed solution.

simplest one, namely that headaches are bad, and not just unwelcome to
the people who have them.

Everything depends on whether the idea makes sense. If the possibility
of real values is admitted, specific values become susceptible to a kind of
observational testing, but it operates through the kind of explanation
appropriate to the subject: normative explanation. In physics, one infers
from factual appearances to their most plausible explanation in a theory
of how the world is. In ethics, one infers from appearances of value to
their most plausible explanation in a theory of what there is reason to
do or want. All the inferences will rely on general ideas of reality that do
not derive from appearance—the most important being the general idea
of objective reality itself. And in both science and ethics some of the
appearances will turn out to be mistaken and to have psychological
explanations of a kind that do not confirm their truth.

My belief that the distinction between appearance and reality applies
here is based not on a metaphysical picture, but on the capacity of a
realistic approach to make sense of our thoughts. If we start by regarding appearances of value as appearances of something, and then step
back to form hypotheses about the broader system of motivational possibilities of which we have had a glimpse, the result is a gradual opening
out of a complex domain which we apparently discover. The method of
discovery is to seek the best normative explanation of the normative
appearances. I believe that the actual results of this method tend to confirm the realistic assumption behind it—though I recognize that a skeptic may object that the results are contaminated by the assumption itself
and cannot therefore supply independent confirmation.

Let me now turn to the second argument against realism. Unlike the
first, it is not based on a misinterpretation of moral objectivity. Instead,
it tries to represent the unreality of values as an objective discovery. The
argument is that if claims of value have to be objectively correct, and if
they are not reducible to any other kind of objective claim, then we can
just see that all positive value claims must be false. Nothing has any
objective value, because objectively nothing matters at all. If we push the
claims of objective detachment to their logical conclusion, and survey
the world from a standpoint completely detached from all interests, we
discover that there is *nothing*—no values left of any kind: things can be
said to matter at all only to individuals within the world. The result is
objective nihilism.

I don't deny that the objective standpoint tempts one in this direction,
and I'll say more about it later, when discussing the meaning of life. But
I believe this can seem like the required conclusion only if one makes
the mistake of assuming that objective judgments of value must emerge

from the detached standpoint alone. It is true that with nothing to go
on but a conception of the world from nowhere, one would have no way
of telling whether anything had value. But an objective view has more to
go on, for its data include the appearance of value to individuals with
particular perspectives, including oneself. In this respect practical reason is no different from anything else. Starting from a pure idea of a
possible reality and a very impure set of appearances, we try to fill in the
idea of reality so as to make some partial sense of the appearances, using
objectivity as a method. To find out what the world is like from outside
we have to approach it from within: it is no wonder that the same is true
for ethics.

And indeed, when we take up the objective standpoint, the problem
is not that values seem to disappear but that there seem to be too many
of them, coming from every life and drowning out those that arise from
our own. It is just as easy to form desires from an objective standpoint
as it is to form beliefs. Probably easier. Like beliefs, these desires and
evaluations must be criticized and justified partly in terms of the appearances. But they are not just further appearances, any more than the
beliefs about the world which arise from an impersonal standpoint are
just further appearances.

The third type of argument against the objective reality of values is an
empirical argument. It is also perhaps the most common. It is intended
not to rule out the possibility of real values from the start, but rather to
demonstrate that even if their possibility is admitted, we have no reason
to believe that there are any. The claim is that if we consider the wide
cultural variation in normative beliefs, the importance of social pressure
and other psychological influences to their formation, and the difficulty
of settling moral disagreements, it becomes highly implausible that they
are anything but pure appearances.

Anyone offering this argument must admit that not every psychological factor in the explanation of an appearance shows that the appearance
corresponds to nothing real. Visual capacities and elaborate training
play a part in explaining the physicist's perception of a cloud-chamber
track, or a student's coming to believe a proposition of geometry, but
the nature of the particle and the truth of the proposition also play an
essential part in these explanations. No one has produced a general
account of the kinds of psychological explanation that discredit an
appearance. But some skeptics about ethics feel that because of the way
we acquire moral beliefs and other impressions of value, there are
grounds for confidence that here, nothing real is being talked about.

I find the popularity of this argument surprising. The fact that morality is socially inculcated and that there is radical disagreement about it

across cultures, over time, and even within cultures at a time is a poor reason to conclude that values have no objective reality. Even where there is truth, it is not always easy to discover. Other areas of knowledge are taught by social pressure, many truths as well as falsehoods are believed without rational grounds, and there is wide disagreement about scientific and social facts, especially where strong interests are involved which will be affected by different answers to a disputed question. This last factor is present throughout ethics to a uniquely high degree: it is an area in which one would expect extreme variation of belief and radical disagreement however objectively real the subject actually was. For comparably motivated disagreements about matters of fact, one has to go to the heliocentric theory, the theory of evolution, the Dreyfus case, the Hiss case, and the genetic contribution to racial differences in I.Q.

Although the methods of ethical reasoning are rather primitive, the degree to which agreement can be achieved and social prejudices transcended in the face of strong pressures suggests that something real is being investigated, and that part of the explanation of the appearances, both at simple and at complex levels, is that we perceive, often inaccurately, that there are certain reasons for action, and go on to infer, often erroneously, the general form of the principles that best account for those reasons.

Again let me stress that this is not to be understood on the model of perception of features of the external world. The subject matter of our investigations is how to live, and the process of ethical thought is one of motivational discovery. The fact that people can to some extent reach agreement on answers which they regard as objective suggests that when they step outside of their particular individual perspectives, they call into operation a common evaluative faculty whose correct functioning provides the answers, even though it can also malfunction and be distorted by other influences. It is not a question of bringing the mind into correspondence with an external reality which acts causally on it, but of reordering the mind itself in accordance with the demands of its own external view of itself.

I have not discussed all the possible arguments against realism about values, but I have tried to give general reasons for skepticism about such arguments. It seems to me that they tend to be supported by a narrow preconception of what sorts of truths there are, and that this is essentially question-begging. Nothing said here will force a reductionist to give up his denial of normative realism, but perhaps it has been shown to be a reasonable position. I should add that the search for objective principles makes sense even if we do not assume that all of ethics or human value is equally objective. Objectivity need not be all or nothing.

So long as realism is true in some of these areas, we can reasonably pursue the method of objective reflection as far as it will take us.

3. Desires and Reasons

There is no preset method of carrying out a normative investigation, though the aim of achieving integration between the subjective and objective standpoints gives the process direction and sets conditions of success and failure. We look at human life from within and without simultaneously, and try to arrive at a reasonable set of attitudes. The process of development can go on indefinitely, as is true in the pursuit of any other type of knowledge. Some aspects of practical reason may prove to be irreducibly subjective, so that while their existence must be acknowledged from an objective standpoint their content cannot be understood except from a more particular perspective. But other reasons will irresistibly engage the objective will.

The initial data are reasons that appear from one's own point of view in acting. They usually present themselves with some pretensions of objectivity to begin with, just as perceptual appearances do. When two things look the same size to me, they look at least initially as if they *are* the same size. And when I want to take aspirin because it will cure my headache, I believe at least initially that this *is* a reason for me to take aspirin.

The ordinary process of deliberation, aimed at finding out what I should do, assumes the existence of an answer to this question. And in difficult cases especially it is often accompanied by the belief that I may not arrive at the correct answer. I do not assume that the correct answer is just whatever will result from consistent application of deliberative methods—even assuming perfect information about the facts. In deliberation we are trying to arrive at conclusions that are correct in virtue of something independent of our arriving at them. So although some of the starting points will be abandoned on the way, the pursuit of an objective account has its basis in the claims of ordinary practical reasoning.

It is important to recognize that the objectivity of reasons may be implied by a great variety of substantive views about what reasons there are, including some that have little or no ethical content. By way of illustration, consider a minimal position that some find plausible and that I shall call, following Parfit, the Instrumental theory: that basic general reasons depend exclusively on the desires of the agent, whatever their objects (Parfit (2), p.117). Roughly, the position is that each person has a reason to do what will satisfy his desires or preferences at the time of

action, where these can to some extent be identified independently of
what he does, so that it is not a tautology that he is always rational relative to his beliefs. The desires need not have experiences as objects, and
their satisfaction need not be experienced, for it can consist simply in
the occurrence of the thing desired, which may be something not involving the agent at all, or something he will not live to see.

This position is reached by a fairly minimal generalization from one's
own case. (I believe it errs in being both too minimal and in another
sense too broad, but let me leave that aside for now.) One translates
one's own reasons into a form that can be accepted by people with different preferences, so that it can be used by anyone to account generally
for his own reasons and those of others. Nothing but the need for an
account that can be understood from no particular perspective would
require the adoption of such general principles.

The point is that even this minimal form of generalization is produced
by a requirement of objectivity. The Instrumental theory makes general
claims about the conditions under which people have reasons, which
provide a basis for regarding some of their acts as irrational. If one were
concerned only to decide what to do oneself, it would be sufficient to
reason practically in terms of the preferences and desires one actually
has. It would not be necessary to ascend to this level of generality.

We wish to formulate our reasons in general terms that relativize them
to interests and desires so that they can be recognized and *accepted* from
outside, either by someone else or by us when we regard the situation
objectively, independent of the preferences and desires we actually have.
From such a point of view we still want to be able to see what reasons
we have, and this is made possible by a general, relativized formulation
which enables us to say what others have reasons to do, and also what
we would ourselves have reasons to do if our desires were different. We
can still apply it after stepping back. It is not enough that our actions be
motivationally explainable by others, and that we should likewise be able
to explain theirs. We assume the justifications are also objectively correct, and this means they must be based on impersonally acceptable principles that allow for more particular variation in desires.

If this is right, then even the apparently subjective Instrumental theory is the thin end of an objective wedge. Even though the reasons it
identifies are based on desires, they will not necessarily be recognized
and acted upon by the subject of those desires. The reasons are real, they
are not just appearances. To be sure, they will be attributed only to a
being that has, in addition to desires, a general capacity to develop an
objective view of what it should do. Thus, if cockroaches cannot think
about what they should do, there is nothing they should do. But this
capacity is open-ended. We cannot replace practical reasoning by the

psychology of our practical reasoning capacity, any more than we can replace mathematical reasoning by the psychology of our mathematical capacity. The pursuit of objective practical principles is not to be conceived of as a psychological exploration of our moral sense, but as an employment of it. We must engage in reasoning to discover what reasons we have, and exercise of the capacity will not always yield the right answer.

The quest for objectivity is responsible for even the limited form of generality found in the Instrumental theory. But once this principle is seen as the solution to a problem, and the problem is described, alternative solutions can also be considered, and some of them may prove superior. Perhaps not all reasons are based on desires, and not all desires generate reasons. More than one hypothesis can account from an objective standpoint for a large range of individual cases. The task of ethical theory is to develop and compare conceptions of how to live, which can be understood and considered from no particular perspective, and therefore from many perspectives insofar as we can abstract from their particularity. All these conceptions will attempt to reconcile the apparent requirement of generality that objectivity imposes with the richness, variety, and reality of the reasons that appear subjectively.

The Instrumental view is conservative because it imposes the minimum generalization compatible with preserving certain premoral subjective reasons that individuals appear to have. It adds essentially nothing to these, but merely subsumes them under an account general enough to be applicable to any person A by any other person B who knows what A's preferences, desires, beliefs, and circumstances are. One is not forced by the formal condition of generality to go any further than this. But that does not mean that the view is correct. One is not forced to stay wherever one cannot be forced to leave. There are too many such places.

In an earlier discussion I argued that motivation by reasons does not always depend on antecedently existing desires (Nagel (1), ch. 5). Sometimes a desire appears only because I recognize that there is reason to do or want something. This is true of prudential motivation, which stems from the expectation of future desires or interests and requires none in the present. It is even more clearly true of altruistic motivation, which stems from recognition of the desires and interests of others, and requires no desires in the agent except those that are motivated by that recognition.[3] But even when a present desire of the agent is among the

---

3. The distinction I am making between unmotivated desires that originate motivation and desires that are themselves rationally motivated has a good deal in common with Kant's distinction between inclination (*Neigung*) and interest (*Interesse*) (Kant (2), p. 413n.)—though Kant believes that a purely rational interest appears only in morality.

grounds for rational action, a purely descriptive causal account of what happens is incomplete. I want my headache to go away—but this doesn't directly cause me to take aspirin. I take aspirin because I recognize that my desire to be rid of the headache gives me a reason to take it, justifies my wanting to take it. That's *why* I take it, and from inside I can't think that it would be no less rational to bang my head against a fire hydrant instead.

If we suppose, then, that I have a reason in this particular case, the question becomes, what kind of reason is it, when we look at the matter objectively? How does it fit into a more general conception of the kinds of reasons there are—a conception that applies not just to me?

4. Types of Generality

The search for generality is one of the main impulses in the construction of an objective view—in normative as in theoretical matters. One takes the particular case as an example, and forms hypotheses about what general truth it is an example of. There is more than one type of generality, and no reason to assume that a single form will apply to every type of value. Since the choice among types of generality defines some of the central issues of moral theory, let me describe the options.

One respect in which reasons may vary is in their breadth. A principle may be general in the sense that it applies to everyone but be quite narrow in content; and it is an open question to what extent narrower principles of practical reason (don't lie; develop your talents) can be subsumed under broader ones (don't hurt others; consider your long-term interests), or even at the limit under a single widest principle from which all the rest derive. Reasons may be universal, in other words, without forming a unified system that always provides a method for arriving at determinate conclusions about what one should do.

A second respect in which reasons vary is in their *relativity to the agent*, the person for whom they are reasons. The distinction between reasons that are relative to the agent and reasons that are not is an extremely important one.[4] If a reason can be given a general form which does not include an essential reference to the person who has it, it is an *agent-neutral* reason. For example, if it is a reason for anyone to do or want

---

4. In Nagel (1) I marked it by speaking of "subjective" and "objective" reasons, but since those terms are being put to different use here, I shall adopt Parfit's terms, "agent-relative" and "agent-neutral" (Parfit (2), p. 143). Often I shall shorten these to "relative" and "neutral"; and sometimes I shall refer to the corresponding values as "personal" and "impersonal."

something that it would reduce the amount of wretchedness in the world, then that is a neutral reason. If on the other hand the general form of a reason does include an essential reference to the person who has it, it is an *agent-relative* reason. For example, if it is a reason for anyone to do or want something that it would be in *his* interest, then that is a relative reason. In such a case, if something were in Jones's interest but contrary to Smith's, Jones would have reason to want it to happen and Smith would have the same reason to want it not to happen. (Both agent-relative and agent-neutral reasons are objective, if they can be understood and affirmed from outside the viewpoint of the individual who has them.)

A third way in which reasons may vary is in their degree of externality, or independence of the concerns of sentient beings. Most of the apparent reasons that initially present themselves to us are intimately connected with interests and desires, our own or those of others, and often with experiential satisfaction. But it seems that some of these interests give evidence that their objects have an intrinsic value which is not merely a function of the satisfaction that people may derive from them or of the fact that anyone wants them—a value which is not reducible to their value *for* anyone. I don't know how to establish whether there are any such values, but the objectifying tendency produces a strong impulse to believe that there are—especially in aesthetics, where the object of interest is external and the interest seems perpetually capable of criticism in light of further attention to the object. The problem is to account for external values in a way which avoids the implausible consequence that they retain their practical importance even if no one will *ever* be able to respond to them. (So that if all sentient life is destroyed, it will still be a good thing if the Frick Collection survives.)

There may be other significant dimensions of variation. I want to concentrate on these because they locate the main controversies about what ethics is. Reasons and values that can be described in these terms provide the material for objective judgments. If one looks at human action and its conditions from outside and considers whether some normative principles are plausible, these are the forms they will take.

The actual acceptance of a general normative judgment will have motivational implications, for it will commit you under some circumstances to the acceptance of reasons to want and do things yourself.

This is most clear when the objective judgment is that something has agent-neutral or impersonal value. That means anyone has reason to want it to happen—and that includes someone considering the world in detachment from the perspective of any particular person within it. Such a judgment has motivational content even before it is brought back down to the particular perspective of the individual who has accepted it objectively.

Relative reasons are different. An objective judgment that some kind of thing has agent-relative value commits us only to believing that someone has reason to want and pursue it if it is related to him in the right way (being in his interest, for example). Someone who accepts this judgment is not even committed to wanting it to be the case that people in general are influenced by such reasons. The judgment commits him to wanting something only when its implications are drawn for the individual person he happens to be. With regard to others, the content of the objective judgment concerns only what *they* should do or want.

Judgments of both these kinds, as well as others, are evoked from us when we take up an objective standpoint, and the pressure to combine intelligibly the two standpoints toward action can lead to the refinement and extension of such judgments.

The choice among normative hypotheses is difficult and there is no general method of making it, any more than there is a general method of selecting the most plausible objective account of the facts on the basis of the appearances. The only "method," here or elsewhere, is to try to generate hypotheses and then to consider which of them seems most reasonable, in light of everything else one is fairly confident of. Since we may assume that not every alternative has been thought of, the best we can hope for is a comparison among those available, not a firm solution.

This is not quite empty, for it means at least that logic alone can settle nothing. We do not have to be shown that the denial of some kind of objective value is self-contradictory in order to be reasonably led to accept its existence. There is no constraint to pick the weakest or narrowest or most economical principle consistent with the initial data that arise from individual perspectives. Our admission of reasons beyond these is determined not by logical entailment, but by the relative plausibility of those normative hypotheses—including the null hypothesis—that are consistent with the evidence.

In this respect ethics is no different from anything else: theoretical knowledge does not arise by deductive inference from the appearances either. The main difference is that our objective thinking about practical reasons is very primitive and has difficulty taking even the first step. Philosophical skepticism and idealism about values are much more popular than their metaphysical counterparts. Nevertheless, I believe they are no more correct. Although no single objective principle of practical reason like egoism or utilitarianism covers everything, the acceptance of some objective values is unavoidable—not because the alternative is inconsistent but because it is not *credible*. Someone who, as in Hume's example (*Treatise*, bk. 2, pt. 3, sec. 3), prefers the destruction of the whole world to the scratching of his finger may not be involved in a contradiction or in any false expectations, but there is something the matter with him nonetheless, and anyone else not in the grip of an overnarrow conception of what reasoning is would regard his preference as objectively wrong.

But even if it is unreasonable to deny that anyone ever objectively has a reason to do anything, it is not easy to find positive objective principles that *are* reasonable. In particular it is not easy to follow the objectifying impulse without distorting individual life and personal relations. We want to be able to understand and accept the way we live from outside, but it may not always follow that we should control our lives from inside by the terms of that external understanding. Often the objective viewpoint will not be suitable as a replacement for the subjective, but will coexist with it, setting a standard with which the subjective is constrained not to clash. In deciding what to do, for example, we should not reach a result different from what we could decide objectively that that *person* should do—but we need not arrive at the result in the same way from the two standpoints.

Sometimes, also, the objective standpoint will allow us to judge how people should be or should live, without permitting us to translate this into a judgment about what they have reasons to do. For in some respects it is better to live and act not for reasons, but because it does not occur to us to do anything else. This is especially true of close personal relations. Here the objective standpoint cannot be brought into the perspective of action without diminishing precisely what it affirms the value of. Nevertheless, the possibility of objective affirmation is important. We should be *able* to view our lives from outside without extreme dissociation or distaste, and the extent to which we should live without considering the objective point of view or even any reasons at all is itself determined largely from that point of view.

It is also possible that some idiosyncratic individual grounds of action, or the values of strange communities, will prove objectively inaccessible. To take an example in our midst: people who want to be able to run twenty-six miles without stopping are not exactly irrational, but their reasons can be understood only from the perspective of a value system that some find alien to the point of unintelligibility.[5] A correct objective view will have to allow for such pockets of unassimilable subjectivity, which need not clash with objective principles but won't be affirmed by them

5. Though one never knows where it will strike next: it's like *Invasion of the Body-Snatchers*.

either. Many aspects of personal taste will come in this category if, as I think, they cannot all be brought under a general hedonistic principle.

But the most difficult and interesting problems of accommodation appear where objectivity can be employed as a standard, and we have to decide how. Some of the problems are these: To what extent should an objective view admit external values? To what extent should it admit agent-neutral values? To what extent should reasons to respect the interests of others take an agent-relative form? To what extent is it legitimate for each person to give priority to his own interests or to the interests of those close to him? These are all questions about the proper form of generality for different kinds of practical reasoning, and the proper relation between objective principles and the deliberations of individual agents.

We shall return to some of them later, but a great deal will be left out. I shall concentrate on the proper form of values or reasons which depend on interests or desires. They can be objectified in more than one way, and I believe different forms of objectification are appropriate for different cases.

5. Pleasure and Pain

Let me begin, however, with a case for which I think the solution is clear: physical pleasure and pain, comfort and discomfort—the pleasures of food, drink, sleep, sex, warmth, and ease; the pains of injury, sickness, hunger, thirst, cold, and exhaustion. Let me leave out of consideration mild pleasures and pains that we don't care about much, and concentrate on those sensory experiences that we strongly—perhaps intensely—like or dislike. I am not an ethical hedonist, but I think pleasure and pain are very important, and that they provide a clearer case for a certain kind of objective value than preferences and desires, which will be discussed later on. I shall defend the unsurprising claim that sensory pleasure is good and pain bad, no matter whose they are. The point of the exercise is to see how the pressures of objectification operate in a simple case.

Physical pleasure and pain do not usually depend on activities or desires which themselves raise questions of justification and value. They are just sensory experiences in relation to which we are fairly passive, but toward which we feel involuntary desire or aversion. Almost everyone takes the avoidance of his own pain and the promotion of his own pleasure as subjective reasons for action in a fairly simple way; they are not backed up by any further reasons. On the other hand if someone pursues pain or avoids pleasure, either it is as a means to some end or it is backed up by dark reasons like guilt or sexual masochism. What sort of general value, if any, ought to be assigned to pleasure and pain when we consider these facts from an objective standpoint? What kind of judgment can we reasonably make about these things when we view them in abstraction from who we are?

We can begin by asking why there is no plausibility in the zero position, that pleasure and pain have no value of any kind that can be objectively recognized. That would mean that I have no reason to take aspirin for a severe headache, however I may in fact be motivated; and that looking at it from outside, you couldn't even say that someone had a reason not to put his hand on a hot stove, just because of the pain. Try looking at it from the outside and see whether you can manage to withhold that judgment. If the idea of objective practical reason makes any sense at all, so that there is some judgment to withhold, it does not seem possible. If the general arguments against the reality of objective reasons are no good, then it is at least possible that I have a reason, and not just an inclination, to refrain from putting my hand on a hot stove. But given the possibility, it seems meaningless to deny that this is so.

Oddly enough, however, we can think of a story that would go with such a denial. It might be suggested that the aversion to pain is a useful phobia—having nothing to do with the intrinsic undesirability of pain itself—which helps us avoid or escape the injuries that are signaled by pain. (The same type of purely instrumental value might be ascribed to sensory pleasure: the pleasures of food, drink, and sex might be regarded as having no value in themselves, though our natural attraction to them assists survival and reproduction.) There would then be nothing wrong with pain in itself, and someone who was never motivated deliberately to do anything just because he knew it would reduce or avoid pain would have nothing the matter with him. He would still have involuntary avoidance reactions, otherwise it would be hard to say that he felt pain at all. And he would be motivated to reduce pain for other reasons—because it was an effective way to avoid the danger being signaled, or because pain interfered with some physical or mental activity that was important to him. He just wouldn't regard the pain as *itself* something he had any reason to avoid, even though he hated the feeling just as much as the rest of us. (And of course he wouldn't be able to justify the avoidance of pain in the way that we customarily justify avoiding what we hate without reason—that is, on the ground that even an irrational hatred makes its object very unpleasant!)

There is nothing self-contradictory in this proposal, but it seems nevertheless insane. Without some positive reason to think there is nothing in itself good or bad about having an experience you intensely like or dislike, we can't seriously regard the common impression to the contrary as a collective illusion. Such things are at least good or bad *for us*, if anything is. What seems to be going on here is that we cannot from an objective standpoint withhold a certain kind of endorsement of the most direct and immediate subjective value judgments we make concerning the contents of our own consciousness. We regard ourselves as too close to those things to be mistaken in our immediate, nonideological evaluative impressions. No objective view we can attain could possibly overrule our subjective authority in such cases. There can be no reason to reject the appearances here.

It is clear that the reasons we must recognize here are broad rather than narrow: if I have a reason to take aspirin for a headache or to avoid hot stoves, it is not because of something specific about those pains but because they are examples of pain, suffering, or discomfort. So long as we stick with basic physical pleasures and pains, there is no reason to count some of them as good or bad and not others—hence any principle of practical reason short of the broadest, "Seek pleasure and avoid pain," would be arbitrary. To be precise, the broadest principle is that we have reason to seek/avoid sensations we immediately and strongly like/dislike. (This includes feelings like nausea, which are not pains, and experiences to which not everyone reacts in the same way, like the sound of squeaking chalk.)

An alternative hypothesis would be that the operative reason is broader still: "Seek what you want and avoid what you don't want," (the Instrumental theory mentioned earlier). But I don't believe we would be justified in going that far on the basis of these examples. Admittedly people usually want pleasure and don't want pain, but we may not be equally ready to admit that they have objective reason to go after everything they want; we regard some compulsions as irrational, for example. The fact that physical pleasures and pains are experiences, and that our desires and aversions for them are immediate and unreflective, puts them in a special category. I shall say more about the relation between preferences and reasons eventually, and about why the increasing reliance on preferences in the formulation of ethical theories is not an advance. The Instrumental theory is not even part of the truth.

If I am right so far, primitive pleasures and pains provide at least agent-relative reasons for pursuit and avoidance—reasons that can be affirmed from an objective standpoint and that do not merely describe the actual motivation of the agent.

What interests me is the next question. Do pleasure and pain have merely agent-relative value or do they provide neutral reasons as well?

If the avoidance of pain has only relative value, then people have reason to avoid their own pain, but not to relieve the pain of others (unless other kinds of reasons come into play). If the relief of pain has neutral value as well, then anyone has a reason to want any pain to stop, whether or not it is his. From an objective standpoint, which of these hypotheses is more plausible? Is the value of sensory pleasure and pain relative or neutral? The relation between agent-relative and agent-neutral reasons is probably the central question of ethical theory.

I once claimed that there could be no reasons that were *just* agent-relative—that there had to be a neutral reason corresponding to every relative one, because otherwise recognition of the relative reason from the objective standpoint would be incomplete. I even suggested that all apparently relative reasons were really subsumable under neutral ones. The argument was, roughly, that unless the ascription of a reason for action to someone else had motivational content for me when I viewed him objectively, it was incompatible with full recognition of him as a person like myself. This would also imply a radical dissociation with respect to myself, for I wouldn't even recognize my own reality properly from the objective standpoint. Neutral reasons were necessary to avoid a practical analogue of solipsism (Nagel (1), chs. 11 and 12).

Though I no longer think the argument works,[6] I don't think there was nothing in it. Integration of the two standpoints and full recognition that one is only a person among others are the essential forces behind the development of a moral position. But they do not in every case require the acceptance of neutral reasons: some values are agent-relative and full recognition of the reality of other persons does not require that we accord these values any greater objective range than that. I shall discuss some cases later. The point here is that no completely general argument about reasons can show that we must move from the admission that pleasure and pain have relative value to the conclusion that they have neutral value as well.

Nevertheless, for reasons related to the attempted general argument, I believe the conclusion is true for this case: it is conceivable, but false, that pleasure and pain provide only agent-relative reasons for action. In other words, pleasure is a good thing and pain is a bad thing, and the most reasonable objective principle which admits that each of us has reason to pursue his own pleasure and avoid his own pain will acknowledge that these are not the only reasons present. This is a normative claim. Unreasonable, as I have said, does not mean inconsistent.

In arguing for this claim, I am somewhat handicapped by the fact that

6. See Sturgeon for some effective criticisms.

I find it self-evident. Since I can't find anything still more certain with which to back it up, I face the danger of explaining the obvious in terms of the obscure. I have already argued that the *possibility* of assigning agent-neutral value to pleasure and pain should be admitted. The issue then is whether this hypothesis or the hypothesis of purely relative value is more credible.

What overall system of practical judgments makes the most sense from an objective standpoint? If we admit the general principle that each person has a reason to care about his own pleasure and pain, how does this consort with alternative objective judgments about the rational bearing of one person's pleasure and pain on the actions of another? We have to decide whether the kind of reason people have to avoid pain for themselves can be plausibly combined with impersonal indifference to it. Here the argument from dissociation seems to me persuasive. If we assign impersonal value to pleasure and pain, then each person can think about his own suffering not just that he has reason to want it gone, but that it's bad and should be got rid of. If on the other hand we limit ourselves to relative reasons, he will have to say that though he has a reason to want an analgesic, there is no reason for him to have one, or for anyone else who happens to be around to give him one.

While this may be all right for reasons connected with individual projects, which express personal values that others cannot be expected to share, it is a very peculiar attitude to take toward the primitive comforts and discomforts of life. Suppose I have been rescued from a fire and find myself in a hospital burn ward. I want something for the pain, and so does the person in the next bed. He professes to hope we both will be given morphine, but I fail to understand this. I understand why he has reason to want morphine for himself, but what reason does he have to want *me* to get some? Does my groaning bother him?

The dissociation here is a split attitude toward my own suffering. As objective spectator, I acknowledge that TN has a reason to want it to stop, but I see no reason why it should stop. My evaluation of it is entirely confined within the framework of a judgment about what it is rational *for this person* to want.

But the pain, though it comes attached to a person and his individual perspective, is just as clearly hateful to the objective self as to the subjective individual. I know what it's like even when I contemplate myself from outside, as one person among countless others. And the same applies when I think about anyone else in this way. The pain can be detached in thought from the fact that it is mine without losing any of its dreadfulness. It has, so to speak, a life of its own. That is why it is natural to ascribe to it a value of its own.

The claim that we must grant objective reality at least to agent-relative reasons for avoiding pain was based on the evaluative authority of the sufferer. He is closer to it than anyone else, after all. The question now is whether the same authority should extend to the conclusion that suffering is a bad thing, period, and not just for the sufferer. From the objective standpoint, can I stop with an endorsement of the sufferer's efforts to avoid or alleviate it, without going on to acknowledge an impersonal reason to want it to go away? It seems to me that to do this—to say that there is no agent-neutral objection to suffering at all—would again be to overrule the clearest authority present in the situation. We are thinking from no particular point of view about how to regard a world which contains points of view. What exists inside those points of view can be considered from outside to have some sort of value simply as part of what is happening in the world, and the value assigned to it should be that which it overwhelmingly appears to have from the inside.

When the objective self contemplates pain, it has to do so through the perspective of the sufferer, and the sufferer's reaction is very clear. Of course he wants to be rid of *this pain* unreflectively—not because he thinks it would be good to reduce the amount of pain in the world. But at the same time his awareness of how bad it is doesn't essentially involve the thought of it as his. The desire to be rid of pain has only the pain as its object. This is shown by the fact that it doesn't even require the idea of *oneself* in order to make sense: if I lacked or lost the conception of myself as distinct from other possible or actual persons, I could still apprehend the badness of pain, immediately. So when I consider it from an objective standpoint, the ego doesn't get between the pain and the objective self. My objective attitude toward pain is rightly taken over from the immediate attitude of the subject, and naturally takes the form of an evaluation of the pain itself, rather than merely a judgment of what would be reasonable for its victim to want: "*This experience* ought not to go on, *whoever* is having it." To regard pain as impersonally bad from the objective standpoint does not involve the illegitimate suppression of an essential reference to the identity of its victim. In its most primitive form, the fact that it is mine—the concept of myself—doesn't come into my perception of the badness of my pain.

Of course I may easily form an explicitly egocentric desire to be rid of my pain—if for example there is only one dose of morphine available and I hope the doctor gives it to me rather than to my fellow sufferer in the next bed. But this is not a pure response to the badness of my pain, and it would be a flagrant misobjectification to convert this, from the objective standpoint, into a judgment that the doctor has a reason to prefer me to my neighbor. The desire is essentially egocentric, and if it supports any objective value judgment at all, it will be an agent-relative one—perhaps that I have a reason to try to bribe or persuade the doctor to favor me (but then my neighbor has exactly the same agent-relative reason to get the doctor to favor him).

If there are such exclusively relative reasons for pursuing pleasure and avoiding pain for oneself, they must compete with the neutral reasons which seem immediately apparent when we regard these things objectively. There's a reason for me to be given morphine which is independent of the fact that the pain is mine—namely that it's awful. The first and most natural generalization of the value that any individual perceives in his pleasure or suffering is an agent-neutral one—whatever else may be added later on.

As I said, this conclusion seems to me self-evident, and in trying to explain why it's true, and why the alternatives are less plausible, I may not have gone far beyond this. That pleasure is impersonally good and pain impersonally bad are propositions that one really needs reasons to doubt rather than reasons to believe, but it does assist understanding to relate them to the integration of subjective and objective standpoints toward one's own motives.

6. Overobjectification

It will be obvious from the way the argument has gone so far that I don't believe all objective reasons have the same form. The interaction between objectivity and the will yields complex results which cannot necessarily be formed into a unified system. This means that the natural ambition of a comprehensive system of ethics may be unrealizable.

I have argued against skepticism, and in favor of realism and the pursuit of objectivity in the domain of practical reason. But if realism is admitted as a possibility, one is quickly faced with the opposite of the problem of skepticism, namely the problem of overobjectification: the temptation to interpret the objectivity of reasons in too strong a way.

In ethics, as in metaphysics, the allure of objectivity is very great: there is a persistent tendency in both areas to seek a single complete objective account of reality. In the area of value that means a search for the most objective possible account of all reasons for action: the account which engages us from a maximally detached standpoint.

This idea underlies the fairly common moral assumption that the only real values are impersonal values, and that someone can really have a reason to do something only if there is an agent-neutral reason for it to happen. That is the essence of traditional forms of consequentialism: the only reason for anyone to do anything is that it would be better in itself, considering the world as a whole, if he did it. The idea also finds reflection in Hare's view about the only kind of judgment that moral language can be used to express: for his claim that moral judgments are universally prescriptive means that they depend on what one would *want to happen*, considering the question from all points of view—rather than on what one would think people had *reason to do*, considering the question in this way. In fact he doesn't acknowledge the possibility of prescriptions that say what someone else ought to do but don't commit the prescriber to wanting what is prescribed to happen. Consequently any principle that was moral in his sense would have to be agent-neutral.

In the next chapter I shall try to explain why ethics is not based solely on impersonal values like those that attach to pleasure and pain. We can no more assume that all values are impersonal than that all reality is physical. I argued earlier that not everything there is can be gathered into a uniform conception of the universe from nowhere within it. If certain perspectives evidently exist which cannot be analyzed in physical terms, we must modify our idea of objective reality to include them. If that is not enough, we must admit to reality some things that cannot be objectively understood. Similarly, if certain reasons for action which appear to exist cannot be accommodated within a purely neutral system—or even perhaps within a general but relative system—then we may have to modify our realist idea of value and practical reason accordingly. I don't mean to suggest that there is no conflict here. The opposition between objective reasons and subjective inclinations may be severe, and may require us to change our lives. I mean only that the truth, if there is any, will be arrived at by the exploration of this conflict rather than by the automatic victory of the most transcendent standpoint. In the conduct of life, of all places, the rivalry between the view from within and the view from without must be taken seriously.

IX

ETHICS

1. Three Kinds of Agent-relativity

In this chapter I want to take up some of the problems that must be faced by any defender of the objectivity of ethics who wishes to make sense of the actual complexity of the subject. The treatment will be general and very incomplete. Essentially I shall discuss some examples in order to suggest that the enterprise is not hopeless.

The discussion will revolve around the distinction between agent-relative and agent-neutral values. I won't try to set forth a full ethical theory, even in outline, but I will try to say something in this chapter and the next about the central problem of ethics: how the lives, interests, and welfare of others make claims on us and how these claims, of various forms, are to be reconciled with the aim of living our own lives. My assumption is that the shape of a moral theory depends on the interplay of forces in the psychic economy of complex rational beings. (I shall not say anything about aesthetic values, whose relation to human interests is obscure, though they are revealed to us by the capacity of certain things outside us to command our interest and respect.)

There is one important component of ethics that is consequentialist and impersonal. If what I said in the last chapter is right, some kind of hedonistic, agent-neutral consequentialism describes a significant form of concern that we owe to others. Life is filled with basic pleasures and pains, and they matter. Perhaps other basic human goods, such as health and survival, have the same status, but let me put that aside for the moment. I want now to examine other sorts of objective reasons that complicate the picture. Ethics is concerned not only with what should happen, but also independently with what people should or may *do*. Neutral reasons underlie the former; but relative reasons can affect the latter. In philosophical discussion, the hegemony of neutral reasons and impersonal values is typically challenged by three broad types of reasons that are relative in form, and whose existence seems to be independent of impersonal values.

The first type of reason stems from the desires, projects, commitments, and personal ties of the individual agent, all of which give him reasons to act in the pursuit of ends that are his own. These I shall collect under the general heading of reasons of autonomy (not to be confused with the autonomy of free will).

The second type of reason stems from the claims of other persons not to be maltreated in certain ways. What I have in mind are not neutral reasons for everyone to bring it about that no one is maltreated, but relative reasons for each individual not to maltreat others himself, in his dealings with them (for example by violating their rights, breaking his promises to them, etc.). These I shall collect under the general, ugly, and familiar heading of deontology. Autonomous reasons would limit what we are obliged to do in the service of impersonal values. Deontological reasons would limit what we are *permitted* to do in the service of either impersonal or autonomous ones.

The third type of reason stems from the special obligations we have toward those to whom we are closely related: parents, children, spouses, siblings, fellow members of a community or even a nation. Most people would acknowledge a noncontractual obligation to show special concern for some of these others—though there would be disagreement about the strength of the reasons and the width of the net. I'll refer to them as reasons of obligation, even though they don't include a great many obligations that are voluntarily undertaken. I mention them here only for completeness and won't discuss them in detail. I have less confidence here than with regard to the other two categories that in ordinary thought they resist agent-neutral justification.

I am not sure whether all these agent-relative reasons actually exist. The autonomous ones and perhaps the obligatory ones are fairly intelligible; but while the idea behind the deontological ones can I think be explained, it is an explanation which throws some doubt on their validity. The only way to find out what limits there are to what we may or must do in the service of impersonal values is to see what sense can be made of the apparent limits, and to accept or reject them according to whether the maximum sense is good enough.

Taken together, autonomous, obligatory, neutral, and deontological reasons cover much of the territory of unreflective bourgeois morality. Common sense suggests that each of us should live his own life (autonomy), give special consideration to certain others (obligation), have some significant concern for the general good (neutral values), and treat the people he deals with decently (deontology). It also suggests that these aims may produce serious inner conflict. Common sense doesn't have the last word in ethics or anywhere else, but it has, as J. L. Austin said about ordinary language, the first word: it should be examined before it is discarded.

Attempts have been made to find room for some version of all three types of apparent exception to impersonal ethics in a more complex impersonal system, using developments of consequentialism like rule-utilitarianism and motive-utilitarianism. A recent example is Hare's two-level version of utilitarianism in *Moral Thinking*. And T. M. Scanlon offers a consequentialist but nonutilitarian justification of deontological rights in "Rights, Goals, and Fairness." I shall not try to show that these reductions of the agent-relative to the agent-neutral fail, since I believe they are partly correct. They just aren't the whole truth. I shall try to present an alternative account of how the exceptions might make sense independently. My aim is to explain what it is that eludes justification in neutral terms. Since this is most conspicuous with regard to autonomy and deontology, I shall concentrate on them. The account in both cases depends on certain discrepancies between what can be valued from an objective standpoint and what can be seen from an objective standpoint to have value from a less objective standpoint.

2. Reasons of Autonomy

Not all the sources of subjective reasons are as simple as sensory pleasure and pain. I believe that the most reasonable objectification of the value that we all recognize in our own encounter with these experiences is an impersonal one. Difficult as it may be to carry out, each of us has reason to give significant weight to the simple sensory pleasure or pain of others as well as to his own. When these values occur in isolation, the results can be demanding. If you and a stranger have both been injured, you have one dose of painkiller, and his pain is much more severe than yours, you should give him the painkiller—not for any complicated reasons, but simply because of the relative severity of the two pains, which provides a neutral reason to prefer the relief of the more severe. The same may be said of other basic elements of human good and ill.

But many values are not like this. Though some human interests (and not only pleasure and pain) give rise to impersonal values, I now want to argue that not all of them do. If I have a bad headache, anyone has a reason to want it to stop. But if I badly want to climb to the top of Mount Kilimanjaro, not everyone has a reason to want me to succeed. I have a reason to try to get to the top, and it may be much stronger than my reason for wanting a headache to go away, but other people have very little reason, if any, to care whether I climb the mountain or not. Or suppose I want to become a pianist. Then I have a reason to practice, but other people have little or no reason to care if I practice or not. Why is this?

Why shouldn't the satisfaction of my desire to climb the mountain have impersonal value comparable to the value it has for me—just like the elimination of my headache? As it happens, you may have to put up with severe altitude headaches and nausea to get to the top of a mountain that high: it has to be worth it to you. Why doesn't the objectification of these values preserve the relation among them that exists in the perspective of the climber? This problem was originally formulated by Scanlon. He makes a strong case against the view that the satisfaction of preferences as such provides the raw material for ethics—the basis of our claims to the concern of others. The impersonal value of things that matter to an individual need not correspond to their personal value to him. "The fact that someone would be willing to forgo a decent diet in order to build a monument to his god does not mean that his claim on others for aid in his project has the same strength as a claim for aid in obtaining enough to eat" (Scanlon (1), pp. 659–60).

There are two ways in which a value may be conditional on a desire: the value may lie either outside or inside the conditional, so to speak. In the former case, a person's having X if he desires X has neutral value: satisfaction of the desire has objective utility that everyone has reason to promote. In the latter case, if a person desires X, his having X has relative value for him: susceptibility to the value is conditional on having the desire, and satisfaction of the desire does not have impersonal utility.

It isn't easy to state a general rule for assigning desires to one category or the other. I have claimed that sensory experiences which we strongly like or dislike simply in themselves have agent-neutral value because of those desires. Such immediate likes and dislikes, not resulting from any choice or underlying reason, are very different from the desires that define our broader aims and ambitions. The former result in mental states that are transparently good or bad, because the attitude of the subject is decisive. The latter require more complicated evaluation.

Most of the things we pursue, if not most of the things we avoid, are optional. Their value to us depends on our individual aims, projects, and concerns, including particular concerns for other people that reflect our relations with them; they acquire value only because of the interest we develop in them and the place this gives them in our lives, rather than evoking interest because of their value. When we look at such desires objectively, from outside, we can acknowledge the validity of the reasons they give for action without judging that there is a neutral reason for any of those things to be done. That is because when we move to the objective standpoint, we leave behind the perspective from which the values have to be accepted.

The crucial question is how far the authority of each individual runs in determining the objective value of the satisfaction of his own desires and preferences. From the objective standpoint we see a world which contains multiple individual perspectives. Some of the appearances of value from within those perspectives can just be taken over by the objective self. But I believe that others must remain essentially perspectival— appearances of value only *to the subject*, and valid only from within his life. Their value is not impersonally detachable, because it is too bound up with the idiosyncratic attitudes and aims of the subject, and can't be subsumed under a more universal value of comparable importance, like that of pleasure and pain.

Anyone may of course make the ends of another person his own, but that is a different matter: a matter of personal sympathy rather than of objective acknowledgment. So long as I truly occupy the objective standpoint, I can recognize the value of one of these optional ends only vicariously, through the perspective of the person who has chosen it, and not in its own right.

This is true even if the person is myself. When I regard my life from outside, integration of the two standpoints cannot overcome a certain form of detachment. I can't directly appreciate the value of my climbing Mount Kilimanjaro just because I want to, as I appreciate the value of my being adequately fed and clothed. The *fact* that I want to, viewed from outside, has none of the importance of *wanting to*, experienced from within. I can see a reason here only through the perspective of TN, who has chosen an optional goal which adds to the values operating within his life something beyond the reasons that simply come at him independently of his choices. I cannot see it except as a value for him, and I cannot therefore take it on without qualification as an impersonal value.

While this seems to me true, there is a natural way to dispute it. I have acknowledged that in the case of sensations, a strong desire or aversion can confer agent-neutral value, and it doesn't require that I have the desire or even fully understand it. Even if, for example, I don't mind the sound of squeaking chalk, I can acknowledge that it is impersonally bad for someone who hates it to be subjected to that sound. The impersonal badness attaches not to the experience conceived merely as a certain sound, but to someone's *having an experience he hates*. The evident awfulness is enough. Now someone might ask, why shouldn't a comparable impersonal value attach to someone's *having (or doing) something he wants*—whatever the desire is? Even if I can't objectively identify with the desire, and therefore can't assign any value to the achievement as such, why can't I judge it to have impersonal value under this more complex description? This would be the universal value under which one could objectively favor all preference-satisfaction.

It isn't easy to make the case convincingly, but I don't believe there is such a universal value. One reason is that the personal projects we are talking about generally involve things happening in the world outside our minds. It seems too much to allow an individual's desires to confer impersonal value on something outside himself, even if he is to some extent involved in it. The impersonal authority of the individual's values diminishes with distance from his inner condition. We can see this clearly, I think, in the limiting case of a personal desire for something which will never impinge on his consciousness: posthumous fame, for example. If someone wants posthumous fame, he may have a reason to do what he thinks will achieve it but one cannot see it as anything but a good *for him*. There is no agent-neutral value whatever in the realization of his hope: the only reason anyone else could have for caring about it would be a specific personal concern for him and his ambitions.

On the other hand, the more a desire has as its object the quality of the subject's experience, and the more immediate and independent of his other values it is, the more it will tend to generate impersonal as well as personal reasons. But to the extent that it transcends his own experience, the achievement of a typical personal project or ambition has no value except from the perspective of its subject—at least none in any way comparable to the value reasonably placed on it by the person whose ambition it is. (I am assuming here that we can abstract from any intrinsic value the achievement may have which does not depend on his interest at all—or else that we are dealing with projects whose actual value, whatever it is, derives entirely from the interest of the subject.) Whereas one clearly can find value in the occurrence/nonoccurrence of a sensory experience that is strongly liked/disliked for itself, whether or not one has or even empathizes with the reaction. To put it in a way that sounds paradoxical: the more subjective the object of the desire, the more impersonal the value of its satisfaction.

If this is right, then a certain amount of dissociation is inevitable when we bring the two standpoints together. From within I am directly subject to certain agent-relative reasons. From without all I can do is to acknowledge the reasonableness for the person I am of being motivated by those reasons—without being motivated by them myself, qua objective self. My objectivity shows up in the acknowledgment that these relative reasons are examples of something general, and could arise for any other agent with optional goals of his own. From a point of view outside the perspective of the ambition to climb Kilimanjaro or become a pianist, it is possible to recognize and understand that perspective and so to acknowledge the reasons that arise inside it; but it is not possible to accept those reasons as one's own, unless one occupies the perspective rather than merely recognizing it.

There is nothing incoherent in wanting to be able to climb Kilimanjaro or play all the Beethoven piano sonatas, while thinking that impersonally it doesn't matter whether one can do this. In fact one would have to be dotty to think it did matter impersonally. It doesn't even matter much impersonally that *if* someone wants to play all the Beethoven sonatas by heart, he should be able to. It matters a little, so that if he is incapable of achieving it, it might be better if he didn't want to—leaving aside whatever value there may be in the ambition itself. The neutral values of pleasure and pain come into effect here. But even that is a rather weak neutral value, since it is not the neutral correlate of the agent-relative reasons deriving directly from the ambition, whose object is not pleasure. If an interest is developed by the agent himself through his choices and actions, then the objective reasons it provides are primarily relative.

Any neutral reasons stemming from it must express values that are independent of the particular perspective and system of preferences of the agent. The general values of pleasure and pain, satisfaction and frustration, fill this role to some extent, as I have said, though only to the extent that they can be detached from the value of the object of desire whose acquisition or loss produces the feeling. (This, incidentally, explains the appeal of hedonism to consequentialists: it reduces all value to the impersonal common denominator of pleasure and pain.) But what there is not, I believe, is a completely general impersonal value of the satisfaction of desires and preferences. The strength of an individual's personal preferences in general determines what they give him reason to do, but it does not determine the impersonal value of his getting what he wants. There is no independent value of preference-satisfaction per se, which preserves its force even from an impersonal standpoint.

3. Personal Values and Impartiality

This may seem harsh, and if we left it at that, it would be. For if agent-neutral reasons derived only from pleasure and pain, we would have no reason to care about many fundamental aspects of other people's welfare which cannot easily be given a hedonistic interpretation—their freedom, their self-respect, their access to opportunities and resources that enable them to live fulfilling lives.

But I believe there is another way in which these things can be seen as having impersonal value—without giving carte blanche to individual preferences. These very general human goods share with the much more specific goods of pleasure and freedom from pain a characteristic that generates neutral reasons. Their value does not have to be seen through the particular values of the individual who has or lacks them, or through the particular preferences or projects he has formed.[1] Also, though they do not involve solely the contents of consciousness, such goods are very "close to home": they determine the character of life from the inside, and this lends authority to the value placed on them by the subject. For both these reasons, when we contemplate our own lives and those of others from outside, the most plausible objectification of these very general goods is not agent-relative.

From the objective standpoint, the fundamental thing leading to the recognition of agent-neutral reasons is a sense that no one is more important than anyone else. The question then is whether we are all equally unimportant or all equally important, and the answer, I think, is somewhere in between. The areas in which we must continue to be concerned about ourselves and others from outside are those whose value comes as close as possible to being universal. If impersonal value is going to be admitted at all, it will naturally attach to liberty, general opportunities, and the basic resources of life, as well as to pleasure and the

1. This is the rationale behind the choice of primary goods as the common measure of welfare for distributive justice in Rawls (1). See Rawls (2) for a much fuller treatment. That essay, Scanlon (1), and the present discussion are all treatments of the "deep problem" described in Rawls (1), pp. 173–5. Dworkin's defense of resources rather than welfare as the correct measure of equality is also in part a response to this problem.

absence of suffering. This is not equivalent to assigning impersonal value to each person's getting whatever he wants.

The hypothesis of two levels of objectification implies that there is not a significant reason for something to happen corresponding to every reason for someone to do something. Each person has reasons stemming from the perspective of his own life which, though they can be publicly recognized, do not in general provide reasons for others and do not correspond to reasons that the interests of others provide for him. Since the relative reasons are general and not purely subjective, he must acknowledge that the same is true of others with respect to him. A certain objective distance from his own aims is unavoidable; there will be some dissociation of the two standpoints with respect to his individual concerns. The ethical results will depend on the size of the impersonal demands made on him and others by the actual circumstances, and how strongly they weigh against more personal reasons.

One difficult question is whether such a two-tier system implies a significant limit to the degree to which ethics requires us to be impartial between ourselves and others.[2] It would imply this if the agent-relative reasons coming from our personal aims were simply added on to the neutral reasons derived from more universal values. For then I would be permitted to pursue my personal projects in preference to the impersonal good of others just as I can pursue those projects in preference to my own health, comfort, etc.; and I wouldn't have to sacrifice myself in return for the furtherance of *their* personal projects—only for their impersonal good. So it looks as though each person's agent-relative reasons would give him a margin of protection against the claims of others—though of course it could be overridden by sufficiently strong impersonal reasons.

However, there is some reason to doubt that the result will be this straightforward. In weighing our agent-relative reasons against the impersonal claims of others, we may not be able to use the same standards we use within our own lives. To take Scanlon's example again: just as we have more reason to help someone get enough to eat than to help him build a monument to his god—even if he is willing to forgo the food for the monument—so he may have more reason to help feed others than to build the monument, even if he cannot be faulted for starving himself. In other words, we have to give basic impersonal goods more

2. Impartiality should not be confused with equality. Nothing I say here bears on the question of how much equality is required in the allocation of what has impersonal value. Absolute impartiality is consistent with a denial that equality should be an independent factor at all in settling distributive questions.

weight when they come from other people's needs than when they compete with personal reasons within our own lives.

I am not sure of the best account of this, or how far it would go toward requiring impartiality. Full impartiality would seem to demand that any tendency toward self-favoritism on the basis of personal reasons be offset by a corresponding decrease in the weight given in one's interpersonal decisions to impersonal reasons deriving from one's own basic needs— so that one's total is not increased, so to speak. All reasons would have to be weighted so that everyone was equally important. But I don't know whether a credible system of this kind could be described, at any rate for the purposes of individual decision making. It seems more likely that interpersonal impartiality, both among others and between oneself and others, would have to be defined in terms of agent-neutral values, and that this would leave room for some partiality toward oneself and one's personal concerns and attachments, the extent of it depending on the comparative importance of relative and neutral reasons in the overall system. A stronger form of impartiality, if one is required, would have to appear at a higher level, in the application of practical reason to the social and political institutions that provide a background to individual choice.

There is one objection to this approach which ought to be mentioned, though probably few people would make it. I have claimed that a neutral objectification of the bulk of individualistic subjective reasons does not make sense. But of course that doesn't entail that a relative objectification is correct instead. There is a radical alternative: it could be that these reasons have no objective validity at all, relative or neutral. That is, it might be said by an uncompromising utilitarian that if there isn't a neutral reason for me to climb Kilimanjaro or learn the Beethoven sonatas—if it wouldn't be a good thing in itself, if the world wouldn't be a better place for my getting to the top of the mountain or being able to play the sonatas—then I have no reason of any kind to do those things, and I had better get rid of my desire to do them as soon as possible. I may not, in other words, accord more personal value to anything in my life than is justified by its impersonal value.

That is a logically possible move, but not a plausible one. It results from the aim of eliminating perspective from the domain of real value to the greatest possible extent, and that aim is not required of us by objectivity, so far as I can see. We should certainly try to harmonize our lives to some extent with how we think the world should be. But there is no necessity, I now believe, to abandon all values that do not correspond to anything desirable from an impersonal standpoint, even though this may be possible as a personal choice—a choice of self-transcendence.

If there are, objectively, both relative and neutral reasons, this raises a problem about how life is to be organized so that both can be given their due. One way of dealing with the problem is to put much of the responsibility for securing impersonal values into the hands of an impersonal institution like the state. A well designed set of political and social institutions should function as a moral buffer to protect personal life against the ravenous claims of impersonal good, and vice versa. I shall say a bit more about the relation between ethics and political theory later.

Before leaving the subject of autonomy, let me compare what I have said with another recent treatment of the relation between personal and impersonal values in ethical theory: Samuel Scheffler's *The Rejection of Consequentialism*. He proposes an "agent-centred prerogative," which would permit each individual to accord extra weight to all of his interests in deciding what to do, above that which they contribute to the neutral value of the total outcome of his actions, impersonally viewed.

> More specifically, I believe that a plausible agent-centred prerogative would allow each agent to assign a certain proportionately greater weight to his own interests than to the interests of other people. It would then allow the agent to promote the non-optimal outcome of his own choosing, provided only that the degree of its inferiority to each of the superior outcomes he could instead promote in no case exceeded, by more than the specified proportion, the degree of sacrifice necessary for him to promote the superior outcome. (p. 20)

This proposal is different from mine but not strictly incompatible with it. Scheffler does not make the distinction I have made between those interests and desires that do and those that do not generate impersonal values. He is not committed to a particular method of ranking the impersonal value of states of affairs, but his discussion suggests that he believes the satisfaction of most types of human preferences could be counted in determining whether one state of affairs or outcome was impersonally better than another. But whether or not he would accept my distinction, one could accept it and still formulate the proposal of an agent-centered prerogative; for that proposal describes a limit on the requirement always to produce the impersonally best outcome, which is independent of how the comparative impersonal value of outcomes is determined. It might be determined not by all interests but only by some. Then the prerogative would allow an individual to give those interests extra weight if they were his.

The trouble is that on the autonomy view I have put forward, he may already have some unopposed reasons which favor himself, arising from those desires whose satisfaction yields personal but not impersonal value. Perhaps it's going too far in moral indulgence to add to these a further prerogative of favoring himself with respect to the fundamental goods and evils whose impersonal value is clear.

An alternative position, which combines aspects of Scheffler's and mine, might be this. The division between interests that give rise to impersonal values and interests that don't is not sharp; it is a matter of degree. Some interests generate only relative reasons and no neutral ones; some generate neutral reasons that are just as strong as the relative ones; but some generate both relative reasons and somewhat weaker neutral ones. An individual is permitted to favor himself with respect to an interest to the degree to which the agent-relative reason generated by that interest exceeds the corresponding agent-neutral reason. There is no uniform prerogative of assigning a single proportionately greater weight to the cure of one's headaches, the realization of one's musical or athletic ambitions, and the happiness of one's children.

A variable prerogative of this kind would accord better than a uniform prerogative with Scheffler's account of the motivation behind it: the wish to give moral significance to the personal point of view by permitting morality to reflect the way in which concerns and commitments are naturally generated from within a particular point of view. If some interests are more dependent on a particular normative point of view than others, they will more naturally resist assimilation to the unifying claims of impersonal value in the construction of morality. All this emerges from the attempt to combine subjective and objective standpoints toward action and its motives.

On the other hand, even after such adjustments there will still be claims of impersonal morality that seem from an individual point of view excessive, and it may be that the response to this will have to include a more general agent-centered prerogative. I shall take up the problem in the next chapter.

4. Deontology

Let me turn now to the obscure topic of deontological constraints. These are agent-relative reasons which depend not on the aims or projects of the agent but on the claims of others. Unlike autonomous reasons, they are not optional. If they exist, they restrict what we may do in the service of either relative or neutral goals.

They complicate an already complicated picture. If there are agent-relative reasons of autonomy that do not give rise to agent-neutral interpersonal claims, then the claims of others must compete with these personal reasons in determining what one should do. Deontological constraints add further agent-relative reasons to the system—reasons not to treat others in certain ways. They are not impersonal claims derived from the interests of others, but personal demands governing one's relations with others.

Whatever their explanation, they are conspicuous among the moral appearances. Here is an example to focus your intuitions.

You have an auto accident one winter night on a lonely road. The other passengers are badly injured, the car is out of commission, and the road is deserted, so you run along it till you find an isolated house. The house turns out to be occupied by an old woman who is looking after her small grandchild. There is no phone, but there is a car in the garage, and you ask desperately to borrow it, and explain the situation. She doesn't believe you. Terrified by your desperation she runs upstairs and locks herself in the bathroom, leaving you alone with the child. You pound ineffectively on the door and search without success for the car keys. Then it occurs to you that she might be persuaded to tell you where they are if you were to twist the child's arm outside the bathroom door. Should you do it?

It is difficult not to see this as a dilemma, even though the child's getting its arm twisted is a minor evil compared with your friends' not getting to the hospital. The dilemma must be due to a special reason against *doing* such a thing. Otherwise it would be obvious that you should choose the lesser evil and twist the child's arm.

Common moral intuition recognizes several types of deontological reasons—limits on what one may do to people or how one may treat them. There are the special obligations created by promises and agreements; the restrictions against lying and betrayal; the prohibitions against violating various individual rights, rights not to be killed, injured, imprisoned, threatened, tortured, coerced, robbed; the restrictions against imposing certain sacrifices on someone simply as means to an end; and perhaps the special claim of immediacy, which makes distress at a distance so different from distress in the same room. There may also be a deontological requirement of fairness, of evenhandedness or equality in one's treatment of people. (This is to be distinguished from an impersonal value thought to attach to equality in the distribution of benefits, considered as an aspect of the assessment of states of affairs.)

In all these cases it appears that the special reasons, if they exist, cannot be explained simply in terms of neutral values, because the particular relation of the agent to the outcome is essential. Deontological constraints may be overridden by neutral reasons of sufficient strength, but they are not themselves to be understood as the expression of neutral values of any kind. It is clear from the way such reasons work that they cannot be explained by the hypothesis that the violation of a deontological constraint has high negative impersonal value. Deontological reasons have their full force against your doing something—not just against its happening.

For example, if there really are such constraints, the following things seem to be true. It seems that you shouldn't break a promise or tell a lie for the sake of some benefit, even though you would not be required to forgo a comparable benefit in order to prevent someone else from breaking a promise or telling a lie. And it seems that you shouldn't twist the arm of a small child to get its grandmother to do something, even something important enough so that you would not be required to forgo a comparable benefit in order to prevent someone else from twisting a child's arm. And it may be that you shouldn't engage in certain kinds of unfair discriminatory treatment (in an official role, for example) even to produce a good result which you would not be required to forgo in order to prevent similar unfairness by others.

Some may simply deny the plausibility of such moral intuitions. Others may say that their plausibility can be subtly accounted for in terms of impersonal values, and that they appear to involve a fundamentally different type of reason for action only if they are inadequately analyzed. As I have said, I don't want to take up these alternative accounts here. They may provide the best hope of rationally justifying something that has the rough shape of a set of deontological restrictions; but offered as complete accounts they seem to me essentially revisionist. Even if from that point of view they contain a good deal of truth, they do not shed light on the independent deontological conceptions they are intended to replace. Those conceptions still have to be understood, even if they will eventually be rejected.

Sometimes, particularly when institutions and general practices are involved in the case, there is a neutral justification for what looks initially like an agent-relative restriction on action. And it is certainly a help to the acceptance of deontological constraints that general adherence to them does not produce disastrous results in the long run. Rules against the direct infliction of harm and against the violation of widely accepted rights have considerable social utility, and if it ceased to be so, those rules would lose much of their moral attractiveness.

But I am convinced that a less indirect, nonstatistical form of evaluation is also at work in support of deontological constraints, and that it underlies the central, most puzzling intuitions in this area. This is what would produce a sense of dilemma if it turned out that general adherence to deontological restrictions worked consistently contrary to impersonal utility. Right or wrong, it is this type of view that I want to explore and understand. There is no point in trying to show in advance that such dilemmas cannot arise.

One reason for the resistance to deontological constraints is that they are formally puzzling, in a way that the other reasons we have discussed are not. We can understand how autonomous agent-relative reasons might derive from the specific projects and concerns of the agent, and we can understand how neutral reasons might derive from the interests of others, giving each of us reason to take them into account. But how can there be relative reasons to respect the claims of others? How can there be a reason not to twist someone's arm which is not equally a reason to prevent his arm from being twisted by someone else?

The relative character of the reason cannot come simply from the character of the interest that is being respected, for that alone would justify only a neutral reason to protect the interest. And the relative reason does not come from an aim or project of the individual agent, for it is not conditional on what the agent wants. Deontological restrictions, if they exist, apply to everyone: they are mandatory and may not be given up like personal ambitions or commitments.

It is hard to understand how there could be such a thing. One would expect that reasons stemming from the interests of others would be neutral and not relative. How can a claim based on the interests of others apply to those who may infringe it directly or intentionally in a way that it does not apply to those whose actions may damage that same interest just as much indirectly? After all, it is no worse *for the victim* to be killed or injured deliberately than accidentally, or as an unavoidable sideeffect of the dangerous rescue operation. In fact the special features of action that bring these reasons into effect may not add to the impersonal badness of the occurrence at all. To use an example of T. M. Scanlon, if you have to choose between saving someone from being murdered and saving someone else from being killed in a similar manner accidentally, and you have no special relation to either of them, it seems that your choice should depend only on which one you're more likely to succeed in saving. Admittedly the wickedness of a murder is in some sense a bad thing; but when it is a matter of deciding which of them there is more reason to prevent, a murder does not seem to be a significantly worse event, impersonally considered, than an accidental or incidental death. Some entirely different kind of value must be brought in to explain the idea that one should not kill one person even to prevent a number of accidental deaths: murder is not just an evil that everyone has reason to prevent, but an act that everyone has reason to *avoid*.

In any case, even if a murder were a worse event, impersonally considered, than an accidental death, this could not be used to explain the deontological constraint against murder. For that constraint prohibits murder even if it is necessary to prevent other *murders*—not only other deaths.

There is no doubt that ideas of this kind form an important part of common moral phenomenology. Yet their paradoxical flavor tempts one to think that the whole thing is a kind of moral illusion resulting either from innate psychological dispositions or from crude but useful moral indoctrination. Before debunking the intuition, however, we ought to have a better grasp of what it is. No doubt it's a good thing for people to have a deep inhibition against torturing children even for very strong reasons, and the same might be said of other deontological constraints. But that does not explain why we find it almost impossible to regard it as a merely useful inhibition. An illusion involves a judgment or a disposition to judge, and not a mere motivational impulse. The phenomenological fact to be accounted for is that we seem to apprehend in each individual case an extremely powerful agent-relative *reason* not to harm an innocent person. This presents itself as the apprehension of a normative truth, not just as a psychological inhibition. It needs to be analyzed and accounted for, and accepted or rejected according to whether the account gives it an adequate justification.

I believe that the traditional principle of double effect, despite problems of application, provides a rough guide to the extension and character of deontological constraints, and that even after the volumes that have been written on the subject in recent years, this remains the right point of convergence for efforts to capture our intuitions.[3] The principle says that to violate deontological constraints one must maltreat someone else intentionally. The maltreatment must be something that one does or chooses, either as an end or as a means, rather than something one's actions merely cause or fail to prevent but that one doesn't aim at.

It is also possible to foresee that one's actions will cause or fail to prevent a harm that one does not intend to bring about or permit. In that case it does not come under a deontological constraint, though it may still be objectionable for neutral reasons. The precise way to draw this distinction has been the subject of extensive debate, sometimes involving ingenious examples of a runaway trolley which will kill five people unless you . . . , where the dots are filled in by different ways of saving the five, all of which in some way involve one other person's death. I won't try to draw the exact boundaries of the principle. Though I say it with trepi-

3. A good statement of a view of this type is found in Fried.

dation, I believe that for my purposes they don't matter too much, and I suspect they can't be drawn more than roughly: my deontological intuitions, at least, begin to fail above a certain level of complexity. But one point worth mentioning is that the constraints apply to intentionally permitting as well as to intentionally doing harm. Thus in our example there would be the same kind of objection if with the same end in view you permitted someone else to twist the child's arm. You would have let it happen intentionally, and that would be different from a failure to prevent such an occurrence because you were too engaged in doing something else, which was more important.

5. Agents and Victims

So far this is just moral phenomenology: it does not remove the paradox. Why should we consider ourselves far more responsible for what we do (or permit) intentionally than for consequences of action that we foresee and decide to accept but that do not form part of our aims (intermediate or final)? How can the connection of ends and means conduct responsibility so much more effectively than the connection of foresight and avoidability?

It is as if each action produced a unique normative perspective on the world, determined by intention. When I twist the child's arm intentionally I incorporate that evil into what I do: it is my deliberate creation and the reasons stemming from it are magnified and lit up from my point of view. They overshadow reasons stemming from greater evils that are more "faint" from this perspective, because they do not fall within the intensifying beam of my intentions even though they are consequences of what I do.

That is the picture, but can it be correct? Isn't it a normatively distorted picture?

This problem is an instance of the collision between subjective and objective points of view. The issue is whether the special, personal perspective of agency has legitimate significance in determining what people have reason to do—whether, because of this perspective, I can have sufficient reason not to do something which, considered from an external standpoint, it would be better if I did. That is, *things* will be better, what *happens* will be better, if I twist the child's arm than if I do not. But I will have done something worse. If considerations of what I may do, and the correlative claims of my victim against me, can outweigh the substantial impersonal value of what will happen, that can only be because the perspective of the agent has an importance in practical reasoning that resists domination by a conception of the world as a place where good and bad things happen whose value is perspective-free.

I have already claimed that the dominance of this neutral conception of value is not complete. It does not swallow up or overwhelm the relative reasons arising from those individual ambitions, commitments, and attachments that are in some sense chosen. But the admission of what I have called autonomous reasons does not imply the possibility of deontological reasons.[4] The two are very different. The peculiarity of deontological reasons is that although they are agent-relative, they do not express the subjective autonomy of the agent at all. They are demands, not options. The paradox is that this partial, perspectival respect for the interests of others should not give way to an agent-neutral respect free of perspective. The deontological perspective seems primitive, even superstitious, by comparison: merely a stage on the way to full objectivity. How can what we *do* in this narrow sense be so important?

Let me try to say where the strength of the deontological view lies. We may begin by considering a curious feature of deontological reasons on which I have not yet remarked. Intention appears to magnify the importance of evil aims by comparison with evil side-effects in a way that it does not magnify the importance of good aims by comparison with good side-effects. We are supposed to avoid using evil means to produce a good end, even though it would be permissible to produce that good end by neutral means with comparably evil side-effects. On the other hand, given two routes to a legitimate end, one of which involves good means and neutral side-effects and the other of which involves neutral means and equally good side-effects, there is no reason to choose the first route. Deontological reasons tell us only not to aim at evil; they don't tell us to aim at good, as a means. Why should this be? What is the relation between evil and intention, or aiming, that makes them clash with such force?

The answer emerges if we ask ourselves what it is to aim at something, what differentiates it from merely producing the result knowingly.

The difference is that action intentionally aimed at a goal is guided by that goal. Whether the goal is an end in itself or only a means, action aimed at it must follow it and be prepared to adjust its pursuit if deflected by altered circumstances—whereas an act that merely produces an effect does not follow it, is not *guided* by it, even if the effect is foreseen.

What does this mean? It means that to aim at evil, even as a means, is to have one's action guided by evil. One must be prepared to adjust it

4. This is emphasized by Scheffler, who has a cautiously skeptical discussion of deontological constraints under the heading of "agent-centred restrictions."

to insure the production of evil: a falling-off in the level of the desired evil becomes a reason for altering what one does so that the evil is restored and maintained. But the essence of evil is that it should *repel* us. If something is evil, our actions should be guided, if they are guided by it at all, toward its elimination rather than toward its maintenance. That is what evil *means*. So when we aim at evil we are swimming head-on against the normative current. Our action is guided by the goal at every point in the direction diametrically opposite to that in which the value of that goal points. To put it another way, if we aim at evil we make what we do in the first instance a positive rather than a negative function of it. At every point, the intentional function is simply the normative function reversed, and from the point of view of the agent, this produces an acute sense of moral dislocation.

If you twist the child's arm, your aim is to produce pain. So when the child cries, "Stop, it hurts!" his objection corresponds in perfect diametrical opposition to your intention. What he is pleading as your reason to stop is precisely your reason to go on. If it didn't hurt you would twist harder, or try the other arm. There may be cases (e.g. of justified punishment or obloquy) when pain is not intrinsically evil, but this is not one of them: the victim is innocent. You are pushing directly and essentially against the intrinsic normative force of your goal, for it is the production of his pain that guides you. It seems to me that this is the phenomenological nerve of deontological constraints. What feels peculiarly wrong about doing evil intentionally even that good may come of it is the headlong striving against value that is internal to one's aim.

I have discussed a simple case, but naturally there can be complications. One is the possibility of someone volunteering to be subjected to some kind of pain or damage, either for his own good or for some other end which is important to him. In that case the particular evil that you aim at is swallowed up in the larger aim for deontological purposes. So the evil at which we are constrained not to aim is *our victim's* evil, rather than just a particular bad thing, and each individual has considerable authority in defining what will count as harming him for the purpose of this restriction. [5]

All this still leaves unsettled the question of justification. For it will be objected that if one aims at evil as a means only, then even if several people's interests are involved one's action is really being guided not by

---

5. The same seems to apply even when informed consent is impossible, as when we cause suffering or damage to a young child for its own greater good—though here there may be a residual inhibition: if we imagine in the case described that the *child's* safety depends on getting the car keys, it doesn't altogether remove the revulsion against twisting his arm to get them.

evil but by overall good, which includes a balance of goods and evils. So when you twist the child's arm, you are guided by the aim of rescuing your injured friends, and the good of that aim dominates the evil of the child's pain. The immediacy of the fact that you must try to produce evil as a subsidiary aim is phenomenologically important, but why should it be morally important? Even though it adds to the personal cost to you, why should it result in a prohibition?

I don't believe there is a decisive answer here. The question is whether to disregard the resistance encountered by my immediate pursuit of what is evil for my victim, in favor of the overall value of the results of what I do. When I view my act from outside and think of it as resulting from a choice of the impersonally considered state of the world in which it occurs, this seems rational. In thinking of the matter this way, I abstract my will and its choices from my person, as it were, and even from my actions, and decide directly among states of the world, as if I were taking a multiple choice test. If the choice is determined by what on balance is impersonally best, then I am guided by good and not by evil.

But the self that is so guided is the objective self, which regards the world impersonally, as a place containing TN and his actions, among other things. It is detached from the perspective of TN, for it views the world from nowhere within it. It chooses, and TN, its instrument, or perhaps one could say its agent, carries out the instructions as best he can. *He* may have to aim at evil, for the impersonally best alternative may involve the production of good ends by evil means. But he is only following orders.

To see the matter in this light is to see both the appeal of agent-neutral, consequentialist ethics and the contrary force of agent-relative, deontological ethics. The detached, objective view takes in everything and provides a standpoint of choice from which all choosers can agree about what should happen. But each of us is not only an objective self but a particular person with a particular perspective; we act in the world from that perspective, and not only from the point of view of a detached will, selecting and rejecting world-states. So our choices are not merely choices of states of the world, but of actions. Every choice is two choices, and from the internal point of view, the pursuit of evil in twisting the child's arm looms large. The production of pain is the immediate aim, and the fact that from an external perspective you are choosing a balance of good over evil does not cover up the fact that this is the intrinsic character of your action.

I have concentrated on the point of view of the agent, as seems suitable in the investigation of an agent-relative constraint. But there is also something to be said about the point of view of the victim. There too we encounter problems having to do with the integration of the two stand-points, and further support for the analysis. Moral principles don't sim-ply tell agents what they may and may not do. They also tell victims what sort of treatment they may and may not object to, resist, or demand.

If I were justified in killing one innocent person to save five others, then he would have no right to object, and on a fully consequentialist view he would have no right to resist. The other five, by contrast, would have the right to object if I *didn't* kill him to save them. A thoroughly impersonal morality would require that victims as well as actors be dom-inated by impersonal, agent-neutral values in their judgments about how others treat them.

But this seems an excessive demand to make of individuals whose per-spective on the world is inherently complex and includes a strong sub-jective component. Of course none of the six people in this dilemma wants to die, but only one of them is faced with me trying to kill him. This person is not permitted, on a purely agent-neutral consequentialist view, to appeal for his life against my deliberate attempt to take it from him. His special position as my victim doesn't give him any special stand-ing to appeal to me.

Of course the deontological position has a parallel feature. On a deon-tological view, the five people I could save by killing the one cannot appeal to me for their lives, against my refusal to save them. (They may appeal against *their* killers, if that's the nature of the death threat, but not against me.) But this does not make the two positions symmetrical, for there is a difference. The deontological constraint permits a victim always to object to those who aim at his harm, and this relation has the same special character of normative magnification when seen from the personal perspective of the victim that it has when seen from the per-sonal perspective of the agent. Such a constraint expresses the direct appeal to the point of view of the agent from the point of view of the person on whom he is acting. It operates through that relation. The vic-tim feels outrage when he is deliberately harmed even for the greater good of others, not simply because of the quantity of the harm but because of the assault on his value of having my actions guided by his evil. What I do is immediately directed against his good: it doesn't just in fact harm him.

The five people I could save by killing him can't say the same, if I refrain. They can appeal only to my objective acknowledgment of the impersonal value of their lives. That is not trivial, of course, but it still seems less pressing than the protest available to my victim—a protest he can make not to them but to me, as the possessor of the life I am aiming to destroy.

This merely corroborates the importance of the internal perspective in accounting for the content of deontological intuitions. It does not prove the correctness of those intuitions. But it confirms that a purely impersonal morality requires the general suppression of the personal perspective in moral motivation, not only in its rejection of relative reasons of autonomy but also in its refusal to accept agent-relative deontological restrictions. Such restrictions need not be absolute: they can be thought of as relative reasons with a certain weight, that are among the sources of morality but do not exhaust it. When we regard human relations objectively, it does not seem irrational to admit such reasons at the basic level into the perspective of both agents and victims.

6. Moral Progress

This account of the force of deontological reasons applies with special clarity to the constraint against doing harm as a means to your ends. A fuller deontological theory would have to explain the different types of normative grain against which one acts in breaking promises, lying, discriminating unfairly, and denying immediate emergency aid. It would also have to deal with problems about what exactly is being aimed at, in cases of action that can be described in several different ways. But I believe that the key to understanding any of these moral intuitions is the distinction between the internal viewpoint of the agent or victim and an external, objective viewpoint which both agent and victim can also adopt. Reasons for action look different from the first two points of view than from the third.

We are faced with a choice. For the purposes of ethics, should we identify with the detached, impersonal will that chooses total outcomes, and act on reasons that are determined accordingly? Or is this a denial of what we are really doing and an avoidance of the full range of reasons that apply to creatures like us? This is a true philosophical dilemma; it arises out of our nature, which includes different points of view on the world. When we ask ourselves how to live, the complexity of what we are makes a unified answer difficult. I believe the human duality of perspectives is too deep for us reasonably to hope to overcome it. A fully agent-neutral morality is not a plausible human goal.

On the other hand, it is conceivable that deontological restrictions now widely accepted may be modified under the pressure of conflict with the impersonal standpoint. Some degree of skepticism about our current moral intuitions is not unreasonable, in light of the importance to moral belief of our starting points, the social influences pressing on us, and the confusion of our thought. If we aspire to objective truth in this area—that is, truth that is independent of our beliefs—we would be wise to hold many of our views more tentatively than we are naturally inclined to do. In ethics, even without the benefit of many clear examples, we should be open to the possibility of progress as we are in other areas, with a consequent effect of reduced confidence in the finality of our current understanding.[6]

It is evident that we are at a primitive stage of moral development. Even the most civilized human beings have only a haphazard understanding of how to live, how to treat others, how to organize their societies. The idea that the basic principles of morality are *known*, and that the problems all come in their interpretation and application, is one of the most fantastic conceits to which our conceited species has been drawn. (The idea that if we cannot easily know it, there is no truth here is no less conceited.) Not all of our ignorance in these areas is ethical, but a lot of it is. And the idea of the possibility of moral progress is an essential condition of moral progress. None of it is inevitable.

The pursuit of objectivity is only a method of getting closer to the truth. It is not guaranteed to succeed, and there is room for skepticism about its specific results in ethics as elsewhere. How far it can take us from the appearances is not clear. The truth here could not be radically inaccessible in the way that the truth about the physical world might be. It is more closely tied to the human perspective and the human motivational capacity because its point is the regulation of human conduct. It has to be suited to govern our lives day by day, in a way in which theoretical understanding of the physical world does not. And to do its work it must be far more widely accepted and internalized than in areas where the public is willing to defer to expert opinion.

There might be forms of morality incommensurable with our own that are appropriate for Martians but to which we do not have access for the same reason that we do not have access to the minds of such creatures. Unless we can understand their lives, experiences, and motives from inside, we will be unable to appreciate the values to which they respond in a way that allows us to objectify them accurately. Objectivity needs subjective material to work on, and for human morality this is found in human life.

How far outside ourselves we can go without losing contact with this essential material—with the forms of life in which values and justifications are rooted—is not certain. But I believe that ethics, unlike aesthetics, requires more than the purification and intensification of inter-

6. See Parfit (2), pt. 1, for discussion of some ways commonsense morality might be revised to bring it closer to consequentialism.

nal human perspectives. It requires a detachment from particular perspectives and transcendence of one's time and place. If we did not have this capacity then there would be no alternative to relativism in ethics. But I believe we do have it, and that it is not inevitably a form of false consciousness.

Even the very primitive stage of moral development we have reached was arrived at only by a long and difficult journey. I assume a much longer one lies ahead of us, if we survive. It would be foolish to try to lay down in advance the outlines of a correct method for ethical progress, but it seems reasonable at present to continue the awkward pursuit of objectivity described here. This does not mean that greater detachment always takes us closer to the truth. Sometimes, to be sure, objectivity will lead us to regard our original inclinations as mistaken, and then we will try to replace them or bracket them as ineliminable but illusory. But it would be a mistake to try to eliminate perspective from our conception of ethics entirely—as much of a mistake as it would be to try to eliminate perspective from the universe. This itself must be objectively recognized. Though it may be equally tempting, it would be no more reasonable to eliminate all those reasons for action that cannot be assimilated to the most external, impersonal system of value than it would be to eliminate all facts that cannot be assimilated to physics.

Yet in defending the legitimacy of agent-relative principles, we must guard against self-deception and the escalation of personal claims simply to resist burdensome moral demands. It is not always easy to tell, for example, whether a morality that leaves extensive free space in each individual life for the pursuit of personal interests is not just a disguise for the simplest form of badness: selfishness in the face of the legitimate claims of others. It is hard to be good, as we all know.

I suspect that if we try to develop a system of reasons which harmonizes personal and impersonal claims, then even if it is acknowledged that each of us must live in part from his own point of view, there will be a tendency for the personal components to be altered. As the claims of objectivity are recognized, they may come to form a larger and larger part of each individual's conception of himself, and will influence the range of personal aims and ambitions, and the ideas of his particular relations to others and the claims they justify. I do not think it is utopian to look forward to the gradual development of a greater universality of moral respect, an internalization of moral objectivity analogous to the gradual internalization of scientific progress that seems to be a feature of modern culture.

On the other hand there is no reason to expect progress to be reductive, though here as elsewhere progress is too easily identified with reduction and simplification. Distinct individuals are still the clients of ethics, and their variety guarantees that pluralism will be an essential aspect of any adequate morality, however advanced.

There have to be principles of practical reason that allow us to take into account values that we do not share but whose force for others we must acknowledge. In general, the problem of how to combine the enormous and disparate wealth of reasons that practical objectivity generates, together with the subjective reasons that remain, by a method that will allow us to act and choose in the world, is dauntingly difficult.

This brings us to a final point. There can be no ethics without politics. A theory of how individuals should act requires a theory—an ethical theory, not just an empirical one—of the institutions under which they should live: institutions which substantially determine their starting points, the choices they can make, the consequences of what they do, and their relations to one another. Since the standpoint of political theory is necessarily objective and detached, it offers strong temptations to simplify, which it is important to resist. A society must in some sense be organized in accordance with a single set of principles, even though people are very different.

This is inconvenient: it may seem that political theory must be based on a universal human nature, and that if we cannot discover such a thing we have to invent it, for political theory must exist. To avoid such folly, it is necessary to take on the much more difficult task of devising fair uniform social principles for beings whose nature is not uniform and whose values are legitimately diverse. If they were diverse enough, the task might be impossible—there may be no such thing as intergalactic political theory—but within the human species the variation seems to fall within bounds that do not rule out the possibility of at least a partial solution. This would have to be something acceptable from a standpoint external to that of each particular individual, which at the same time acknowledges the plurality of values and reasons arising within all those perspectives. Even though the morality of politics is rightly more impersonal than the morality of private life, the acknowledgment of personal values and autonomy is essential even at the level that requires the greatest impersonality.

There is no telling what kinds of transcendence of individuality will result over the long term from the combined influence of moral and political progress, or decline. A general takeover of individual life from the perspective of the universe, or even from the perspective of humanity, seems premature—even if some saints or mystics can manage it. Reasons for action have to be reasons for individuals, and individual perspectives can be expected to retain their moral importance so long as diverse human individuals continue to exist.

X

LIVING RIGHT AND
LIVING WELL

1. Williams's Question

The admission of a variety of motivational elements among the sources of morality results in a system that reflects the divisions of the self. It does not resolve or eliminate those divisions. The discussion so far has not been detailed enough to provide the basis for a substantive moral theory: it has been concerned with foundations and with certain contrasts among the ways the rights and interests of others can impinge on us. While I have argued that moral claims have an objective basis, this doesn't mean that they are radically impersonal. As I have emphasized, objectivity requires that we recognize substantial elements of personal value in practical reasoning, and hence in morality.

Still, the impersonal element in any objective morality will be significant and depending on circumstances may become very demanding: it may overshadow everything else. In this chapter I want to discuss the tension between subjective and objective standpoints that results when these demands of impersonal morality are addressed to individuals who have their own lives to lead.

This is a problem that faces us after the reality of objective moral claims is admitted, and it will be treated differently depending on one's views of the sources of morality, the conditions of practical rationality, and the overall motivational economy of the soul. But it is a problem of

real life and not just of philosophical theory, as most of us can attest
from experience. And it does not depend on one specific form of impersonal morality. To take an example close to home: the bill for two in a
moderately expensive New York restaurant equals the annual per capita
income of Bangladesh. Every time I eat out, not because I have to but
just because I feel like it, the money could do noticeably more good if
contributed to famine relief. The same could be said of many purchases
of clothing, wine, theater tickets, vacations, gifts, books, records, furni-
ture, stemware, etc. It all adds up. It adds up both to a form of life and
to quite a lot of money.

If one is near the upper end of a very unequal world economic distribution, the difference in cost between the life to which one is probably
accustomed and a much grubbier but perfectly tolerable existence is
enough to feed several dozen starving families, year in, year out. Doubts
about the best way to combat famine and other evils are beside the point.
It is clear that a strongly impersonal morality, with any significant
requirements of impartiality, can pose a serious threat to the kind of
personal life that many of us take to be desirable.

This is true not only of purely impersonal moralities like utilitarianism
or other consequentialist views. Provided a morality admits substantial
agent-neutral reasons arising from the interests of others, it will face this
problem even if it also grants significant weight to agent-relative reasons
of autonomy and obligation. In the previous chapter I left the question
of the required degree of impartiality open. But even if personal interests whose value is tied to my own perspective do not have to compete
in my practical deliberations with the corresponding personal values of
others, they do have to compete with the impersonal value that attaches
to satisfaction of the most basic needs of others—a value I can't think
of as relative when I regard it objectively. I may not be concerned that
the money I pay for a three-course meal would allow someone else to
complete his stamp collection, build a monument to his god, or spend a
couple of days at the track, even if he cares much more about those
things than I do about the meal; but I can't be similarly blasé about the
fact that it could save someone from malnutrition, malaria—or perhaps
more indirectly, illiteracy or imprisonment without trial. The magnitude
of the world's problems and the inequality in access to its resources produce a weight of potential guilt that may, depending on one's temperament, require considerable ingenuity to keep roped down.

Most of us won't find comfort in Mill's claim that "the occasions on
which any person (except one in a thousand) has it in his power to . . .
be a public benefactor, are but exceptional; and on these occasions alone
is he called on to consider public utility; in every other case, private util-

ity, the interest and happiness of some few persons, is all he has to attend to" (Mill, ch. 2, par. 19). We are more likely to agree with Susan Wolf that "no plausible argument can justify the use of human resources involved in producing *pâté de canard en croûte* against possible alternative beneficent ends to which these resources might be put" (Wolf (2), p. 422).

One attitude toward this problem is that it's just too bad: no one ever said morality was going to be easy. But there is another response, which takes the problem as a basis for criticism of impersonal moral demands. An important development in recent moral philosophy has been Williams's challenge to the claims of impersonal morality from the point of view of the individual agent to whom those claims are addressed. He objects not only to utilitarianism and other consequentialist theories but also to Kantian theories.[1] The general objection is that impersonal moralities demand too much of us, and that if we accept and act on those demands, we cannot lead good lives. I want to discuss the assumptions about the conditions on morality that are implied by this criticism. It is not always clear whether Williams's argument is about the content of morality or about its authority, but I shall discuss both—both the idea that the true morality cannot be so demanding and the idea that if it is so demanding we should refuse to obey it.

The problem is not just that an impersonal morality may from time to time require us to act contrary to our interests. Its effect on our lives is deeper than that: an impersonal morality requires of us not only certain forms of conduct but also the motives required to produce that conduct. This much is I think true of any morality properly worked out. If we are required to do certain things, then we are required to be the kinds of people who will do those things. And adherence to different versions of impersonal morality requires a set of motives, and of priorities among them, that is according to Williams incompatible with other motives necessary for a good human life. In particular, he claims that impersonal demands rule out the commitment to personal projects that is a condition for the integrity of one's life, and that they undermine the commitment to particular other persons that is a condition of love and friendship. The cost in alienation from one's projects and one's life is too high.[2]

1. See Williams (4) and (6) and some of the other essays in (8).
2. I shall use the expression "a good life" throughout, even though Williams doesn't put his position in these terms and though it may be somewhat inexact. "Living well" might be better, since it doesn't so strongly suggest the maximization of a person's interests over the course of his life as a whole. This would accord better with Williams's position that

Those against whom this argument is directed are unlikely to be convinced. Utilitarians could reply, first, that their system is perfectly capable of taking the value of individual projects and personal commitments into account in determining what is good for individuals and therefore what is good for the totality of individuals whose welfare is the standard of morality. Second, they might say that utilitarianism places no obstacle in the way of the integrity of anyone's life, provided he chooses projects and commitments that do not conflict with the general welfare: for example, someone whose governing project is to maximize the general welfare will obviously not find himself frustrated by utilitarian requirements. Third, they might say that insofar as any objection remains which cannot be accommodated by utilitarianism, it begs the question. For utilitarianism is a theory about how it is right to live, and cannot be refuted on the basis of independent claims about how it is good to live.

This last reply, which could also be made by a Kantian, can take either of two forms, depending on whether or not it acknowledges the possibility of a conflict between morality and the good life. The no-conflict view would hold that a moral theory like utilitarianism or Kantianism, in telling us what we ought to do, reveals an essential aspect of the good life that cannot be known independent of morality. Not to do what we have decisive moral reasons to do is ipso facto to live badly. And even if morality requires sacrifices of us, the fact that they are required implies that it would be even *worse for us* if in those circumstances we did not make them. On this view, since the best life *is* the moral life, a morality cannot be refuted on the ground of its conflict with the good life.

The other form of reply, by contrast, admits the possibility of conflict. On this other view, it would be said that while there is a distinction and possible divergence between living a good life and doing right, a moral theory is a theory about how it is right to live, and cannot be refuted by pointing out that living this way may make the good man's life worse than it otherwise would be. Such a refutation would assume, falsely, that morality should tell you how to have the best life you can. The truth is that a morality takes the agent's personal interests into account as only one factor among others in determing how he should live.

---

the appropriate standpoint of decision is *from now*, rather than from a timeless vantage point that overlooks your whole life. It would also remove the suggestion that what opposes impersonal morality is only self-interest, rather than any of a range of things that an individual may be personally concerned with at any given time—including the interests of particular others and perhaps not including his own long-term self-interest at all. But the main issues don't depend on the choice among these interpretations of living well. The general opposition we are concerned with is that between the claims of impersonal morality and the personal perspective of the agent to whom they are addressed. Putting it in terms of the good life enables us to connect Williams's point with earlier discussions.

I want to explore this dispute about the relative positions of the good life and the moral life—or living well and doing right—in ethical theory. I won't attempt to define these terms, for their analysis is part of the problem. But I will assume a rough grasp of the prima facie distinction between the concepts. Let me say only that by the moral life I mean a life that complies with moral requirements. Later I shall say something about supererogatory virtue, which goes beyond these requirements.

The dispute has more than two sides, for there are several competing positions, distinguished by the way they answer three questions. (1) To what extent are the ideas of the good life and the moral life logically independent? (2) If they are not independent, which of them has priority in determining the content of the other? Must the good life be moral or must the moral life be good? (3) To the extent that they are independent, which of them has priority in determining how it is reasonable or rational for a person to live? Should he resist morality if it conflicts with the good life, or should he sacrifice the good life to morality, or is it reasonable to do either; or does the answer vary with the strength of the conflicting claims? We therefore have to consider the relation among three concepts: the good life, the moral life, and the rational life.

What interests me especially is the assumption that a morality must attempt to tell people how they can live a good life, or at least how they can live a moral life that is not also a bad life—and that in taking this responsibility it opens itself to possible criticism from the point of view of a more comprehensive idea of what it is to live well—an idea that includes more than morality. When the target of such criticism is an impersonal morality, we have a prime example of the clash between the personal standpoint of each individual and the more objective, detached standpoint with which such a morality is naturally connected. This clash presents moral theory with a fundamental task.

2. Antecedents

The problem of how to deal with the individual's rebellion against the claims of morality is an ancient one. In different ways, many philosophical defenders of morality have tried to harmonize it with the largest good of each individual, either by making it part of human good or by tailoring it to avoid conflict. A few examples. Plato's *Republic* is a heroic attempt to reconcile the two standpoints by showing that moral virtue forms an indispensable part of the good for each person. Kant, on the other hand, says the harmony is something whose necessity we cannot demonstrate but must for moral reasons postulate as having noumenal reality even though we cannot find it in the world of experience. So we may hope that outside of our temporal lives, in virtue of the immortality of the soul and the existence of God, the highest good is realized and happiness is perfectly correlated with worthiness to be happy.[3]

There are also those who explicitly deny the correlation—like Nietzsche, whose rejection of impersonal morality is an assertion of the dominance of the ideal of living well. (See for example *The Genealogy of Morals*, first essay.) It is important that this ideal is not to be identified just with the successful pursuit of one's long-term interests or one's pleasure. That is clear in the case of Nietzsche. The ideal of a good life must be understood very broadly in thinking about this conflict.

Among defenders of impersonal morality, Bentham is conspicuous in denying any internal connection between what is right for an individual to do and what is good for that individual. According to Bentham, each person is ruled entirely by the pursuit of his own pleasure and the avoidance of his own pain, and the only way in which he can be led to act in accordance with the principle of utility is by bringing it about—through internal or external sanctions and social or political institutions—that what gives him happiness also serves the general welfare (Bentham, ch. 1). Since this is a highly contingent matter, there is no necessary connection between doing right and living well, and in a showdown the individual's happiness will automatically win, by the iron laws of psychology.

I suspect that most contemporary utilitarians would not entirely agree with Bentham, but would claim instead that the principle of utility tells us not only what it would be right to do (supposing we had some adequate reason to do it), but what we have decisive reason to do simply *because* it is right, even if it conflicts with our individual happiness. The further question is whether they would also reject the demand for reconciliation, or accept it and claim that in some other way it is still best, for the individual, to live this way. Sidgwick doubted that such harmony could be generated, and thought that without it morality was on a doubtful footing.[4]

For contemporary Kantians, we have the question whether in the absence of hope for a balancing out in the hereafter, they would still try to meet Williams's challenge by maintaining that someone who obeys the moral law at a cost to his other interests has a better life than someone who breaks it. Both utilitarians and Kantians, if they wished to support this reconciliation of the two values, would probably have to appeal to the good of a higher self that expresses itself through impersonal morality. That is also the general form of the solution offered by Plato.

3. Kant (3), pp. 110–33; Kant (1), p. B839.
4. Sidgwick, bk. 2, ch. 5, and concluding chapter.

The idea would be that recognition of impersonal moral claims, which take into account everyone's interests or the requirements of universal law, is the function of an aspect of each one of us that is so important that its proper functioning and dominance in our lives overshadows in value for us all the other goods and evils that may befall us. On any view there *are* other goods and evils. For example, two equally moral people may be unequally well off because one has arthritis and the other doesn't. But on the reconciliationist view, these other values can never make an immoral life better than a moral one. Even if what is required of us is the acceptance of death, that only shows that a short moral life is better than a long immoral one.

I suspect that such a reconciliation is not possible, and that for the defense of morality it is not necessary. Morality does not fall if Kant's "highest good" is unattainable. And while I agree with Williams that it is the task of a moral theory to tell us not only what we are morally required to do but also how to lead a good life, I do not believe that a theory can be rejected on the ground that under some conditions it requires us to live a life less good than we could if we ignored its demands. Perhaps Williams would not hold morality to such a strict standard, but he does seem to put more ethical weight than I would on living well rather than doing right. I believe both these aspects of moral theory are important, and that the conflict between them probably cannot be eliminated from any plausible view. If that is true, then a third important aspect of moral theory will be how it resolves the conflict.

3. Five Alternatives

To approach the issue systematically, let me distinguish several positions concerning the relative priority of the good life and the moral life. The view I am drawn to will emerge, but it can be best defended by contrast with the alternatives.

(1) *The moral life is defined in terms of the good life.* This is Aristotle's position, more or less. It doesn't mean that the two ideas are equivalent, but it does mean that the content of morality is defined in terms of the necessary· conditions for a good life, so far as this depends on certain aspects of the individual's conduct, such as his relations with other people, the fulfillment of his social role, and the expression and control of his emotions. The test of moral principles will be their contribution, either instrumental or constitutive, to the good life as a whole; but since we are social beings, this may entail some of the familiar moral virtues.

(2) *The good life is defined in terms of the moral life.* This is Plato's posi-

tion. It can allow that there is more to the good life than morality so long as it assigns absolute priority to the moral component—so that though two moral lives may not be equally good (because of differences in health, for example), a moral life is always better than an immoral one, however good the immoral one is in other respects.

Both these positions imply that conflict between the two kinds of life is logically impossible, because of their internal relation. The next two positions admit the possibility of conflict and say how it is to be resolved in rational choice.

(3) *The good life overrides the moral life.* This is Nietzsche's position. It is expressed also by Thrasymachus in the *Republic*, and has recently been adopted by Philippa Foot in preference to her earlier espousal of position (1).[5] This position can admit that morality is *a* human good, so long as it is not allowed to be dominant. The view is that if, taking everything into consideration, a moral life will not be a good life for the individual, it would be a mistake to lead it. Of course it may be held, as by Thrasymachus and Nietzsche, that morality is in itself bad for its possessor.

(4) *The moral life overrides the good life.* This would I think hold in the most natural form of utilitarianism, and also in most nonreligious deontological theories, including rights theories. The idea is not that morality will necessarily conflict with the good life but that it can, and when it does it provides us with sufficient reason to sacrifice our own good. In utilitarianism the possibility of conflict follows directly from the way in which moral right is defined in terms of individual good. Not in the manner of position (1), where what is moral for an individual is defined in terms of the good life for that individual—rather what is morally required of each individual is defined in terms of what is optimal for the totality of individuals. Any coincidence between this and what is best for him in particular will be a matter of luck, or political and social arrangement. And if he is in a position to benefit others sufficiently at some cost to himself, he will have to sacrifice his income, his personal relations, his health, his happiness, and even his life if that will have more utility than anything else he can do. Morality, in other words, may require him to give up a good life; and something similar may occur in a deontological system, if he is prohibited from saving himself from ruin or death by wronging someone else.

This position, like position (3), can count morality as a part of the good life so long as it does not say that a moral life is always better than an immoral one. When the immoral one would be better, the moral one must be adopted, not because it is a better life but in spite of the fact that it is worse.

5. The change occurs between Foot (1) and (2).

Finally, there is a position in the middle:

(5) *Neither the good life nor the moral life consistently overrides the other.* This assumes, like (3) and (4), that the two are not interdefinable, and that each of them is supported by reasons that may vary in relative strength.

My own view is that the first three positions are just wrong and that the really difficult choice is between (4) and (5), though I incline to (4). The view that moral considerations are overriding is a common one. But if it is correct, this is not a matter of definition. Rather it depends on the truth about ethics.

What I think is this. While doing the right thing is part of living well it is not the whole of it, nor even the dominant part: because the impersonal standpoint that acknowledges the claims of morality is only one aspect of a normal individual among others. And there are times when doing the right thing may cost more in terms of other aspects of the good life than it contributes to the good life in its own right.[6]

Position (1) is wrong, in my view, because moral requirements have their source in the claims of other persons, and the moral force of those claims cannot be strictly limited by their capacity to be accommodated within a good individual life. This is inevitable so long as ethics includes any significant condition of impartiality.

Position (2) is wrong because there is much more to us, and therefore much more to what is good and bad for us, than what is directly involved in morality. It may be that the extremes of immorality constitute a dominant evil—that to be horribly wicked is so bad that no rewards of other kinds could imply that such a person would be worse off if he were not wicked. But the relation between morality and the good life in general is not determined by such cases.

Living well and doing right are both things we have reason to want, and while there may be some overlap, those reasons are generally of different kinds and come from different sources. Even if the reasons for each take all the facts into account, they don't each include all the reasons there are.

---

6. My position resembles that of Wolf. She discusses the relation between the moral point of view and the point of view of individual perfection, and calls into question "the assumption that it is always better to be morally better" (Wolf (2), p. 438). She also concludes that it is not necessarily a defect in a moral theory that someone who is morally perfect by its standards would have to be a flawed person—since the moral point of view does not provide a way of comprehensively evaluating a person's life. Wolf focuses on the distasteful aspects of moral perfection, but her position could also apply to the problem of adherence to lesser moral requirements (see Wolf (3)). Where I part from her, as I explain below, is in my hope that there is some way of preserving the priority of moral requirements—if not of moral considerations generally—in determining how it is rational to live, though not how it is good to live.

That the moral life is at least part of the good life seems to be true on any view that does not regard morality as a purely instrumental second best, or else as a positive evil. If there are intrinsic reasons to be moral, then being moral will be to that extent a good for the individual, even if he doesn't pursue it out of self-interest.

This can be made more specific, if we consider Williams's claim that impersonal morality requires the alienation of the individual from his projects and commitments. I believe this is the opposite of the truth. If the impersonal standpoint is an important aspect of the self, then it would be left in the role of a pure, detached spectator of one's life if it could not enter into practical reasoning and action in the way that impersonal morality envisions.

This form of alienation can be avoided only to the extent that personal projects and individual action can be harmonized with universal requirements, requirements that are apprehended from an impersonal standpoint and typically expressed by certain moralities. Those universalistic moralities are supposed, after all, to answer to something very important in us. They are not imposed from outside, but reflect our own disposition to view ourselves, and our need to *accept* ourselves, from outside. Without such acceptance we will be in a significant way alienated from our lives.[7]

Still, the impersonal standpoint is not the whole of human life. There are other parts as well, and this makes it likely that under some circumstances a moral life would be worse than an immoral life with other compensations. Acting in accordance with moral reasons, and even acting in accordance with the decisive overall balance of reasons of all kinds, is not the whole of what is good in an individual life, because reasons are not everything. Morality might provide overriding reasons, stemming from the interests of others, to choose a worse life, without that choice really making one's life better after all.

But it cannot be assumed that if the possibility of conflict between morality and the good life is admitted, the weight of reasons will always fall on the side of morality, in accordance with position (4). On any view that takes the existence of independent moral reasons seriously, they will often outweigh the good of the individual, contrary to position (3), which assigns absolute priority to the good life. But sometimes perhaps they will not: it depends on the nature of moral reasons, and of human rationality. This brings us to the choice between alternatives (4) and (5).

It is clear how alternative (5) could be realized on some theories of

7. Railton provides a persuasive discussion of these issues, though from a more consequentialist position than I can accept.

morality and of human good. For example, if one identifies morality with the expression of certain detached and impartial judgments of approval and disapproval, as Hume did, then it is still an open question (a) what part obedience to those judgments has in the good life as a whole, and (b) how much weight they should carry in rational decisions (assuming one believes that there is such a thing as rational decision). Theories of morality as a system of social practices or rules or conventions also meet condition (5). But I am more interested in whether it can be met by impersonal moralities with universal pretensions, like utilitarianism and some forms of Kantianism.

Such moralities purport to derive their content from a view of one's own actions *sub specie aeternitatis*, though they interpret this in different ways. A universal standpoint that does not distinguish between oneself and anyone else reveals general principles of conduct that apply to oneself because they apply to everyone. There is a natural tendency to identify this higher standpoint with the true self, weighed down perhaps by individualistic baggage. There is a further tendency to accord absolute priority in the governance of life to its judgments. This is found in ideals of moral transcendence. Is it possible to resist these tendencies, and to have such a conception while believing not only that the good life includes more than morality, and may conflict with it, but also that morality can sometimes rationally be rejected for nonmoral reasons, including those having to do with the good life? Everything depends on the place one assigns to the impersonal standpoint in a larger conception of human life.

This question is admittedly, in a broad sense, a question of ethical theory, as is any question about the relation of moral requirements to anything else. And it might be said that an answer which allows the impersonal standpoint not to be dominant is better understood as a rejection of impersonal morality and substitution of a more complex morality. But I think that would depend on whether the overall system worked in such a way that it could plausibly be described as an alternative morality, instead of as a combination of morality and other things. The factors that outweigh impersonal morality, either in determining the good life or in governing practical reason, may simply be too personal and nonuniversal to form an alternative moral system. They may be reasons that cannot be endorsed from outside as valid for anyone.

As a matter of moral conviction, I myself am inclined against this possibility—against position (5). I am inclined strongly to hope, and less strongly to believe, that the correct morality will always have the preponderance of reasons on its side, even though it needn't coincide with the good life. There is a danger here that in wishing to guarantee the coincidence between morality and rationality I may fall into an error analogous to the one I have condemned in the attempts to secure coincidence between good and moral lives, by defining the first in terms of the second or vice versa. I think the important thing is that the convergence between rationality and ethics should not be achieved too easily, and certainly not by a simple definition of the moral as the rational or the rational as the moral. It's not clear that I can avoid this form of trivialization, but let me try.

4. The Moral, the Rational, and the Supererogatory

There is an ambiguity in the idea of the rational which bears on the issue. "Rational" may mean either rationally required or rationally acceptable. If someone says that the moral must be rational he may mean that to be immoral is always irrational, or he may mean something weaker—that to be moral is never irrational. Strictly speaking, it is only the first of these that would make position (4) true.

Where a number of different and opposing reasons bear on a decision, there are three possible outcomes with regard to the rationality of the alternatives. Either the reasons against may be decisive enough so that the act would be irrational; or the reasons for may be decisive enough so that the act is rationally required; or there may be enough reasons both for and against so that although the act is not rationally required, it would not be irrational either—in other words, it would be rational in the weak sense: rationally acceptable.

I am strongly disposed to the view that morality must at least be rational in this weak sense—not *ir*rational—though I should be more satisfied with a theory that showed it to be rational in the strong sense.

One or both of these conclusions can I think be supported, without obvious circularity, by an argument within ethical theory, whose result is a modification of the impersonal demands of morality. (I return here to the problem of impartiality discussed briefly in the previous chapter.) This modification reduces the size of the clash between the moral life and the good life, without removing it entirely—and thereby also reduces, and perhaps even eliminates, the gap between what is morally required and what is rationally required. But even if this latter gap is not entirely closed, the argument should make the weak rationality of the moral life more secure—should insure, in other words, that it is never irrational to prefer the moral life to the good life when they conflict.

The argument depends on the idea that valid moral requirements must take account of the common motivational capacities of the individuals to whom they apply. Moral reasoning must be applied to the question of how to draw rational conclusions from conflicts between impersonal reasons and personal ones.

We might think of impersonal morality as developing in stages. Its source is a wish to be able to endorse or accept one's actions and their justifications from a standpoint outside of one's particular situation, which is not that of any other particular person either. Such a standpoint must be not only detached but universal, and it must engage the will. Initially this may seem to produce the result that the welfare and the projects of others should be accorded as much weight as my own and those of people I care about: that I should be as impartial between myself and others as I would be between people I don't know. Even if adjustments are made to exclude from this condition certain interests which may continue to move me but whose personal nature makes them unsuitable objects of impersonal concern, such as individual ambitions for achievement, or romantic love, the remaining weight of impersonal reasons stemming from the good of everyone will be very substantial by comparison with my own interests, in most cases. I must recognize that objectively I am no more important than anyone else—my happiness and misery matter no more than anyone else's. And the part of me that recognizes this is central—no less a part of me than my personal perspective.

At the next stage, the conflict between these two forces itself becomes an ethical problem, to be solved by seeing what resolution can be endorsed from an external standpoint. I am not referring to the obvious point that moral requirements which, if generally accepted, would seriously worsen people's lives, not through the consequences of the resulting actions but through the inner character of the lives so led themselves, will be to that extent defective. This much is a direct consequence of any impersonal morality, realistically worked out. It does not exclude principles which require extreme self-sacrifice provided the lives of others can be made sufficiently better thereby.

But reflection on human motives may yield a further modification in the demands of impersonal morality—a modification based on tolerance and the recognition of limits. Viewing the situation from outside, I may recognize that the weight of impersonal reasons, however fully they are faced, will still have to contend with the immediate pressure of more personal motives, which remain active in their own right even though they have been taken into account from an impersonal standpoint as the desires of one person among others. It isn't just that my personal interests will cause me to rebel against impersonal demands—though that may happen. It's that this resistance will get some support from the objective standpoint itself. When we regard people objectively and think about how they should live, their motivational complexity is a consideration. If we are trying to answer from the objective standpoint the question how personal and impersonal motives are to be integrated, the result will not just be a rubber stamp for the dominance of impersonal values, despite the fact that it is the objective standpoint that reveals those values. We can take conflict between subjective and objective standpoints back to the objective standpoint on appeal. The result is likely to be that at some threshold, hard to define, we will conclude that it is unreasonable to expect people in general to sacrifice themselves and those to whom they have close personal ties to the general good.

The hard question is whether this understanding—this condition of "reasonableness"—will show itself in a modification of moral requirements, or merely in acceptance of the fact that most of us are miserable sinners, which is probably true in any case. One might take the severe line that moral requirements result from a correct assessment of the weight of good and evil, impersonally revealed, that it is our job to bring our motives into line with this, and that if we cannot do it because of personal weakness, this shows not that the requirements are excessive but that we are bad—though one might refrain from being too censorious about it.

I don't believe this because even though morality has to emerge from an impersonal standpoint, that standpoint must take into account the kind of complex beings for whom it is being devised. The impersonal is only one aspect of their nature, not the whole of it. What it is reasonable to ask of them, and what is impersonally expected of them, should reflect this. We must so to speak strike a bargain between our higher and lower selves in arriving at an acceptable morality. In this way the gap between moral and more comprehensively rational requirements can be narrowed. It means that there is impersonal sanction for striking the balance between personal and impersonal reasons in a certain way.

Wolf says that the standpoint from which such a judgment should be made is not the impersonal standpoint of morality—nor the standpoint of personal perfection—but "a perspective that is unattached to a commitment to any well-ordered system of values" (Wolf (2), p. 439). She believes morality cannot be judge in its own case, and that we should expect that there will sometimes be good reasons for resisting its claims. But I believe an answer can be sought from the impartial standpoint of morality, which will give to everyone a dispensation for a certain degree of partiality—in recognition of the fact that it is only one aspect of the human perspective. Like reason, the moral standpoint should try to recognize and explain its own limits.[8]

Does my argument avoid circularity? I believe it does, at least in the outright sense of defining the moral as the rational or vice versa. It does not define moral requirements so as to meet some antecedent standard of rationality that can be known independently of moral argument. Rather it adjusts the requirements of morality to make adherence to them reasonable, taking the moral standpoint into account—both in the generation of impersonal reasons and in the determination of how the balance between them and personal reasons is to be struck, that is, how much should be demanded of rational individuals. And it does not define the rational simply in terms of the moral, because morally derived reasons supply only one of the factors determining what people can reasonably be required to do. This is a fairly strong interdependence of the moral and the rational, but it does not make them coincide at all costs, though it brings them closer together.

Even without knowing the content of such a principle, we can observe something else about its character. It is an attempt to make the best of an unsatisfactory situation. Insofar as it reduces the requirements of impersonal morality, this will reflect an attitude of tolerance and realism about human nature, rather than the conviction that to act on a more demanding requirement would be irrational or wrong. The idea is that certain demands on the ordinary individual—to overcome his own needs, commitments, and attachments in favor of impersonal claims that he can also recognize—are unreasonable in a way that can be impersonally acknowledged.

But this does not necessarily mean that it would be irrational for someone who can do so to accept such demands, or rather to impose them on himself. So this aspect of impersonal morality may throw light on the puzzling subject of supererogation. Supererogatory virtue is shown by acts of exceptional sacrifice for the benefit of others. Such acts are praiseworthy and not regarded as irrational, but they are not thought to be either morally or rationally required. What is it about them that makes them good, indeed exceptionally good, and provides a reason for doing them, without at the same time providing a reason against not doing them that would make such failure rationally unjustified and bad?

8. For a different and fascinating response to Wolf see Adams, who criticizes the "strong temptation to make morality into a substitute for religion, and in so doing to make morality the object of a devotion that is maximal, at least in aspiration, and virtually religious in character" (p. 400). This, he says, would be a form of idolatry.

After all, someone who does not make these sacrifices is failing to do something that he does have a morally estimable reason to do. Morality is not *indifferent* between his doing it and his not doing it. So why should the difference be of this peculiar, "optional" kind?

The answer, I think, is that supererogatory virtue is adherence to the claims of impersonal morality prior to their modification to accommodate the normal limitations of human nature. This modification takes the form of a relaxation of these requirements through tolerance, as it were, rather than the discovery of new moral reasons that outweigh the original impersonal ones. If they had been outweighed, then there would be reasons against the type of sacrifice that displays supererogatory virtue: it would be *wrong*. As things are, it is merely not required. And those who undertake it nonetheless are praiseworthy for submitting themselves to the true strength of reasons that they could not reasonably be required to follow strictly, given the mixed character of human motives. The appearance of supererogation in a morality is a recognition from an impersonal standpoint of the difficulties with which that standpoint has to contend in becoming motivationally effective in the real life of beings of whom it is only one aspect.[9]

The result for the relation between morality and the good life is that some of the starker conflicts will be softened by these reductions of moral demands due to tolerance. But the conflict will certainly not disappear, and that brings us back to the original problem of whether, in such cases, morality will always have the net balance of reasons on its side, as against the good life. I believe that the self-limiting modifications of impersonal morality that let in supererogation make this more likely, though they do not guarantee it. Insofar as reasons are universal, the repeated application of impersonal standards seems to yield the most integrated set of requirements that can be hoped for, taking into account reasons derived from all perspectives.

5. Politics and Conversion

I have claimed that the requirements of morality can conflict with the good life, and that this is not a legitimate ground for rejecting a morality. On the other hand, my own view is that the correctness of a morality is

9. Hare offers an account of supererogation in *Moral Thinking* that is in some ways similar to this—except that he believes that it is compatible with utilitarianism, because given human nature, the less demanding principles may be the ones whose inculcation has the greatest utility.

put in doubt if it would sometimes be irrational to accede to its demands (though the idea of such a morality is not incoherent). There is pressure from the moral standpoint itself to adjust those demands so that they converge with the condition of full human rationality, though not the condition of a good life.

Yet there remains something deeply unsatisfying about conflict between the good life and the moral life and the compromises between them, which produces constant pressure to reinterpret one or both of them so that the two are guaranteed to coincide. In saying that such conflicts are possible I do not mean to treat them lightly. Williams has put his finger on a fundamental and neglected problem of ethics. If it is the function of an ethical theory to identify both the moral life and the good life, and to reveal the reasons we have to lead each of them, then a theory that allows them to diverge will be claiming something that is hard to accept, given the importance of each of these ideals.

Since we don't want life to be like that, it is natural to hope that such theories are false, but this cannot refute them. Only a more radical defect, or a better alternative, can do that. It may seem impossible that living as we have decisive reason to live should constitute a bad life, or a life that is less than optimal given our circumstances. It may seem impossible that an immoral life should be better than a moral one, or that a moral life should be a bad one. But I believe that what lies behind these impossibility claims is not ethics or logic but the conviction that things should not be that way—that it would be bad if they were. So it would. But it is not a necessary truth that the best life is always realized by doing everything right. Moral rationality is not a dominant enough part of individual human good for that. If it has a dominant role in determining what we should do, that is because of goods that lie outside us.

Like Williams, I find utilitarianism too demanding and hope it is false. But these problems will not disappear if utilitarianism is rejected. The basic moral insight that objectively no one matters more than anyone else, and that this acknowledgment should be of fundamental importance to each of us even though the objective standpoint is not our only standpoint, creates a conflict in the self too powerful to admit an easy resolution. I doubt that an appealing reconciliation of morality, rationality, and the good life can be achieved within the boundaries of ethical theory, narrowly understood. The dilemmas revealed here can arise for most ethical theories, and in particular for theories with a significant impersonal element. Whether the dilemmas are not only possible but actual will depend on the way the world is, and the way we are.

This leads to a different way of dealing with them, not theoretically, but in life. The clash between morality and the good life is an unsatisfactory condition that presents us with a task, and while theory may be required for its solution, the solution itself is not just a new theory but a change in the conditions of life. I shall mention two possible approaches.

The first is personal conversion. Someone who finds himself convinced of the truth of a morality that makes impossible demands on him—such as utilitarianism if he is an affluent individual in a world of extreme inequality—may be able by a leap of self-transcendence to change his life so radically from the inside that service to this morality—to the welfare of mankind or of all sentient beings—becomes his overwhelming concern and his dominant good. This might be either a personal choice or something that he thinks everyone should do: a demand of human transformation.

From the point of view of someone facing the prospect of such a leap it naturally seems like a terrible sacrifice or even a form of self-immolation. But that is by the standards of a good life as defined by his preconverted condition. If the leap is successful, what constitutes a good life for him will be different when he lands on the other side, and harmony will be restored. The problem is to find the strength to make the leap, given the very different personal values he now has. If his sense of alienation over the clash between his morality and his life is acute enough, this may help provide the needed impetus; but obviously such conversions, like others, may be very painful.

The second alternative is political. I have said something in the last chapter about the role of political institutions in externalizing the clash of standpoints. An important, perhaps the most important task of political thought and action is to arrange the world so that everyone can live a good life without doing wrong, injuring others, benefiting unfairly from their misfortune, and so forth. Moral harmony and not only civil peace is the right aim of politics, and it would be desirable to achieve it without putting everyone through the type of deep personal conversion needed to make a clash between morality and the good life impossible.

Some degree of alteration of individual personality is a legitimate part of the ambition of reconciliation through politics, but it need not be so radical as what is hoped for in pure personal conversion, where all the work is done within a single soul and a great deal may have to be abandoned. Instead we take the clash between personal values and impersonal morality to be a clash between ideals neither of which we should want to abandon, so that it presents us with the constructive task of creating a world in which the effective clash will be contingently reduced, if not eliminated, and the institutions under which we live will make it possible for us to lead rich personal lives without denying the impersonal claims that derive from the needs of our billions of fellow inmates. This is not yet an ethical or a political theory, but it describes the form that I think a theory must take which harmonizes morality and the good life without abandoning too much of either.

Given a choice between these two methods of dealing with the clash of perspectives I prefer the second, which brings a normative division of labor into human life and therefore requires less heroic unification. But in the present state of the world we may not have a choice, for the task of creating a political order with the desired moral harmony seems so large and so urgent that it may demand radical personal conversion by many individuals in order to begin to carry it out.

Still, it makes sense to ask what should serve as our moral ideal, and to this question I would give a pluralistic, anticommunitarian reply.

The world that I dream would emerge from a process of political reconstruction would not contain "new men" unrecognizably different from ourselves in being dominated by impersonal values, so that their individual happiness consists in serving humanity. That might be better than the world we have now, but quite apart from the problem of whether such a thing is possible, it would be a poorer world than one in which the great bulk of impersonal claims were met by institutions that left individuals—including those that supported and operated those institutions—free to devote considerable attention and energy to their own lives and to values that could not be impersonally acknowledged.

XI

BIRTH, DEATH, AND
THE MEANING OF LIFE

1. Life

One summer more than ten years ago, when I taught at Princeton, a large spider appeared in the urinal of the men's room in 1879 Hall, a building that houses the Philosophy Department. When the urinal wasn't in use, he would perch on the metal drain at its base, and when it was, he would try to scramble out of the way, sometimes managing to climb an inch or two up the porcelain wall at a point that wasn't too wet. But sometimes he was caught, tumbled and drenched by the flushing torrent. He didn't seem to like it, and always got out of the way if he could. But it was a floor-length urinal with a sunken base and a smooth overhanging lip: he was below floor level and couldn't get out.

Somehow he survived, presumably feeding on tiny insects attracted to the site, and was still there when the fall term began. The urinal must have been used more than a hundred times a day, and always it was the same desperate scramble to get out of the way. His life seemed miserable and exhausting.

Gradually our encounters began to oppress me. Of course it might be his natural habitat, but because he was trapped by the smooth porcelain overhang, there was no way for him to get out even if he wanted to, and no way to tell whether he wanted to. None of the other regulars did anything to alter the situation, but as the months wore on and fall turned to winter I arrived with much uncertainty and hesitation at the decision

208

to liberate him. I reflected that if he didn't like it on the outside, or didn't find enough to eat, he could easily go back. So one day toward the end of the term I took a paper towel from the wall dispenser and extended it to him. His legs grasped the end of the towel and I lifted him out and deposited him on the tile floor.

He just sat there, not moving a muscle. I nudged him slightly with the towel, but nothing happened. I pushed him an inch or two along the tiles, right next to the urinal, but he still didn't respond. He seemed to be paralyzed. I felt uneasy but thought that if he didn't want to stay on the tiles when he came to, a few steps would put him back. Meanwhile he was close to the wall and not in danger of being trodden on. I left, but when I came back two hours later he hadn't moved.

The next day I found him in the same place, his legs shriveled in that way characteristic of dead spiders. His corpse stayed there for a week, until they finally swept the floor.

It illustrates the hazards of combining perspectives that are radically distinct. Those hazards take many forms; in this final chapter I shall describe some that arise in connection with our attitude toward our own lives.

The pursuit of objectivity with respect to value runs the risk of leaving value behind altogether. We may reach a standpoint so removed from the perspective of human life that all we can do is to observe: nothing seems to have value of the kind it appears to have from inside, and all we can see is human desires, human striving—human *valuing*, as an activity or condition. In chapter 8 I alluded to the fact that if we continue along the path that leads from personal inclination to objective values and ethics, we may fall into nihilism. The problem is to know where and how to stop, and it shows itself in some of the more personally disturbing questions of philosophy.

The uneasy relation between inner and outer perspectives, neither of which we can escape, makes it hard to maintain a coherent attitude toward the fact that we exist at all, toward our deaths, and toward the meaning or point of our lives, because a detached view of our own existence, once achieved, is not easily made part of the standpoint from which life is lived. From far enough outside my birth seems accidental, my life pointless, and my death insignificant, but from inside my never having been born seems nearly unimaginable, my life monstrously important, and my death catastrophic. Though the two viewpoints clearly belong to one person—these problems wouldn't arise if they didn't—they function independently enough so that each can come as something of a surprise to the other, like an identity that has been temporarily forgotten.

The subjective view is at the core of everyday life, and the objective develops initially as a form of extended understanding; much of what it reveals can be used instrumentally in the pursuit of subjective aims. But taken far enough, it will undermine those aims: to see myself objectively as a small, contingent, and exceedingly temporary organic bubble in the universal soup produces an attitude approaching indifference. My attitude toward TN's life from that perspective is the same as toward any other creature's life. My attitude toward myself is quite different, and the two collide. The same person who is subjectively committed to a personal life in all its rich detail finds himself in another aspect simultaneously detached; this detachment undermines his commitment without destroying it—leaving him divided. And the objective self, noticing that it is personally identical with the object of its detachment, comes to feel trapped in this particular life—detached but unable to disengage, and dragged along by a subjective seriousness it can't even attempt to get rid of.

Some of the attitudes that lead to these conflicts may be mistaken; others may be modifiable by a process of reconciliation in which detachment is reduced and engagement is modified, so that the clash is lessened; but some of the conflicts are impossible to eliminate. No doubt many who have experienced the discomfort of objective detachment from themselves simply forget about it and live inside the world as if there were no external view. Some may dismiss these existential worries as bogus or artificial. I find both these responses unacceptable, because the objective standpoint, even at its limit, is too essential a part of us to be suppressed without dishonesty and because the effort to find a form of individual life that acknowledges and includes it can be fruitful, even if complete integration inevitably eludes us.

The wish to live so far as possible in full recognition that one's position in the universe is not central has an element of the religious impulse about it, or at least an acknowledgment of the question to which religion purports to supply an answer. A religious solution gives us a borrowed centrality through the concern of a supreme being. Perhaps the religious question without a religious answer amounts to antihumanism, since we cannot compensate for the lack of cosmic meaning with a meaning derived from our own perspective. We have to accomplish what reconciliation we can inside our own heads, and the possibilities are limited. The problem is not merely intellectual. The external standpoint and the contemplation of death lead to loss of equilibrium in life. Most of us have felt suddenly giddy at the thought of the extreme unlikelihood of our own birth or the thought of the world sailing on after we are dead. Some of us feel a constant undertow of absurdity in the projects and ambitions that give our lives their forward drive. These jarring displacements of the external view are inseparable from the full development of consciousness.

Let me start with the problem of birth—the problem of what attitude to take toward the fact that we exist at all. This is less familiar than the problems of death and the meaning of life, but its form is similar. From an objective standpoint two things, neither of them easy to assimilate, strike me about my own birth: its extreme contingency and its unimportance. (The same can be said of anyone's birth; and if it is someone I care about, many of the same difficulties will arise as a result.) Let me discuss these two points in turn, contingency first.

Subjectively, we begin by taking our existence for granted: it is a given of the most basic kind. When in childhood each of us first learns of the contingency of his existence, even the simple fact that it depends on his parents having met, the result is a lessening of his unreflectively secure footing in the world. We are here by luck, not by right or by necessity.

Rudimentary biology reveals how extreme the situation is. My existence depends on the birth of a particular organism that could have developed only from a particular sperm and egg, which in turn could have been produced only by the particular organisms that produced them, and so forth. In view of the typical sperm count, there was very little chance of my being born given the situation that obtained an hour before I was conceived, let alone a million years before, unless everything that happens in the world is determined with absolute rigidity—which appears not to be the case. The natural delusion of my own inevitability collides with the objective fact that *who* exists and has existed is radically contingent, my own existence in particular being one of the most inessential things in the world. Almost every possible person has not been born and never will be, and it is sheer accident that I am one of the few who actually made it.

The subjective effects of this information are complex: it is not just a sobering thought. There is amazement and relief, plus the giddiness or retrospective alarm that comes from learning about a very close call only after the risk is past. There can also be a taste of survivor's syndrome, guilt toward all those others who will never be born. Yet at the same time, the sense of subjective inevitability doesn't completely disappear; these indisputable objective facts about myself provoke emotional incredulity. I can imagine having died at the age of five, but it is not easy to grasp in full consciousness the fact that the history of the universe might have run its course without my ever putting in an appearance *at all*. When I do get my mind properly around this idea, it produces a sinking feeling which reveals that a powerful but unnoticed support has been removed from my world.

My own existence looms large at the center of my prereflective world picture, since this life is the source and avenue for my understanding of everything else. It is unnerving to be led through it to the discovery that it is totally inessential—one of the least "basic" things in the world. A world without me at any point in its history seems like a world with a crucial piece missing, a world that has suddenly lost its moorings. If you concentrate hard on the thought that you might never have been born— the distinct possibility of your eternal and complete absence from this world—I believe you too will find that this perfectly clear and straight- forward truth produces a positively uncanny sensation.

There is a solipsistic tendency at work here, which attaches curiously enough to the objective rather than to the subjective viewpoint—like the solipsism of Wittgenstein's *Tractatus*. The objective standpoint, which considers everything *sub specie aeternitatis*, easily slips into regarding itself as the condition of the world or the frame of all existence, rather than as an aspect of a particular individual within the world.

If I forget who I am, I can imagine TN's never having existed without a qualm; but there is a risk of doing this only halfway, by imagining *my world* without TN in it—the objective self being held in reserve, so to speak. To fully imagine the world without me, I have to get rid of the objective self as well, and this begins to feel like getting rid of the world itself rather than of something in it. It is as if there were a natural illusion that the world is not completely detachable from my conception of it.

The appeal of this illusion is mysterious. I know perfectly well that the world is not essentially my world: it is not a necessary truth that it can be or could ever have been referred to or thought about by me. Just as the room I am now in, which I can refer to as this room, might never have borne the relation to me that makes that reference possible— because I might never have been in it—so it is with this world and every- thing about it. The fact that I must exist in it to think that it might not have contained me does not make the possibility any less real. Even if some of the respects in which the world can be objectively described are essential to it, I as a particular possessor of the objective view am not, and I can think of the world in abstraction from my connection with it.

But even if we firmly reject the solipsistic assumption as a mistake, a pale version of it remains. Although the world is not essentially my world, the objective recognition of my contingency has to coexist in my head with a total world picture whose subject *is* inescapably me. The person whose contingency I recognize is the epicenter not just of the world as it looks from here, but of my entire world view. To suppose that he should never have existed is to suppose that my world should never have existed.

This makes it seem as if the existence of my world depends on the existence of something in it. But of course that is not the case. The real me is not merely part of *my* world. The person who I am is a contingent bit of a world that is not just mine. So my world depends for its existence on me, I depend for my existence on TN, and TN depends on *the world* and is inessential to it. This is another of the discomforts of being someone in particular: my world depends for its existence on his birth, even though he also appears in it as a character. It is eerie to see oneself and one's entire world in this way as a natural product.

The second thing that emerges from an objective view of my birth is its unimportance. While importance and unimportance will be more thoroughly discussed in the following section, let me say a bit about it here.

Setting aside broader questions about the value of human existence as such, when we look at the world from a general vantage point it seems not to matter who exists. My own existence or that of any other particular person is entirely gratuitous. There may be some reason for my continued existence now that I am here, but there is absolutely no reason why I should have come into existence in the first place: if I hadn't, the world would have been none the worse; I certainly wouldn't have been *missed*! There may be a few people like Mozart and Einstein whose nonexistence would have been a real loss, but for the most part there is no reason why anyone in particular should exist. We might go further and say there is no reason why human beings and their form of life should ever have existed: if they hadn't, it would not have been necessary to invent them—in any case there might have been other types of beings instead. But the problem I am talking about here doesn't depend on that wider claim. Let us suppose that the world would be a less interesting and valuable place if there were no people in it. The narrower claim is that objectively it doesn't matter which *particular* persons have come into existence.

This collides with the view we naturally take from within the world. Subjectively we feel that we and those we love belong here—that nothing could undermine our right of admission to the universe. Whatever others may think, the last thing we expect is that *we* may come to see the world in a way that drains our birth of value. But as objectivity increases, detachment sets in and the existence from which all of our concerns and motives and justifications begin becomes a matter of indifference. Anyone else would have done as well as you and I. And because nearly everything that matters to each of us depends on actually existing lives, what matters is firmly rooted in something whose nonexistence wouldn't have mattered in the least.

The obvious reply is that something can matter even if it didn't matter in advance whether it would exist and wouldn't have mattered if it hadn't: however gratuitous its original appearance, once it exists it brings its own value with it and its survival and well-being become important.

There is something in this. When we look at the actual world, even the particular trees in it appear to have a value that is not canceled by their intersubstitutability or their gratuitousness. But it isn't enough to reconcile the two standpoints. From an external view of the universe, which abstracts from our own position in it, it still wouldn't have mattered if we had never existed—and that is not something we can simply accept from the standpoint of real life. It forces on us a kind of double vision and loss of confidence which is developed more fully in doubts about the meaning of life. It is easy to have these thoughts about someone else, and they are not disturbing when we abstract from who in particular we are. But when we bring them back home they cannot be assimilated. Neither as objective self nor as TN can I comfortably think of myself as utterly inessential.

There is a recognizable human desire to find our existence significant no matter how cosmic a view we take, and a consequent discomfort with the partial disengagement that objectivity induces. But perhaps these are mistakes, both intellectual and emotional. Perhaps we are just too demanding, and confer too much authority on the objective standpoint by permitting its lack of independent concern for our existence to support a judgment of insignificance. Perhaps the detachment of the objective self is empty, because justifications come to an end within life and if it makes no sense to seek them outside it we cannot be disappointed by the failure to find them there. Perhaps, as Williams claims, the view *sub specie aeternitatis* is a very poor view of human life, and we should start and end in the middle of things. Or perhaps there is something to be said on both sides.

2. Meaning

In seeing ourselves from outside we find it difficult to take our lives seriously. This loss of conviction, and the attempt to regain it, is the problem of the meaning of life.

I should say at the outset that some people are more susceptible to this problem than others, and even those who are susceptible to it vary over time in the degree to which it grips them. Clearly there are temperamental and circumstantial factors at work. Still, it is a genuine problem which we cannot ignore. The capacity for transcendence brings with it a liability to alienation, and the wish to escape this condition and to find a larger meaning can lead to even greater absurdity. Yet we can't abandon the external standpoint because it is our own. The aim of reaching some kind of harmony with the universe is part of the aim of living in harmony with ourselves.

To the subjective view, the conditions that determine whether life makes sense are simply given, as part of the package. They are determined by the possibilities of good and evil, happiness and unhappiness, achievement and failure, love and isolation that come with being human, and more specifically with being the particular person you are in the particular social and historical setting in which you find yourself. From inside no justification can coherently be sought for trying to live a good and meaningful life by those standards; and if it were needed, it couldn't be found.

Serious problems about the meaning of a life can arise entirely within it, and these should be distinguished from the completely general philosophical problem of the meaning of life, which arises from the threat of objective detachment. A life may be absurd, and felt to be absurd, because it is permeated by trivia or dominated by a neurotic obsession or by the constant need to react to external threats, pressures, or controls. A life in which human possibilities for autonomy and development are largely unrealized and untested will seem deficient in meaning; someone faced with such a life may lack the significant will to live as a purely internal matter, not because of any objective detachment. But all these forms of meaninglessness are compatible with the possibility of meaning, had things gone differently.

The philosophical problem is not the same, for it threatens human life even at its subjective best with objective meaninglessness, and with absurdity if it cannot stop taking itself seriously. This problem is the emotional counterpart of that sense of arbitrariness which the objective self feels at being someone in particular.

Each of us finds himself with a life to lead. While we have a certain amount of control over it, the basic conditions of success and failure, our basic motives and needs, and the social circumstances that define our possibilities are simply given. Shortly after birth we have to start running just to keep from falling down, and there is only limited choice as to what will matter to us. We worry about a bad haircut or a bad review, we try to improve our income, our character, and our sensitivity to other people's feelings, we raise children, watch Johnny Carson, argue about Alfred Hitchcock or Chairman Mao, worry about getting promoted, getting pregnant, or becoming impotent—in short we lead highly specific lives within the parameters of our place, time, species, and culture. What could be more natural?

Yet there is a point of view from which none of it seems to matter.

When you look at your struggles as if from a great height, in abstraction from the engagement you have with this life because it is yours—perhaps even in abstraction from your identification with the human race—you may feel a certain sympathy for the poor beggar, a pale pleasure in his triumphs and a mild concern for his disappointments. And of course given that this person exists, there is little he can do but keep going till he dies, and try to accomplish something by the standards internal to his form of life. But it wouldn't matter all that much if he failed, and it would matter perhaps even less if he didn't exist at all. The clash of standpoints is not absolute, but the disparity is very great.

This kind of detachment is certainly possible for us, but the question is whether *it* matters. What am I doing out there, pretending to be a visitor from outer space—looking at my life from a great height in abstraction from the fact that it is mine, or that I am human and a member of this culture? How can the unimportance of my life from that point of view have any importance for *me*? Perhaps the problem is a purely philosophical artefact, and not real.

I'll return to this objection later, but first let me pose another: Even if the problem can't be dismissed as unreal, it may have a simple solution. Is it so certain that the attitudes really conflict as they appear to? Since the two judgments arise from different perspectives, why isn't their content appropriately relativized to those perspectives, rendering the conflict illusory? If that were true, it would be no more problematic that the course of my life should matter from inside but not from outside than that a large mouse should be a small animal, or that something should look round from one direction and oval from another.

I do not believe this solution is available, logical as it may seem. The trouble is that the two attitudes have to coexist in a single person who is actually leading the life toward which he is simultaneously engaged and detached. This person does not occupy a third standpoint from which he can make two relativized judgments about his life. If all he had were two relativized judgments, they would leave him with no attitude toward his life at all—only information about the appropriate attitude from two points of view, neither of which was his. But in fact he occupies both of the conflicting points of view and his attitudes derive from them both.

The real problem is with the external point of view, which cannot remain a mere spectator once the self has expanded to accommodate it. It has to join in with the rest and lead this life from which it is disengaged. As a result the person becomes in significant part detached from what he is doing. The objective self is dragged along by the unavoidable engagement of the whole person in the living of a life whose form it recognizes as arbitrary. It generates a demand for justification which it at the same time guarantees to be unsatisfiable, because the only available justification depends on the view from inside.

Some philosophers have held that the soul is trapped in the body. To Plato this meant not just that the soul is housed in the body, but that the needs of the body invade and compromise the soul, threatening it with domination by its basest portion, the appetites. I am talking about something different but analogous, the inevitable engagement of the objective self in a particular contingent life, whose consequence is not depravity but absurdity. It isn't so much the animal aspects of life which generate the absurd, for no judgment of importance need attach to an instinctive effort to survive. The problem comes especially with those more developed human projects that pretend to significance and without which life would not be human. It is heightened by the equally human involvement we all have with our *own* lives and ambitions.

This invites a quick solution to the problem. Perhaps we can avoid the absurd if we devote ourselves to providing only for the basic needs of everyone. There is a great deal of misery in the world, and many of us could easily spend our lives trying to eradicate it—wiping out starvation, disease, and torture.

Such aims do indeed seem to give life a meaning that is hard to question. But while they are certainly worthy and perhaps imperative goals, they cannot eliminate the problem. Granted, one advantage of living in a world as bad as this one is that it offers the opportunity for many activities whose importance can't be questioned. But how could the main point of human life be the elimination of evil? Misery, deprivation, and injustice prevent people from pursuing the positive goods which life is assumed to make possible. If all such goods were pointless and the only thing that really mattered was the elimination of misery, that really *would* be absurd. The same could be said of the idea that helping others is the only thing that really gives meaning to life. If no one's life has any meaning in itself, how can it acquire meaning through devotion to the meaningless lives of others?

No, even if the problem of meaning can be postponed until all misery is wiped out, it will not go away permanently. In any case, most of us face it in our own lives. Some of us have bigger egos than others, and a dominant obsession with personal standing or success is recognized as absurd even without the benefit of philosophy. But everyone who is not either mystically transformed or hopelessly lacking in self-esteem regards his life and his projects as important, and not just to him.

From outside we do indeed tend to see most of our pursuits as important only relatively. Watching the human drama is a bit like watching a Little League baseball game: the excitement of the participants is perfectly understandable but one can't really enter into it. At the same time, since one *is* one of the participants, one is caught up in the game directly, in a way that cannot include an admission of relativity. When you are considering a career, marriage, children, or even whether to go on a diet, review a book, or buy a car, the external standpoint is excluded and you face the matter directly, from the internal standpoint of ordinary life. The detached external view just has to come along, and accommodate itself to the unqualified concerns that it can't internalize. At the same time there is a temptation to resist this detachment by inflating the sense of objective importance inside one's life, either by overvaluing one's own significance or by attributing a wider significance to one's pursuits.

It is the same phenomenon we have discussed in other connections—in epistemology, for example. The internal view resists the reduction to a subjective interpretation of its contents which the external view tries to force on it. But this puts the objective standpoint in conflict with itself. Finding my life objectively insignificant, I am nevertheless unable to extricate myself from an unqualified commitment to it—to my aspirations and ambitions, my wishes for fulfillment, recognition, understanding, and so forth. The sense of the absurd is the result of this juxtaposition.

This is not an artificial problem created by a philosophical misstep, any more than epistemological skepticism is. Just as we can't evade skepticism by denying the pretensions of our beliefs about the world and interpreting them as entirely relative to a subjective or personal point of view, so we can't evade the impact of objective detachment by denying the objective pretensions of our dominant aims in life. This would simply falsify the situation. The problem of the meaning of life is in fact a form of skepticism at the level of motivation. We can no more abandon our unqualified commitments at will than we can abandon our beliefs about the world in response to skeptical arguments, however persuasive we may find them, as Hume famously observed. Nor, I believe, can we avoid either problem by refusing to take that step outside ourselves which calls the ordinary view into question.

Several routes might be attempted out of this impasse. I don't believe there is a way out, though there are adjustments we can make to live with the conflict. But it is worth considering what would be required to eliminate it entirely. I'll discuss two proposals which try to meet the problem head-on and one which tries to dissolve it.

The first solution to consider is the most Draconian: to deny the claims of the subjective view, withdraw from the specifics of individual human life as much as possible, minimize the area of one's local contact with the world and concentrate on the universal. Contemplation, meditation, withdrawal from the demands of the body and of society, abandonment of exclusive personal ties and worldly ambition—all this gives the objective standpoint less to be disengaged from, less to regard as vain. I gather this response is recommended by certain traditions, though I don't know enough to be sure that it isn't a caricature: the loss of self in the individual sense is thought to be required by the revelations of an impersonal view, which takes precedence over the view from here. And apparently it is possible for some individuals to achieve this withering away of the ego, so that personal life continues only as a vehicle for the transcendent self, not as an end in itself.[1]

I cannot speak from experience, but this seems to me a high price to pay for spiritual harmony. The amputation of so much of oneself to secure the unequivocal affirmation of the rest seems a waste of consciousness. I would rather lead an absurd life engaged in the particular than a seamless transcendental life immersed in the universal. Perhaps those who have tried both would laugh inscrutably at this preference. It reflects the belief that the absurdity of human life is not such a bad thing. There are limits to what we should be prepared to do to escape it—apart from the point that some of these cures may be more absurd than the disease.

The second solution is the opposite of the first—a denial of the objective unimportance of our lives, which will justify full engagement from the objective standpoint. While this response to detachment has some merit, the truth in it is not enough to resolve the conflict.

As I argued in chapter 8, an impersonal perspective doesn't necessarily lead to nihilism. It may fail to discover *independent* reasons to care about what subjectively concerns us, but much that is of value and significance in the world can be understood directly only from within the perspective of a particular form of life, and this can be recognized from an external standpoint. The fact that the point of something can't be understood from the objective standpoint alone doesn't mean it must be regarded objectively as pointless, any more than the fact that the value of music is not directly comprehensible to someone deaf from birth means he has to judge it worthless. His knowledge of its value must depend on others. And the objective standpoint can recognize the authority of particular points of view with regard to worth as it can with regard to essentially perspectival facts. This includes recognizing the worth of what is of value only to a particular creature—who may be one-

1. Or perhaps alternatively, each particular element, whatever its character, is seen as a manifestation of the universal.

self. We might say that absolute value is revealed to the objective view through the evidence available to particular perspectives, including one's own. So even if there is no externally appreciable reason for the existence of any particular form of life, including my own, at least some of the values, positive and negative, that are defined by reference to it can be externally acknowledged. Playing in a Little League baseball game, making pancakes, or applying a coat of nail polish are perfectly good things to do. Their value is not necessarily canceled by the fact that they lack external justification.

This is not enough, however, to harmonize the two standpoints, because it doesn't warrant a particular objective interest in the individual life that happens to be mine, or even in the general form of human life of which it is an instance. These things have been handed to me and they demand my full attention. But to the external view, many different actual and possible subjective values must be acknowledged. Those arising within my life may evoke sympathy, but that is not the same as true objective engagement. My life is one of countlessly many, in a civilization that is also not unique, and my natural devotion to it is quite out of proportion to the importance I can reasonably accord it from outside.

From there I can accord it no more importance than it merits in a global view which includes all possible forms of life and their value on an equal footing. It is true that my life is the one among all these that I am in the best position to devote attention to, and it could be argued that the traditional principle of division of labor warrants my concentrating on it in the usual way as the best method of contributing to the cosmic pool. But while there is something in this, it should not be exaggerated. The argument would not really justify us in engaging fully with our personal aims from an objective standpoint, and such engagement as it warranted would be on sufferance from an objective concern for the whole of which we were a part. This is at best a method of partial reconciliation between inner and outer views: we can try to avoid assigning ourselves a personal importance grotesquely out of line with our objective value, but we can't realistically hope to close the gap completely. So while the acknowledgment of objective worth inside human life may make the conflict of standpoints less extreme, it doesn't eliminate it.

The third candidate solution I want to discuss can be thought of as an argument that the problem is unreal. The objection is that to identify with the objective self and find its detachment disturbing is to forget who you are. There is something deranged in looking at one's existence from so far outside that one can ask why it matters. If we were actually detached spirits about to be thrown into the world by embodiment in a particular creature whose form of life had so far been only externally observed by us, it would be different: we might well feel a threat of impending captivity. But it isn't like that. We are first of all and essentially individual human beings. Our objectivity is simply a development of our humanity and doesn't allow us to break free of it. It must serve our humanity and to the extent that it does not we can forget about it.

The point here is to force withdrawal of the external demand which gives rise to the problem. This is a natural and in some ways appealing response, but as a conclusive argument it will not work. Objectivity is not content to remain a servant of the individual perspective and its values. It has a life of its own and an aspiration for transcendence that will not be quieted in response to the call to reassume our true identity. This shows itself not only in the permanent disaffection from individual life that is the sense of the absurd, but in the demands for objective justification which we sometimes *can* meet, as in the development of ethics. The external standpoint plays an important positive role in human motivation as well as a negative one, and the two cannot be separated. Both depend on the independence of the external view and the pressure it puts us under to bring it into our lives. The sense of the absurd is just a perception of the limits of this effort, reached when we ascend higher on the transcendental ladder than our merely human individuality can follow, even with the help of considerable readjustment. The objective self is a vital part of us, and to ignore its quasi-independent operation is to be cut off from oneself as much as if one were to abandon one's subjective individuality. There is no escape from alienation or conflict of one kind or another.

In sum, I believe there is no credible way of eliminating the inner conflict. Nonetheless, we have a motive for reducing it, and it is possible to promote a degree of harmony between the two standpoints without taking drastic measures. The attitude toward one's own life is inevitably dominated by the fact that it, unlike all those others, is one's own. But the domination should not be so complete that the objective standpoint treats the values defined by that life as ultimate. While objective reason does naturally fall into the service of the subjective passions, it can retain its recognition, however sympathetic, that they are the passions of a particular individual and whatever importance they may have derives from that. So objectivity itself is split into spectator and participant. It devotes itself to the interests and the ambitions, including the competitive ambitions, of one person while at the same time recognizing that he is no more important than anyone else and that the human form of life is not the embodiment of all value.

One of the devices by which these two attitudes are combined is morality, which seeks a way to live as an individual that affirms the equal worth of other individuals and is therefore externally acceptable. Morality is a form of objective reengagement. It permits the objective assertion of subjective values to the extent that this is compatible with the corresponding claims of others. It can take various forms, some of which I have discussed. All of them involve, to one degree or another, occupying a position far enough outside your own life to reduce the importance of the difference between yourself and other people, yet not so far outside that all human values vanish in a nihilistic blackout.

But there is more to integration than that. The most general effect of the objective stance ought to be a form of humility: the recognition that you are no more important than you are, and that the fact that something is of importance to you, or that it would be good or bad if you did or suffered something, is a fact of purely local significance. Such humility may seem incompatible with full immersion in one's life and in the pursuit of those enjoyments and goods that it makes possible. It may sound like a form of deadening self-consciousness, or self-denigration, or asceticism; but I don't think it has to be.

It does not create self-consciousness but simply gives it content. Our capacity for taking an external view of ourselves poses the problem; we cannot get rid of it, and we must find some attitude or other that reckons with it. Humility falls between nihilistic detachment and blind self-importance. It doesn't require reflection on the cosmic arbitrariness of the sense of taste every time you eat a hamburger. But we can try to avoid the familiar excesses of envy, vanity, conceit, competitiveness, and pride—including pride in our culture, in our nation, and in the achievements of humanity as a species. The human race has a strong disposition to adore itself, in spite of its record. But it is possible to live a complete life of the kind one has been given without overvaluing it hopelessly. We can even resist the tendency to overvalue the historical present, both positively and negatively; what is going on in the world right now is not for that reason especially important. The present is where we are, and we cannot see it only in timeless perspective. But we can forget about it now and then, even if it won't forget about us.

Finally, there is an attitude which cuts through the opposition between transcendent universality and parochial self-absorption, and that is the attitude of nonegocentric respect for the particular.[2] It is conspicuous as an element in aesthetic response, but it can be directed to all kinds of things, including aspects of one's own life. One can simply look hard at a ketchup bottle, and the question of significance from different stand-

2. I am grateful to Jacob Adler for making me see this.

points will disappear. Particular things can have a noncompetitive completeness which is transparent to all aspects of the self. This also helps explain why the experience of great beauty tends to unify the self: the object engages us immediately and totally in a way that makes distinctions among points of view irrelevant.

It is hard to know whether one could sustain such an attitude consistently toward the elements of everyday life. It would require an immediacy of feeling and attention to what is present that doesn't blend well with the complex, forward-looking pursuits of a civilized creature. Perhaps it would require a radical change in what one did, and that would raise the question whether the simplification was worth it.

Apart from this, the possibilities for most of us are limited. Some people are genuinely unworldly, but if it doesn't come naturally, the attempt to achieve this condition is likely to be an exercise in dishonesty and self-distortion. Most of us care a great deal about forms of individual success that we can see from an impersonal standpoint to be much less significant than we cannot help taking them to be from inside our lives. Our constitutional self-absorption together with our capacity to recognize its excessiveness make us irreducibly absurd even if we achieve a measure of subjective-objective integration by bringing the two standpoints closer together. The gap is too wide to be closed entirely, for anyone who is fully human.

So the absurd is part of human life. I do not think this can be basically regretted, because it is a consequence of our existence as particular creatures with a capacity for objectivity. Some philosophers, such as Plato, have been unhappy that the higher self was trapped in a particular human life, and others, such as Nietzsche, have denigrated the role of the objective standpoint; but I believe the significant diminution of either of them in force or importance would lessen us and is not a reasonable aim. Repression can operate effectively and damagingly not just against the instincts but against the objective intelligence. These civil wars of the self result in an impoverished life. It is better to be simultaneously engaged and detached, and therefore absurd, for this is the opposite of self-denial and the result of full awareness.

3. Death

The desire to go on living, which is one of our strongest, is essentially first-personal: it is not the desire that a particular, publicly identifiable human being survive, though its fulfillment of course requires the survival of someone like that, and therefore it collides with objective indifference about the survival of anyone in particular. Your relation to your own death is unique, and here if anywhere the subjective standpoint holds a dominant position. By the same token, the internal standpoint will be vicariously dominant in your attitude toward the deaths of those to whom you are so close that you see the world through their eyes.

Some people believe in an afterlife. I do not; what I say will be based on the assumption that death is nothing, and final. I believe there is little to be said for it: it is a great curse, and if we truly face it nothing can make it palatable except the knowledge that by dying we can prevent an even greater evil. Otherwise, given the simple choice between living for another week and dying in five minutes I would always choose to live for another week; and by a version of mathematical induction I conclude that I would be glad to live forever.

Perhaps I shall eventually tire of life, but at the moment I can't imagine it, nor can I understand those many distinguished and otherwise reasonable persons who sincerely assert that they don't regard their own mortality as a misfortune.[3]

I can't take the kind of metaphysical consolation offered by Parfit (who observes that his view has parallels with Buddhism). By breaking down the metaphysical boundaries between himself and other persons, and loosening the metaphysical bonds that connect him now with his future self, he claims to have become less depressed about his own death, among other things. His death will be the termination of a certain connected sequence of activities and experiences, but not the annihilation of a unique underlying self. "Instead of saying, 'I shall be dead', I should say, 'There will be no future experiences that will be related, in certain ways, to these present experiences'. Because it reminds me what this fact involves, this redescription makes this fact less depressing" (Parfit (2), p. 281). As I've said in chapter 3, I can't accept the metaphysical revision, but I'm not sure that if I did, I'd find the conclusion less depressing. I actually find Parfit's picture of *survival* depressing—but that of course is by comparison with what *I* take survival to be. By comparison with Parfitian survival, Parfitian death may not seem so depressing; but that may owe as much to the deficiencies of the former as to the advantages of the latter. (See his remarks on p. 280.)

I am not going to concentrate here on explaining why death is a bad thing. Life can be wonderful, but even if it isn't, death is usually much worse. If it cuts off the possibility of more future goods than future evils for the victim, it is a loss no matter how long he has lived when it hap-

3. For example Williams (3), ch. 6, "The Makropulos Case; Reflections on the Tedium of Immortality." Can it be that he is more easily bored than I?

pens. And in truth, as Richard Wollheim says, death is a misfortune even when life is no longer worth living (p. 267). But here I want to say something about what it means to look forward to our own deaths, and how, if at all, we can bring the inner and outer views together. The best I can hope to offer is a phenomenological account. I hope it is not simply idiosyncratic. Like the contingency of our birth, the inevitability of our death is easy to grasp objectively, but hard to grasp from within. Everyone dies; I am someone, so I will die. But it isn't just that TN will be killed in a plane crash or a holdup, have a stroke or a heart attack or lung cancer, the clothes going to the Salvation Army, the books to the library, some bits of the body to the organ bank and the rest to the crematorium. In addition to these mundane objective transitions, my world will come to an end, as yours will when you die. That's what's hard to get hold of: the internal fact that one day this consciousness will black out for good and subjective time will simply stop. My death as an event in the world is easy to think about; the end of my world is not.

One of the difficulties is that the appropriate form of a subjective attitude toward my own future is expectation, but in this case there is nothing to expect. How can I expect nothing *as such*? It seems that the best I can do is to expect its complement, a finite but indeterminate amount of something—or a determinate amount, if I am under definite sentence of death. Now a good deal could be said about the consequences of the finiteness of my future, but that is relatively banal and something most of us automatically allow for, particularly after reaching the age of forty. I am concerned with the adequate recognition of my eventual annihilation itself. There will be a last day, a last hour, a last minute of consciousness, and that will be it. Off the edge.

To grasp this it isn't enough to think only of a particular stream of consciousness coming to an end. The external view of death is psychological as well as physical: it includes the idea that the person who you are will have no more thoughts, experiences, memories, intentions, desires, etc. That inner life will be finished. But the recognition that the life of a particular person in the world will come to an end is not what I am talking about. To grasp your own death from within you must try to look *forward* to it—to see it as a *prospect*.

Is this possible? It might seem that there could be no form of thought about your own death except either an external view, in which the world is pictured as continuing after your life stops, or an internal view that sees only this side of death—that includes only the finitude of your expected future consciousness. But this is not true. There is also something that can be called the expectation of nothingness, and though the mind tends to veer away from it, it is an unmistakable experience, always startling, often frightening, and very different from the familiar recognition that your life will go on for only a limited time—that you probably have less than thirty years and certainly less than a hundred. The positive prospect of the end of subjective time, though it is logically inseparable from these limits, is something distinct.

What is the specific object of this feeling? In part, it is the idea of the objective world and objective time continuing without me in it. We are so accustomed to the parallel progress of subjective and objective time that there is some shock in the realization that the world will go calmly on without me after I disappear. It is the ultimate form of abandonment.

But the special feeling I am talking about does not depend only on this, for it would be there even if solipsism were true—even if my death brought with it the end of the only world there was! Or even if, reversing the direction of dependence, my death was going to occur *in consequence* of the end of the world. (Suppose I came to believe a crackpot scientific theory that as the result of a spectacular and inexorable rise in matter/ antimatter collisions, the universe was going to annihilate itself completely six months from now.) It is the prospect of nothingness itself, not the prospect that the world will go on after I cease to exist, that has to be understood.

It hardly needs saying that we are accustomed to our own existence. Each of us has been around for as long as he can remember; it seems the only natural condition of things, and to look forward to its end feels like the denial of something which is more than a mere possibility. It is true that various of my possibilities—things I might do or experience— will remain unrealized as a result of my death. But more fundamental is the fact that they will then cease even to be possibilities—when I as a subject of possibilities as well as of actualities cease to exist. That is why the expectation of complete unconsciousness is so different from the expectation of death. Unconsciousness includes the continued possibility of experience, and therefore doesn't obliterate the here and now as death does.

The internal awareness of my own existence carries with it a particularly strong sense of its own future, and of its possible continuation beyond any future that may actually be reached. It is stronger than the sense of future possibility attaching to the existence of any particular thing in the world objectively conceived—perhaps of a strength surpassed only by the sense of possible continuation we have about the world itself.

The explanation may be this. In our objective conception of the world, particular things can come to an end because the possibility of their nonexistence is allowed for. The possibility of both the existence and the nonexistence of a particular object, artefact, organism, or person is given by actualities which underlie either possibility and coexist with both of them. Thus the existence of certain elements and the truth of the laws of chemistry underlie the possibility of synthesizing a particular chemical compound, or of decomposing it. Such possibilities rest on actualities.

But some possibilities seem themselves to be basic features of the world and not to depend on more deep-seated actualities. For example the number of possible permutations of m things taken n at a time, or the number of possible Euclidean regular solids, are possibilities whose existence is not contingent on anything.

Now the various possibilities some of which make up my life, and many of which I will never realize, are contingent on my existence. My existence is the actuality on which all these possibilities depend. (They also depend on the existence of things outside me which I can encounter, but let me leave that aside for the moment.) The problem is that when I think of myself from the inside, there seems to be nothing still more basic which reveals the actuality of my existence as in turn the realization of a possibility of existence which is correlative with a possibility of nonexistence based on the same foundation. In other words the possibilities which define the subjective conditions of my life seem not to be explainable in turn, within a subjective view, as the contingent realization of deeper possibilities. Nothing is subjectively related to them as the existence of the elements is related to the possibility of a compound.

To explain them we have to go outside of the subjective view for an objective account of why TN exists and has the characteristics that determine his subjective possibilities. They rest on an external actuality.

But this gives rise to an illusion when we think about our lives from inside. We can't really make these external conditions part of the subjective view; in fact we have no idea how they generate our subjective possibilities on any view. It is as if the possible contents of my experience, as opposed to the actualities, themselves constituted a universe, a domain within which things can occur but which is not itself contingent on anything. The thought of the annihilation of this universe of possibilities cannot then be thought of as the realization of yet another possibility already given by an underlying subjective actuality. The subjective view does not allow for its own annihilation, for it does not conceive of its existence as the realization of a possibility. This is the element of truth in the common falsehood that it is impossible to conceive of one's own death.

All this is fairly obvious, but I think it explains something. The sense each person has of himself from inside is partly insulated from the external view of the person who he is, and it projects itself into the future autonomously, so to speak. My existence seems in this light to be a universe of possibilities that stands by itself, and therefore stands in need of nothing else in order to continue. It comes as a rude shock, then, when this partly buried self-conception collides with the plain fact that TN will die and I with him. This is a very strong form of nothingness, the disappearance of an inner world that had not been thought of as a contingent manifestation at all and whose absence is therefore not the realization of a possibility already contained in the conception of it. It turns out that I am not the sort of thing I was unconsciously tempted to think I was: a set of ungrounded possibilities as opposed to a set of possibilities grounded in a contingent actuality. The subjective view projects into the future its sense of unconditional possibilities, and the world denies them. It isn't just that they won't be actualized—they will *vanish*.

This is not just a realization about the future. The submerged illusion it destroys is implicit in the subjective view of the present. In a way it's as if I were dead already, or had never really existed. I am told that the fear of flying typically has as its object not just the possibility of crashing, but flying itself: hurtling along in a smallish vehicle miles above the surface of the earth. It's a bit like that, only in this case it's something you can repeatedly forget and rediscover: all along you have been thinking you were safely on the ground and suddenly you look down and notice that you're standing on a narrow girder a thousand feet above the pavement.

I have said nothing so far about the most perplexing feature of our attitude toward death: the asymmetry between our attitudes to past and future nonexistence. We do not regard the period before we were born in the same way that we regard the prospect of death. Yet most of the things that can be said about the latter are equally true of the former. Lucretius thought this showed it was a mistake to regard death as an evil. But I believe it is an example of a more general future-past asymmetry which is inseparable from the subjective view.

Parfit has explored the asymmetry in connection with other values such as pleasure and pain. The fact that a pain (of ours) is in prospect rather than in the past has a very great effect on our attitude toward it, and this effect cannot be regarded as irrational (Parfit (3), sec. 64).

While I have no explanation of the asymmetry, I believe it must be admitted as an independent factor in the subjective attitude toward our own death. In other words it can't be accounted for in terms of some other difference between past and future nonexistence, any more than the asymmetry in the case of pain can be accounted for in terms of some other difference between past and future pains, which makes the latter worse than the former.

It is a fact perhaps too deep for explanation that the cutting off of future possibilities, both their nonactualization and their obliteration even as possibilities, evokes in us a very different reaction from any parallel nonrealization or nonexistence of possibilities in the past. As things are, we couldn't have come into existence earlier than we did, but even if we could, we wouldn't think of prenatal nonexistence as the same kind of deprivation as death. And even though our nonexistence two hundred years ago faces us with the fact that our subjective existence is the realization of a possibility grounded in objective facts about the world, this does not affect us as the prospect of our annihilation does. The sense of subjective possibility does not project itself into the past with the same imaginative reality with which it faces the future. Death is the negation of something the possibility of whose negation seems not to exist in advance.

The incongruity between this and the objective view of death is clear; much of what was said about birth and the meaning of life applies here and need not be repeated. My death, like any other, is an event in the objective order, and when I think of it that way, detachment seems natural: the vanishing of this individual from the world is no more remarkable or important than his highly accidental appearance in it. That applies both to the full inner life of the individual and to the objective standpoint itself. Granted that the death of something that exists seems worse than its not coming into existence, it still seems not a matter of great seriousness, considered as part of the general cosmic flux.

Another reason to regard death without too much concern is that everyone's mortality is part of the general cycle of biological renewal which is an inseparable part of organic life. Particular deaths may be horrible or premature, but human death itself is a given which, like the fact that hawks eat mice, it makes no sense to deplore. This is no more consoling to someone about to die than it would be to a mouse about to be eaten by a hawk, but it is another obstacle to closing the subjective-objective gap.

One could try to close it in the opposite direction by arguing that the impersonal standpoint should take its view of each death from the attitude of the one whose death it is. If for each person his own death is awful, then every death should be regarded objectively as awful. Detached indifference would then be a form of blindness to what is clear from an internal perspective—and not the only example of such blindness.

There is something right about this; certainly it would be a good thing if some people took death more seriously than they do.[4] But if we try to do justice to the fact that death is the ultimate loss for everybody, it isn't clear what the objective standpoint is to do with the thought of this perpetual cataract of catastrophe in which the world comes to an end hundreds of thousands of times a day. We cannot regard all those deaths with the interest with which their subjects regard them: sheer emotional overload prevents it, as anyone who has tried to summon a feeling adequate to an enormous massacre knows. The objective standpoint simply cannot accommodate at its full subjective value the fact that everyone, oneself included, inevitably dies. There really is no way to eliminate the radical clash of standpoints in relation to death.

None of this means one can't subordinate one's life to other things—sometimes it would be indecent not to. People are willing to die for what is external to themselves: values, causes, other people. Anyone incapable of caring enough about something outside himself to sacrifice his life for it is seriously limited. Moreover such external concerns, while they may require the loss of life, often have the effect of diminishing that loss and can even be cultivated for the purpose. The more you care about people and things outside your own life, the less by comparison will be the loss from death, and you can, to a degree, reduce the evil of death by externalizing your interests as it approaches: concentrating on the welfare of those who will survive you and on the success of projects or causes that you care about independently of whether you will be around to see what happens. We see this kind of disinvestment in mortal, individual life all the time—and more ambiguously in the personal desire for posthumous fame, influence, or recognition.

But the effect of these measures should not be exaggerated. There is no way to achieve a fully integrated attitude no matter how much you expand your objective or posthumous interests. The objectively unremarkable death of this creature will terminate both its stream of conscious experience and the particular objective conception of reality in

---

4. The widespread willingness to rely on thermonuclear bombs as the ultimate weapon displays a cavalier attitude toward death that has always puzzled me. My impression is that whatever they may say, most of the defenders of these weapons are not suitably horrified at the possibility of a war in which hundreds of millions of people would be killed. This may be due to monumental lack of imagination, or perhaps to a peculiar attitude toward risk which leads to the discounting of probabilities of disaster substantially below 50 percent. Or it may be a mechanism of defensive irrationality that appears in circumstances of aggressive conflict. But I suspect that an important factor may be belief in an afterlife, and that the proportion of those who think that death is not the end is much higher among partisans of the bomb than among its opponents.

which its death is included. Of course from the objective standpoint the existence or nonexistence of any particular objective self, including this one, is unimportant. But that is a limited consolation. The objective standpoint may try to cultivate an indifference to its own annihilation, but there will be something false about it: the individual attachment to life will force its way back even at this level. Here, for once, the objective self is not in a position of safety. We may see more clearly, but we cannot rise above death by occupying a vantage point that death will destroy.

The objective standpoint can't really be domesticated. Not only does it threaten to leave us behind, but it gives us more than we can take on in real life. When we acknowledge our containment in the world, it becomes clear that we are incapable of living in the full light of that acknowledgment. Our problem has in this sense no solution, but to recognize that is to come as near as we can to living in light of the truth.

BIBLIOGRAPHY

If in addition to place of original publication a reprint or translation is listed, page references in the text are to the latter. Unless there are page references in the text, no editions have been specified for philosophical classics.

Adams, R. M.
    "Saints," *Journal of Philosophy*, 1984.
Anscombe, G. E. M.
    (1) "Causality and Determination," Inaugural lecture, Cambridge University, 1971, in *Metaphysics and the Philosophy of Mind: Collected Philosophical Papers vol. III*, University of Minnesota Press, 1981.
    (2) "The Causation of Action," in C. Ginet and S. Shoemaker (eds.), *Knowledge and Mind*, Oxford University Press, 1983.
Aristotle
    Nicomachean Ethics.
Austin, J. L.
    "A Plea for Excuses," *Proceedings of the Aristotelian Society*, 1956–7.
Bennett, J.
    Kant's Dialectic, Cambridge University Press, 1974.
Bentham, J.
    An Introduction to the Principles of Morals and Legislation, 1788.
Berkeley, G.
    A Treatise Concerning the Principles of Human Knowledge, 1710.
Butler, J.
    The Analogy of Religion, 1736.
Carter, B.
    "Large Number Coincidences and the Anthropic Principle in Cosmology," in

M. S. Longair (ed.), *Confrontation of Cosmological Theories with Observational Data*, Dordrecht: Reidel, 1974.

Chisholm, R.
Person and Object, La Salle, Ill.: Open Court, 1976.

Chomsky, N.
Rules and Representations, Columbia University Press, 1980.

Clarke, T.
"The Legacy of Skepticism", *Journal of Philosophy*, 1972.

Davidson, D.
(1) "Actions, Reasons, and Causes," *Journal of Philosophy*, 1963; rpt. in (4).
(2) "Mental Events," in L. Foster and J. W. Swanson (eds.), *Experience and Theory*, University of Massachusetts Press, 1970; rpt. in (4).
(3) "On the Very Idea of a Conceptual Scheme," *Proceedings and Addresses of the American Philosophical Association*, 1973–4; rpt. in (5).
(4) *Essays on Actions and Events*, Oxford University Press, 1980.
(5) *Inquiries into Truth and Interpretation*, Oxford University Press, 1984.

Dennett, D. C.
Brainstorms, Montgomery, Vt.: Bradford Books, 1978.

Descartes, R.
Meditations on First Philosophy, 1641.

Dummett, M.
(1) "Wittgenstein's Philosophy of Mathematics," *Philosophical Review*, 1959; rpt. in (3).
(2) "A Defence of McTaggart's Proof of the Unreality of Time," *Philosophical Review*, 1960; rpt. in (3).
(3) *Truth and Other Enigmas*, Harvard University Press, 1978.

Dworkin, R.
"What Is Equality? Part 1: Equality of Welfare" and "What Is Equality? Part 2: Equality of Resources," *Philosophy & Public Affairs*, 1981.

Evans, G.
The Varieties of Reference, Oxford University Press, 1982.

Farrell, B. A.
"Experience," *Mind*, 1950.

Farrer, A.
The Freedom of the Will, London: Adam & Charles Black, 1958.

Fodor, J.
The Modularity of Mind, MIT Press, 1983.

Foot, P.
(1) "Moral Beliefs," *Proceedings of the Aristotelian Society*, 1958–9; rpt. in (3).
(2) "Morality as a System of Hypothetical Imperatives," *Philosophical Review*, 1972; rpt. in (3).
(3) *Virtues and Vices*, Oxford: Blackwell, 1978.

Frankfurt, H.
"The Problem of Action," *American Philosophical Quarterly*, 1978.

Fried, C.
Right and Wrong, Harvard University Press, 1978.

Gould, S. J.
(1) "Is a New and General Theory of Evolution Emerging?" *Paleobiology*, 1980.
(2) "Genes on the Brain," *New York Review of Books*, June 30, 1983.

Hampshire, S.

(1) "Spinoza and the Idea of Freedom," *Proceedings of the British Academy*, 1960; rpt. in (3).

(2) "A Kind of Materialism," *Proceedings and Addresses of the American Philosophical Association*, 1969–70; rpt. in (3).

(3) *Freedom of Mind*, Princeton University Press, 1971.

Hare, R. M.

(1) *Freedom and Reason*, Oxford University Press, 1963.

(2) *Moral Thinking*, Oxford University Press, 1981.

Harman, G.

The Nature of Morality, Oxford University Press, 1977.

Harman, P. M.

Energy, Force, and Matter: the Conceptual Development of Nineteenth-Century Physics, Cambridge University Press, 1982.

Hirsch, S. M.

My Lai 4, New York: Random House, 1970.

Hobbes, T.

Leviathan, 1651.

Hume, D.

A Treatise of Human Nature, 1739.

Husserl, E.

Cartesian Meditations, 1929; trans. Dorion Cairns, The Hague: Martinus Nijhoff, 1960.

Jennings, H. S.

The Behavior of the Lower Organisms, 1906; rpt. Indiana University Press, 1976.

Kant, I.

(1) *Critique of Pure Reason*, 1st ed. (A) 1781; 2nd ed. (B) 1787.

(2) *Foundations of the Metaphysics of Morals*, 1785; Prussian Academy ed., vol. IV.

(3) *Critique of Practical Reason*, 1788; Prussian Academy ed., vol. V.

(4) *Religion Within the Limits of Reason Alone*, 1794.

Kripke, S.

(1) "Naming and Necessity," in D. Davidson and G. Harman (eds.), *Semantics of Natural Language*, Dordrecht: Reidel, 1972; rpt. as *Naming and Necessity*, Harvard University Press, 1980.

(2) *Wittgenstein on Rules and Private Language*, Harvard University Press, 1982.

Locke, J.

Essay Concerning Human Understanding, 2nd ed., 1694.

Lucas, J. R.

The Freedom of the Will, Oxford University Press, 1970.

Lucretius

De Rerum Natura

Mackie, J. L.

(1) *Problems from Locke*, Oxford University Press, 1976.

(2) *Ethics*, Harmondsworth: Penguin, 1977.

Madell, G.

The Identity of the Self, Edinburgh University Press, 1983.

McGinn, C.

The Subjective View, Oxford University Press, 1983.

Mill, J. S.
   Utilitarianism, 1863.
Moore, G. E.
   "Proof of an External World," *Proceedings of the British Academy*, 1939.
Nagel, T.
   (1) *The Possibility of Altruism*, Oxford University Press, 1970; rpt. Princeton University Press, 1978.
   (2) "Brain Bisection and the Unity of Consciousness," *Synthese*, 1971; rpt. in (4).
   (3) "What Is It Like to Be a Bat?" *Philosophical Review*, 1974; rpt. in (4).
   (4) *Mortal Questions*, Cambridge University Press, 1979.
   (5) "The Limits of Objectivity," in S. McMurrin (ed.), *The Tanner Lectures on Human Values, vol.I*, University of Utah Press, 1980.
   (6) "The Objective Self," in C. Ginet and S. Shoemaker (eds.), *Mind and Knowledge*, Oxford University Press, 1983.
Neurath, O.
   "*Protokollsätze*", *Erkenntnis*, 1932–3; trans. F. Schick, in A. J. Ayer (ed.), *Logical Positivism*, New York: The Free Press, 1959.
Nietzsche, F.
   The Genealogy of Morals, 1887.
O'Shaughnessy, B.
   The Will, Cambridge University Press, 1980.
Parfit, D.
   (1) "Later Selves and Moral Principles," in A. Montefiore (ed.), *Philosophy and Personal Relations*, London: Routledge, 1973.
   (2) *Reasons and Persons*, Oxford University Press, 1984.
Peirce, C. S.
   "How to Make Our Ideas Clear," 1878; in *The Collected Papers of Charles Sanders Peirce*, Harvard University Press, 1931–62, vol. V.
Plato
   (1) *Meno*.
   (2) *Republic*.
Popper, K.
   Objective Knowledge, Oxford University Press, 1972.
Putnam, H.
   (1) "The Meaning of 'Meaning,'"*Mind Language and Reality: Philosophical Papers vol. 2*, Cambridge University Press, 1975.
   (2) *Reason, Truth and History*, Cambridge University Press, 1981.
Quine, W. V.
   "Epistemology Naturalized," in *Ontological Relativity and Other Essays*, Columbia University Press, 1969.
Railton, P.
   "Alienation, Consequentialism, and the Demands of Morality," *Philosophy and Public Affairs*, 1984.
Rawls, J.
   (1) *A Theory of Justice*, Harvard University Press, 1971.
   (2) "Social Unity and Primary Goods," in A. Sen and B. Williams (eds.), *Utilitarianism and Beyond*, Cambridge University Press, 1982.
Reid, T.
   Essays on the Intellectual Powers of Man, 1785.

Scanlon, T. M.
   (1) "Preference and Urgency," *Journal of Philosophy*, 1975.
   (2) "Rights, Goals, and Fairness," in S. Hampshire (ed.), *Public and Private Morality*, Cambridge University Press, 1978.
Scheffler, S.
   The Rejection of Consequentialism, Oxford University Press, 1982.
Searle, J. R.
   Intentionality, Cambridge University Press, 1983.
Shoemaker, S.
   "Personal Identity: a Materialist's Account," in S. Shoemaker and R. Swinburne, *Personal Identity*, Oxford: Blackwell, 1984.
Sidgwick, H.
   The Methods of Ethics, 7th ed., 1907.
Spinoza, B.
   (1) *On the Improvement of the Understanding*; tr. R. H. M. Elwes, in *The Chief Works of Benedict de Spinoza*, vol. II, New York: Dover, 1951.
   (2) *Ethics*, 1677.
Sprigge, T.
   "Final Causes," *Proceedings of the Aristotelian Society*, suppl. vol. 45, 1971.
Stanton, W. L.
   "Supervenience and Psychophysical Law in Anomalous Monism," *Pacific Philosophical Quarterly*, 1983.
Strawson, P. F.
   (1) *Individuals*, London: Methuen, 1959.
   (2) "Freedom and Resentment," *Proceedings of the British Academy*, 1962; rpt. in *Freedom and Resentment and Other Essays*, London: Methuen, 1974.
   (3) *The Bounds of Sense*, London: Methuen, 1966.
   (4) "Perception and Its Objects," in G. MacDonald (ed.), *Perception and Identity*, London: Macmillan, 1979.
Stroud, B.
   The Significance of Philosophical Skepticism, Oxford University Press, 1984.
Sturgeon, N.
   "Altruism, Solipsism, and the Objectivity of Reasons," *Philosophical Review*, 1974.
Taylor, R.
   Action and Purpose, Englewood Cliffs, N.J.: Prentice-Hall, 1966.
Wachsberg, M.
   "Personal Identity, the Nature of Persons, and Ethical Theory," Ph.D. diss. Princeton University, 1983.
Watson, G.
   "Free Agency," *Journal of Philosophy*, 1975.
Wefald, E. H.
   "Truth and Knowledge: On Some Themes in Tractarian and Russellian Philosophy of Language," Ph.D. diss. Princeton University, 1985.
Wiggins, D.
   (1) "Freedom, Knowledge, Belief and Causality," in *Knowledge and Necessity*, Royal Institute of Philosophy Lectures, vol. III, London: Macmillan, 1970.
   (2) "Towards a Reasonable Libertarianism," in T. Honderich (ed.), *Essays on Freedom of Action*, London: Routledge, 1973.

Williams, B.

(1) "Imagination and the Self," *Proceedings of the British Academy*, 1966; rpt. in (3).

(2) "The Self and the Future," *Philosophical Review*, 1970; rpt. in (3).

(3) *Problems of the Self*, Cambridge University Press, 1973.

(4) "A Critique of Utilitarianism," in J. J. C. Smart and B. Williams, *Utilitarianism: For and Against*, Cambridge University Press, 1973.

(5) "Wittgenstein and Idealism," in G. Vesey (ed.), *Understanding Wittgenstein*, London: Macmillan, 1974; rpt. in (8).

(6) "Persons, Character, and Morality," in A. Rorty (ed.), *The Identities of Persons*, University of California Press, 1976; rpt. in (8).

(7) *Descartes: The Project of Pure Inquiry*, Harmondsworth: Penguin, 1978.

(8) *Moral Luck*, Cambridge University Press, 1981.

Wittgenstein, L.

(1) *Tractatus Logico-Philosophicus*, London: Routledge, 1922.

(2) *Philosophical Investigations*, Oxford: Blackwell, 1953.

Wolf, S.

(1) "Asymmetrical Freedom," *Journal of Philosophy*, 1980.

(2) "Moral Saints," *Journal of Philosophy*, 1982.

(3) "The Superficiality of Duty," unpublished manuscript, 1983.

Wollheim, R.

The Thread of Life, Harvard University Press, 1984.

INDEX

Absolute conception of reality, 15n, 70n
Absolute space-time, 77
Absurdity, 11, 210, 215, 217–23
Action, 32, 38, 111, 116n, 125–26, 135. *See also* Reasons for action
Adams, R. M., 203n
Adler, J., 222
Aesthetics, 109, 153, 164
Afterlife, 224, 230n
Agency, 111; vs. accountability, 111n
Agent-centred prerogative, 174
Agent-centred restrictions, 181n
Agent-neutral reasons, 152–53, 158–63
Agent-relative principles, legitimacy of, 187
Agent-relative reasons, 153, 158–59, 181
Agent-relative values, 154
Agents, deontology and, 180–85
Aiming, 181–82, 184
Alienation, 214, 221
Altruism, 151, 159–62
Ambitions, 201. *See also* Personal projects
Anscombe, G. E. M., 115, 142n
Anthropic principle, 82n
Anthropocentrism, 18
Antihumanism, 210
Antirealism and values, 143–49
Antiverificationism, 108

Appearance, 36, 77, 89, 100, 102–3, 130; objective distancing from, 66; values alleged to be, 147–48. *See also* Phenomenal world
A priori knowledge, 61, 69, 70, 83, 84, 85n
Aristotle, 195
Austin, J. L., 166
Autonomy, 111, 113–20, 123; reasons of, 165, 166–71, 181
Avoidance vs. prevention, 178–80

Beliefs, 88
Behaviorism, 21
Bennett, J., 111n
Bentham, J., 194
Berkeley, G., 93–94, 143–44
Biological renewal, 229
Biology, 9, 51, 52
Birth, unimportance of, 213
Blame, 120–21
Bourgeois morality, 166
Brain, 40–49; split, 44–45, 50–51; in a vat, 71, 72–73
Buddhism, 224
Butler, J., 33–34

Calley, W., 124, 137
Carter, B., 82n

I am grateful to Nicholas Humez for compiling the index.